DAG HAMMARSKJÖLD

The Statesman and His Faith

DAG HAMMARSKJÖLD

Dag Hammarskjöld

THE STATESMAN AND HIS FAITH

By HENRY P. VAN DUSEN

*'In our era, the road to holiness necessarily
passes through the world of action.'*

HARPER & ROW, PUBLISHERS

NEW YORK, EVANSTON, AND LONDON

Acknowledgment is made to Alfred A. Knopf, Inc. for permission to reprint from *Markings* by Dag Hammarskjöld, translated from the Swedish by Leif Sjöberg and W. H. Auden. Copyright © 1964 by Alfred A. Knopf, Inc. and Faber & Faber, Ltd.

FIRST EDITION

LIBRARY OF CONGRESS CATALOG CARD NUMBER: 67–11503

M-Q

In Tribute

to

DAG HAMMARSKJÖLD

who affirmed

'—"The Communion of Saints" and—within it—

an eternal life.'

Contents

Picture section follows page 48

Preface

'Everyone owns Dag Hammarskjöld's *Markings*. Few have read it. Few of these have understood it.'

This statement by a senior bishop of the American Episcopal Church defines the striking contradiction of this book. Its distribution has surprised its publishers and most reviewers and early readers. Within a month after publication, it stood first among non-fiction best-sellers where it continued through another seven months. In less than a year, sales totaled a quarter of a million copies. Six months later, the demand for the book had not abated; circulation was approaching 450,000 copies. On the other hand, almost no one appears really to have read it. To scores of inquiries, 'Have you read Dag Hammarskjöld's *Markings*?', the reply is, 'Well, I've looked at it' or 'I've glanced at it' or 'I tried, but gave up'. A veteran American authority in international affairs who held high office in the League of Nations in its early years admits that, on a first attempt to read *Markings*, he quickly put it down. On returning to it in preparation for a volume to deal in part with Dag Hammarskjöld's service at the United Nations, he found it 'very hard going'.

Hence, the occasion for *this* book.

ii

One reason for this surprising contradiction is that many readers have treated *Markings* as though it were a miscellany of random reflections, without order or pattern, and have dipped in here and there as they might with a conventional anthology of devotional meditations.

They have failed to take seriously Hammarskjöld's own description of his work as a 'diary', a succession of 'notes' set down, with gaps, over a period of more than thirty-five years. Close study reveals two facts which cast the contents of *Markings* in quite different light.

In the first place, it is possible to trace a discernible development in Dag Hammarskjöld's spiritual experience. Not, to be sure, a line of steady and unbroken upward movement, escalator-like. Quite the opposite. In contrast to both his public career and his personal life, both of which were marked from beginning to end by 'consistency' and 'continuity', the movement of his spirit was more like a jagged sequence of ascending thrusts and sharp declines, plunging toward despairing desolation. Then came an abrupt and wholly unexpected crisis, a 'conversion' in the literal meaning of that word, an 'about-face'. As we shall see, Hammarskjöld himself, in long retrospect, affirmed that 'turning-point' and its decisive influence upon his life.

Second, contrary to a widely held assumption, there was an inti-mate interrelation between Dag Hammarskjöld's public career and his private meditations. Beginning with the days of his first election as Secretary-General of the United Nations and increasingly through the rest of his life, Hammarskjöld developed the habit of placing specific dates over individual and groups of 'markings'. By comparing these datings with major public events, his travel calendars, and cher-ished anniversaries, it is often possible to establish the circumstances which occasioned many of his reflections. Thus they glow with fresh and reciprocal illumination.*

Beyond that, it must be borne in mind that these 'Road Marks' were never intended for the eyes of anyone except their author. They record private 'negotiations with myself—and with God', into which the reader is privileged to enter.

iii

The aim of this book is to enable Dag Hammarskjöld himself to speak directly to its readers.

So far as possible, Hammarskjöld's own words are used. They are

---

* To assist the reader, an Appendix provides a detailed 'Correlation' of Ham-marskjöld's 'markings' with important occasions in both his public and his private life, so arranged that one can discover what occasion corresponded with a par-ticular 'marking' or, conversely, what 'marking' was composed on a particular date of special meaning. Pp. 223 ff.

drawn from his published speeches, from quotations in earlier books about him, from unpublished private letters to friends, but of course especially from the primary source for knowledge of Dag Hammarskjöld's interior life, his 'Road Marks'.*

Throughout the writing, a variety of possible readers has been in mind—those who knew Dag Hammarskjöld well and those who had never met him, those who are familiar with his career and those with scant acquaintance with his life, those who have studied *Markings* carefully and those who have never looked at it, and particularly those who have made some gestures toward reading it but confess that they have not understood it or been gripped by it.

iv

'How well did you know Hammarskjöld?' I am often asked. The answer is, 'Not at all' or, more accurately, 'Almost not at all'.

Shortly after Hammarskjöld came to the United Nations, we spent an evening together in a friend's home at a very small dinner in his honor. There must have been much conversation, but I cannot recall a topic discussed or a word he uttered. So far as I carried away any recollection, it was of a quiet, reticent, unimpressive 'civil servant'. This was not untypical. It was the usual result of Hammarskjöld's distaste for even informal social occasions which appears so often in the narrative which follows.

However, this lack of personal acquaintance may not be a handicap. It may make possible freshness of approach and objectivity in interpretation which might prove difficult for those who knew him well. The materials for a study of Hammarskjöld's inner life were unknown even to those who were closest to him but are now open to any reader.

Beyond that, despite very great and obvious contrasts, there were certain similarities in personal background, in temperament and development and predilections—for example, a lifelong distaste for conventional society—and, perhaps most important, in religious pilgrimage and in the faith to which it led which strike deep resonances

---

* Extensive quotations from *Markings* are with the generous permission of Alfred A. Knopf, Inc., to whom I am greatly indebted for their use. To facilitate study, the page reference for each quotation is indicated in small superior figures within parentheses. Fairly complete cross references to the materials in this book are provided in footnotes.

and may have aided understanding. In any event, throughout the greater part of the past two years, I have lived almost continuously with the 'inner person', self-portrayed in what he himself called 'the only true "profile" that can be drawn'.

To place oneself in imagination day after day alongside this amazing man and, so to say, walk with him as he goes his solitary way down the years into secret inmost fastnesses, through engulfing sloughs of despondency, and up to exhilarating heights in which he delighted is a possibility awaiting anyone prepared to give time and effort. It is a harrowing as well as humbling and immensely enriching experience.

v

This book was begun as 'A Spiritual Biography' of Dag Hammarskjöld. Until a late stage, it bore the subtitle 'A Biographical Interpretation of Markings'.

However, repeated and deeper immersion in both his career and his 'diary' has radically altered the perspective. From the outset, it was assumed that it is possible fully to appreciate, in some instances even to understand, many of Dag Hammarskjöld's profoundest and most pivotal 'Road Marks' only against the background of the circumstances in either his public or his personal life which occasioned them—the particular places or forks on his life's pilgrimage where they were set up. It has become clear that it is equally impossible rightly to appraise, in some instances even to understand, Dag Hammarskjöld the Statesman without the light cast by his private reflections upon the events amidst which he moved and which he did so much to shape.

Thus it is hoped that there emerges a portrait of the Man of Affairs and the Man of the World as he understood himself as well as an authentic 'profile' of the 'Inner Person'.

vi

This is being written on Dag Hammarskjöld's sixty-first birthday.

As we shall discover, anniversaries were always occasions of very particular meaning to him. Many of his most intimate and decisive 'Road Marks' bear their dates. Of all these annual observances, the one which touched him most deeply and most often moved him to special reflection was his own birthday, July 29. During his years away from home, he tried to arrange his all too infrequent and brief holidays so as to spend it at his cottage in southern Sweden. As with his reiterated use of certain key words or phrases across a span of years, it is possible to trace the development of his thought by following, year by year, Hammarskjöld's birthday meditations.*

The last of these, his final birthday meditation, probably written en route from Sweden to Paris on July 29, 1959, appropriately brings the series to climax:

'To be nothing in the self-effacement of humility, yet, for the sake of the task, to embody its whole weight and importance in your bearing, as the one who has been called to undertake it. . . . Praise and blame, the winds of success and adversity, blow over such a life without leaving a trace or upsetting its balance. Towards this, so help me, God—'

H.P.V.D.

Sorrento, Maine
July 29, 1966

* See 'Correlation of Dag Hammarskjöld's Birthdays and Corresponding "Markings" ', below, pp. 223 ff.

This book owes much to unstinting gift of time, knowledge and counsel by many. My first debt is to Dean Andrew W. Cordier of Columbia University who, as Executive Assistant, was Dag Hammarskjöld's closest associate throughout his eight and a half years at the United Nations. He has lent encouragement at every point, prepared the way for my visit to Sweden, made available Hammarskjöld's travel calendars and other papers, and interrupted a crowded academic schedule to read and correct the section on Hammarskjöld as Secretary-General.

During a week spent in Sweden in September 1965, I had the privilege of unhurried, utterly frank and, in some instances, exceedingly intimate conversations with virtually all of Dag Hammarskjöld's family and closest friends from childhood who were in the country at that time. Each one gave valuable information and insight.

Governor Bo Hammarskjöld, Dag's eldest brother and head of the family, welcomed me to Stockholm, personally arranged many interviews, has given further assistance through correspondence, and has scrutinized the part of the manuscript on his brother before he came to New York.

Judge Henrik Klackenberg who probably knew young Hammarskjöld more intimately both professionally and personally than anyone else during the early years of the latter's professional career not only drew generously upon this close association but has continued an active correspondent, has likewise criticized the account of Hammarskjöld's time in Sweden, and has responded to my request by preparing and permitting publication of an exceptionally authoritative statement which, I trust, may help to inter some of the most vicious and groundless rumors regarding his friend's private life. Mrs. Klackenberg kindly translated valuable material from the Swedish.

Dr. Leif Belfrage, presently Permanent Under-Secretary for Foreign Affairs in the Swedish Government, to whom Hammarskjöld entrusted decision on the publication of Vägmärken, gave me the opportunity to examine the original manuscript and has checked the account of its discovery, as has the Hon. Per Lind, now Swedish Ambassador to Canada, whom Hammarskjöld had asked to take charge of his papers. Count Wachmeister, Hammarskjöld's Aide in his last years, supervised arrangements for my visit.

Hammarskjöld's close artist friend of later years, Bo Beskow, was lavish with hospitality and reminiscences, and has translated for publication here a number of personal letters from Hammarskjöld which supplement both his public record and his private meditations.

Several of Hammarskjöld's colleagues and friends at the United Nations have given me the benefit of their recollections. Dr. Sture Linner, head of the United Nations Mission in the Congo at the time of Hammarskjöld's final visit there and now of the United Nations Staff in London, has shared memories of many hours with Hammarskjöld both in New York and in Leopoldville shortly before his fatal flight and has also corrected the account of his last days.

Dr. Maurice S. Friedman in Jerusalem has furthered most helpfully my efforts to clarify Hammarskjöld's relations with Martin Buber.

I have drawn freely upon three already published biographies: Joseph P. Lash's admirable *Dag Hammarskjöld: Custodian of the Brushfire Peace*, Sten Söderberg's delightful *Hammarskjöld: A Pictorial Biography* which is much more than its title suggests, and Sven Stolpe's charming personal memoir, *Dag Hammarskjöld: A Spiritual Portrait*. Only the last makes use of *Markings*. For the most part, none of these authors gives sources of his quotations; usually I have followed their example.

A cherished friend and collaborator in writing and publishing over nearly half a century, William L. Savage, has read the entire manuscript with meticulous care and suggested many corrections and improvements.

Special thanks are due my wife for her long-suffering patience. Through most of the past year, she has had to endure an 'absentee husband', absent not in body but in mind and spirit.

Miss Eleanor Jordan of the staff of Harper & Row has given editorial advice and help far beyond the line of duty in preparing an exceptionally difficult manuscript for the press.

My last and deepest gratitude, however, is to my son Hugh Van Dusen who has criticized two successive drafts of the manuscript in its entirety, has watched over it at every stage of preparation, and without whose confidence and support it might not have reached publication. Were a conventional Dedication appropriate, I would have been strongly disposed to dedicate the book to him.

H.P.V.D.

I · PROLOGUE

Public Servant–Private Man–Inner Person

WHEN DEATH SUDDENLY STRUCK DOWN Dag Hammarskjöld through a mysterious plane accident in the heart of Africa near midnight of September 17–18, 1961, the whole world knew that it had lost one of its most dedicated and invaluable public servants.

As the General Assembly of the United Nations reconvened two days later, one after another representative of its more than one hundred Member Nations, of every continent and race and size and political orientation, rose to attest the shock and grief, the admiration and gratitude, of their Governments and Peoples with a depth of feeling which rang with unmistakable sincerity in a corporate eulogy of almost four hours.

The first speaker, Mr. Krag of Denmark in behalf of the Scandinavian countries, voiced the verdict of all: 'Never before in the history of international organizations has one single man played so central a role as did Dag Hammarskjöld or, at his death, left a political vacuum and a grief embracing the globe.'

The tributes from the newly emergent nations were especially poignant. Hammarskjöld had come to conceive of the United Nations as, in a special sense, the spokesman and protector of these fledgling Powers; and, for them, he himself personified that role: 'He was always the friend and defender of the rights of the weak, of the small nations—those very nations which have now come to freedom and independence and which are the most disinherited ones' . . . 'the smaller nations, whose interests he had so much at heart.'

On the other hand, the representative of Poland, speaking officially 'on behalf of the group of socialist countries', declared: 'Saddened and silent we stand at his coffin—a man the sincerity of whose persuasion could not be denied.' And Krishna Menon of India who had often been one of Hammarskjöld's sharpest critics now proclaimed him 'a great world statesman . . . and a friend of all of us'.

[3

Adlai Stevenson as spokesman of the United States summarized the well-nigh universal sentiment: 'In his passing the community of nations has lost one of the greatest servants it ever had—a brilliant mind, a brave and compassionate spirit. I doubt if any living man has done more to further the search for a world in which men solve their problems by peaceful means and not by force than this gallant friend of us all . . . the very embodiment of the international civil servant. . . .'

Indeed, when the dust and mists of immediacy have cleared and our times stand forth in perspective, history is likely to record, as one of the few truly great men of this era, the name of Dag Hammarskjöld. More than any other single influence, his leadership transformed the United Nations from a forum of prolix and often ineffectual talk into an instrument of action by the Community of Nations for the safeguarding of peace and the furtherance of world order. 'It is arguable', suggests Philip Toynbee, 'that Hammarskjöld was the greatest statesman, and the best "matched with his hour", since Abraham Lincoln.'

ii

This, all the world knew.

However, those who enjoyed his companionship, and they were many, knew that the man of affairs was also a man of the world, of immense and wide-ranging culture, at home in the literature of half a dozen languages and a dozen nations and all periods, an ardent and highly literate connoisseur of drama and music, painting and sculpture, both classical and contemporary, himself a poet and translator of poetry, a lover and interpreter of Nature, a mountaineer, withal 'the best of comrades', all his life surrounded by admiring companions of the most diverse types and outlooks and cosmopolitan interests—in sum, a Renaissance man at mid-twentieth century.

iii

What the world did not know, what only a few among his closest associates sensed, was that this gifted and dedicated man whom mankind had come to esteem as one of its most useful servants and whom friends cherished as an exciting companion was, at the same time, a person of quite extraordinary interior life.

What no one knew, what not one of his family or most intimate colleagues or friends so much as suspected, was that for nearly four decades, from his student days at Uppsala University until a few weeks before his tragic end, Dag Hammarskjöld had been in the habit of recording his most intimate reflections on life and destiny, on Nature's grandeur and mystery, on the temptations and dilemmas of public office, all in the context of a resolute search for utter integrity and a viable faith—in his own words 'a diary . . . begun without a thought of anybody else reading it . . . a sort of "white book" concerning my negotiations with myself—and with God'.

Dag Hammarskjöld's 'Road Marks' or 'Signposts', as he himself described them, published in the original Swedish toward the end of 1963* and in English translation a year later,** were acclaimed at once as 'the noblest self-disclosure of spiritual struggle and triumph, perhaps the greatest testament of personal faith, written in this century, worthy to take a place among the dozen classics of Christian devotion of the ages, quite possibly the foremost by a person un-trained in theology and writing in the heat of professional life and amidst the most exacting responsibilities for world peace and order.'

iv

Hammarskjöld himself was fond of distinguishing the 'public servant' and the 'private man'.

Indeed, his first public utterance following his election as Secretary-General of the United Nations—not in the General Assembly at the moment of his induction into his new office but to the Press who met him at International Airport, New York, on the preceding day—consisted of 'a few very general remarks' upon precisely this distinc-tion: 'In my new official capacity the private man should disappear and the international public servant take his place.'†

* Dag Hammarskjöld, *Vägmärken* (Stockholm: Albert Bonniers Förlag, 1963).
** Dag Hammarskjöld, *Markings*, translated from the Swedish by Leif Sjöberg & W. H. Auden, with a Foreword by W. H. Auden (New York: Alfred A. Knopf, 1964).
† 'The International Public Servant' in *Servant of Peace: A Selection of the Speeches and Statements of Dag Hammarskjöld*, edited by Wilder Foote (New York: Harper & Row, 1963), pp. 27–28.

In half a dozen sentences, he sketched his conception of the 'public servant': 'The public servant is there in order to assist, so to say from the inside, those who take the decisions which frame history. He should—as I see it—listen, analyze and learn to understand fully the forces at work and the interests at stake, so that he will be able to give the right advice when the situation calls for it. . . . He is active as an instrument, a catalyst, perhaps an inspirer—he serves.' This was a conception to which Hammarskjöld returned often through the following eight and a half years in office.

However, as the conclusion of his short Press Conference statement, he took a figure from 'the private man's' favorite recreation: 'My experience [in mountain climbing] is limited to Scandinavia where mountaineering calls more for endurance than for equilibristics. . . . However, that much I know of this sport that the qualities it requires are just those which I feel we all need today: perseverance and patience, a firm grip on realities, careful but imaginative planning, a clear awareness of the dangers but also of the fact that fate is what we make it and that the safest climber is he who never questions his ability to overcome all difficulties.'

Thus, the life of Dag Hammarskjöld as it was known to the world and to his friends revolved in near-perfect ellipse around two poles, as every full-orbed life should, in the spheres which Professor William Ernest Hocking once distinguished in almost identical terms as 'the Public Order' and 'the Private Order'*.

In Dag Hammarskjöld's life, however, there was a third focus of being, not a third point of reference after the manner of a triangle, but rather a *center*, a *core*; here the figure of the ellipse breaks down. Behind and beneath and within both the 'public servant' whom the world revered and the 'private man' whom his friends cherished was the 'inner person', known only to himself but now clearly revealed for all to see in his private 'Road Marks'. Far from being separate from or unrelated to either the 'public servant' or the 'private man', as some have maintained, careful study reveals that the 'inner person' was, in fact, in the most intimate and continuous interaction with both—at once a reflection, a mirror of the 'public servant' and the 'private man', and at the same time the determinative prime mover of each.

* 'The Public Order and the Private Order' in W. E. Hocking, *Human Nature and Its Remaking* (New Haven: Yale University Press, 1918), pp. 304 ff.

Indeed, it is not possible rightly to understand either the public servant familiar to all the world or the private individual known to a small circle of confreres except through familiarity with the inner person who was the true Dag Hammarskjöld. It is the interrelations of these three aspects of this exceptionally talented, versatile and influential human being, but especially the reciprocal influence between the Statesman and the inner person, which furnish the subject matter of this study.

II · THE BACKGROUND

Toward the end of March 1953, word reached the United States Department of State in Washington that France and Great Britain were preparing to propose the name of Dag Hammarskjöld of Sweden for election as Secretary-General of the United Nations. The Security Council which nominates the appointee to the General Assembly had been at a standstill for weeks in its search for an acceptable successor to Trygve Lie. Now, since the Soviet Union which had refused all earlier suggestions from the West had acquiesced, Hammarskjöld's election was assured. It is reported that 'Members of the U.S. delegation to the U.N. went out to canvass their Scandinavian colleagues asking, "Who is this guy?" '

Actually, Dag Hammarskjöld then held the highest office open to a civil servant in the Foreign Service of his own Nation as Vice-Minister of Foreign Affairs and non-party Member without Portfolio in the Swedish Cabinet. He was widely and favorably known throughout the chancelleries of Europe as one of the architects of the Organization for European Economic Cooperation administering the Marshall Plan and Vice-Chairman of its Executive Committee. Russia's assent doubtless sprang from the fact that, six months earlier, her statesmen had encountered him as a scrupulously fair as well as quietly firm negotiator over the shooting down of two Swedish planes over the Baltic. And he was not unknown to high-ranking American Government officials. Some had been associated with him in renegotiation of the Swedish-United States Trade Agreement in 1946. As a matter of fact, Hammarskjöld had been in New York only a few weeks before to head the Swedish Delegation to the United Nations. The 'profile' which emerged from rather frantic inquiries regarding Hammarskjöld 'showed a Swedish civil service aristocrat, gifted administratively, unobtrusive rather than flamboyant, a brilliant technician, an executant rather than a political leader,

[11

and, some feared, a compromiser rather than a fighter'*. H. Freeman Matthews, formerly in charge of the State Department's European desk, advised Secretary of State John Foster Dulles: 'If you can get him, grab him.' Thus, apart from, indeed prior to, his career at the United Nations, Hammarskjöld was recognized as a man of exceptional abilities and achievements.

ii

Dag Hammarskjöld fully understood the wellsprings of his mature conviction. Three forces principally molded his mind and spirit— Family, Fatherland, and Nature, especially the rugged mountains and dense forests of northern Sweden.

In particular, he was keenly alive to his parental heritage and its determinative influence upon him. Twice he had occasion to refer to it publicly, in two of the most notable addresses he ever gave.

'Between the nation in history and the individual, the family is the primary tie', he declared when he was inducted into the Swedish Academy in the seat left vacant by his father's death—the first time such a succession had ever occurred—and custom required that his inaugural address take the form of a eulogy of his predecessor. Then, referring explicitly to his father, he spoke of 'an obvious but subtle interdependence between national and family feeling'**.

Shortly after he came to the United Nations as Secretary-General, in the autumn of 1953, Hammarskjöld accepted an invitation from Edward R. Murrow to participate in a series of personal confessions entitled 'This I Believe'. In this radio talk, he spelled out his indebtedness to his parents quite specifically.† Of his paternal inheritance, he said:

'From generations of soldiers and government officials on my father's side I inherited a belief that no life was more satisfactory than one of selfless service to your country—or humanity. This service required a sacrifice of all personal interests, but likewise the courage to stand up unflinchingly for your convictions.'

* Joseph P. Lash, *Dag Hammarskjöld: Custodian of the Brushfire Peace* (Garden City, New York: Doubleday & Company, 1961), pp. 7–8.

** 'Hjalmar Hammarskjöld', Inaugural Address as a member of the Swedish Academy, Stockholm, Dec. 20, 1954, in *Servant of Peace*, p. 65.

† *Servant of Peace*, pp. 23–24. See below, pp. 46–47.

The Hammarskjöld family is among the oldest in Sweden, known and respected through more than three centuries for outstanding service to the Nation. 'The Hammarskjöld family traits are easily recognizable: seriousness, conscientiousness and dauntless energy. Whenever some knotty problem arises within Swedish administration, the response is likely to be: "Try one of the Hammarskjölds" ' —a forecast of the recourse which became commonplace on the world scene whenever the United Nations was bogged down in a peculiarly intractable dilemma: 'Give it to Dag.'

In this notable succession, Dag Hammarskjöld's father was the most distinguished. A scholar by talent and inclination, Hjalmar Hammarskjöld felt compelled to forego his preferred vocation in philology and teaching in favor of law and government in order to recoup the family's impoverished finances and assist his parents and brothers. His private frustration opened the way to an unprecedented career of public responsibility. 'Few of his countrymen have held so many high offices, and discharged their duties with such responsibility. He was conscientiousness itself, and had a juridical and philosophical basis for everything he undertook.'* After a brief tenure as professor of special civil law at his alma mater, Uppsala University, he was drafted into the Swedish Cabinet as Minister of Justice. Following a happy interlude as President of the Gota Court of Appeals, he returned to the Cabinet as Minister of Education and was one of the four Swedish delegates in the negotiations which effected the dissolution of the union with Norway. He cut short an appointment as Minister to Copenhagen for the sake of his children's education in Sweden, and undertook his first term as Governor of Uppland at Uppsala. But his discharge of this office which greatly delighted him was frequently interrupted by special assignments for the national Government mainly as mediator, as a member of the International Court of Arbitration, as first delegate to the second Peace Conference at The Hague, as President of the Court which settled the Casablanca dispute threatening to draw France and Germany into war, and as chairman of commissions of reconciliation between the United States and China, Switzerland and Germany, Belgium and Spain, Switzerland and Portugal, France and Spain. Thus, the senior Hammarskjöld personified the part which Sweden

* Sten Söderberg, *Hammarskjöld: A Pictorial Biography* (New York: The Viking Press, 1962), p. 24.

came to play in the modern period as mediator in international conflicts, anticipating the role which was to become his son Dag's greatest contribution to world order.

In the early days of 1914, when war clouds were already darkening across Europe, the elder Hammarskjöld was in St. Petersburg for negotiations when a 'Peasants' March' to the Royal Palace in Stockholm demanding stronger Swedish defenses brought down the Government and Hjalmar Hammarskjöld, always a non-party Independent as Dag likewise was to become, was summoned by the King to form a Cabinet. He continued as Prime Minister through three years of World War I, holding Sweden to neutrality. But his stern and autocratic rule not only incensed socialists and liberals but alienated many of the populace who blamed him, even if unjustly, for the wartime food shortages. Despite the fact that nearly 600,000 signatures were affixed to an address expressing the wish that he continue as Prime Minister, he was compelled to resign in 1917. He returned to Uppsala as Governor and continued contentedly in that post for another thirteen years until his retirement, serving also in a number of parliamentary capacities and as chairman of the League of Nations committee for the codification of international law and as delegate to the Disarmament Conference.

By a generation rushing toward Socialism, Hjalmar Hammarskjöld was disparaged as 'a forbidding figure, authoritative to the point of being rude . . . with a reputation for extreme conservatism'.

This was the man whom Dag Hammarskjöld was duty bound to memorialize when he took his father's place in the Swedish Academy. It was probably the most difficult address he ever had to compose; Dr. Andrew Cordier, his closest associate in the United Nations Secretariat, reports that 'he devoted more time to this address than to any other in his United Nations career'. And it reveals almost as much about the son as about its subject. 'Hjalmar Hammarskjöld was one of those who are firm in their roots and firm in their faith, those whose changing fates may well deepen the convictions and directions of their early years, but not change them. . . .' Against the allegation of reaction, he characterized his father as 'a reformist of conservative disposition'. He interpreted the elder Hammarskjöld's internationalism thus:

'*Civitas Dei* was a dream of the past. The present-day attempts to form an international organization with common executive organs had not yet been begun. Instead, there is a glimpse here of a world society, where national states live under the protection of an internationalism which gains its strength from the very logic of justice itself, not from dictates of power, and in which, therefore, the only international organs needed are of a judicial nature.' 'For a small country, international law, in the final analysis, is the only remaining argument, and its defense is therefore worth sacrifices.'*

Dag Hammarskjöld's respect, even reverence, for his father was deep, sincere and of far-reaching effect upon his own mind and life. However, that was not the whole story. To a close friend who congratulated him upon the address but queried whether he felt he could tell the truth or was compelled to defend his father's memory, he replied with a rare burst of frankness:

'The Academy speech is not attacking any myths. But it is strictly honest—an attempt at an all through subjective analysis of motives. The picture is true, from a clearly declared aspect, that *also* is mine. I have naturally other aspects, where I myself stand in the center of a perpetual conflict with a dominating father (in many things deeply unlike me) whose pressure I hated and whose weaknesses I always saw very clearly. But that picture tells more about me than about him and is in this case outside the lighted area.'

And, in his private 'diary', reclaiming memories of boyhood more than forty years before, he entered this painful recollection, still vivid:

'A box on the ear taught the boy
That Father's name
Was odious to them.'**

To his father, Dag Hammarskjöld owed much: an exacting and unflinching devotion to duty, a patriotism which held that 'everything is being done, borne or received in love of our fatherland, in humble endeavour to promote its welfare and stave off its misfortune or downfall', a 'strong sense of independence of public administra-

* *Servant of Peace*, pp. 64, 71, 69, 75.
** *Markings*, p. 180.

tion . . . and the duties accompanying the responsibilities of officials', sympathy for the special plight and predicament of small
nations, dedication to the realization of an international order where
'society is welded together by that higher "reason", common to us all,
which is the bearer of justice', above all the ideal and the example of
'a life of faith in justice and of self-effacing service under a responsibility which unites us all'. But also a warning of the price of integrity
and fidelity to conscience which was to become his own fate: 'A
mature man is his own judge. In the end, his only form of support is
being faithful to his own convictions. . . . Therefore, he must run,
with open eyes, the risk of being accused of obdurate self-suffi-
ciency.'*

iii

It would be difficult to imagine two persons more antipodal in
temperament, while at one in basic ideals and loyalties, than Hjalmar
Hammarskjöld and his wife. Their son Dag was sensitive to the
contrast and its bearing upon their life together. In the same
Academy address memorializing his father, he digressed to characterize his mother:

'In his wife he [Hjalmar Hammarskjöld] found a faithfulness to
personal ideals as strong and steadfast as his own. Otherwise, Agnes
Almqvist was very different from him. She held a radically democratic view of fellow humans, "evangelic" if you like; she was as open
to life as a child and possessed of an anti-rationalism with warm
under-currents of feeling. With these qualities, and the personal
generosity toward both intimates and strangers that they induced in
her, she introduced into Hjalmar Hammarskjöld's life elements
which carry great weight in interpreting his subsequent development.'

A number of those who, when young men, were frequent visitors
in the Hammarskjöld household as friends of the sons, first in the
Governor's Castle at Uppsala and later in Stockholm, have sketched
vivid profiles of the 'engaging and original lady' who was their
hostess: 'a wonderful woman . . . exuberantly forthcoming . . .
with good will and friendliness towards everybody around her . . .
great human warmth. . . . An intellectual woman, in many ways she

* *Servant of Peace*, pp. 64–79.

represented the emotional side of the family.' 'She was warm and
gushing; it was hard to tell at times whether she was laughing or
crying; she had so overflowing and generous a heart that no one who
came near her could avoid her eager solicitude. When I married, this
grand and singular lady wired warm wishes "from your motherly old
battleaxe Agnes Hammarskjöld".' The ancient Castle was notorious
for its vast and oppressive chambers; 'but the gloom of those rooms
was never noticeable so long as Agnes Hammarskjöld was there to
dispel it with her vivacity and warmth.' 'It is the duty of a governor's
lady to be active in good works. . . . For Agnes Hammarskjöld this
Lady Bountiful attitude was probably not enough. She had the
faculty of putting herself in another's place and knew that the aim
must be to set people on their feet, and not just feed them.'

In all of her charitable interests and activities, her son Dag was a
loyal, though sometimes amused, companion and lieutenant. 'Every
Sunday he accompanied her to church, and he would patiently wait
while she chatted with friends or acquaintances she chanced to meet
in the street, whether the Archbishop or a poor shoemaker whom she
had recently rescued from bankruptcy.' And he 'accompanied her on
her visits to people in distress'. 'Dag was his mother's gentleman-in-
waiting, her page, her faithful and considerate attendant.' In European society of that day there was often the 'stay-at-home daughter'
who remained to look after her parents, which prompted one of Dag
Hammarskjöld's oldest and most admiring friends to suggest: 'Dag
was the Hammarskjöld family's stay-at-home daughter. The fantastic
thing is that at the same time he could be a boy with the others, pass.
exams as brilliantly as he did and make a great career.'

The youngest of the four Hammarskjöld children, Dag was born
when his mother was already past forty. She was fond of admitting
that, after three sons, she had hoped for a daughter. But, if there was
an initial disappointment, it did not shadow in the slightest degree
her affection for him. On the contrary, their relationship was an
especially intimate, congenial and mutually appreciative one. Indeed,.
this has encouraged some interpreters to suggest that close attachment to his mother prevented Dag's marriage. There is no warrant
for this hypothesis, either in his personal relationships or in his.
private meditations. He enjoyed friendships with women contemporaries. At least once and perhaps more often, he gave serious thought
to the possibility of marriage. As we shall see, his only explicit self-

scrutiny on the subject was composed a dozen years after his mother's death. The altogether adequate explanation of his celibacy, he himself offered on more than one occasion: 'how could he invite a woman to share his kind of life?'

Dag Hammarskjöld's attitude toward his mother was marked by touchingly gentle admiration and gratitude. There was nothing unusual, let alone abnormal, about it. He was above all the dutiful and faithful son. When a close friend of many years heard that Mrs. Hammarskjöld's life was drawing toward its close and sent a note of sympathy, Dag responded:

'Thank you for your note. And thank you for your desire to help me. You could not have done it in a better way than by writing that letter. It was quite right of you to remove the intellectual mask from an inner world in which sentiment determines everything I esteem most. I am too shy to show my colours and I must therefore content myself with the "cragginess" which I perhaps experience on the part of others. But I felt happiness when the wall was razed and that on a day like yesterday.

'My mother ended her life today. She had the qualities I admire most: she was courageous and good.'

Dag Hammarskjöld's principal indebtedness to his mother can best be given in his own words, from the deeply personal and autobiographical radio confession already quoted:

'From scholars and clergymen on my mother's side I inherited a belief that, in the very radical sense of the Gospels, all men were equals as children of God, and should be met and treated by us as our masters in God.'*

Hammarskjöld lived with his parents in the Castle throughout his student days at Uppsala University, moved with them to Stockholm on his father's retirement, and continued as a member of the parental household not only until his mother's death a decade later but for another five years with his widowed father. Not until he was forty, had carried the dual role of Under-Secretary of the Finance Ministry and Chairman of the Bank of Sweden and was about to transfer to the Foreign Office, did he establish his own home. It is an indication

* *Servant of Peace*, p. 23.

of both the character and the quality of his filial devotion that all through those years of mounting and increasingly demanding responsibilities, it was his unfailing practice unless prevented by special circumstances to leave the Ministry in good time to dine with his parents, stay on for an hour of conversation, and then be back at his desk by nine and work on in solitude until near daybreak. And, in later years when he was much in Paris at the Organization for European Economic Cooperation, again unless held there by urgent tasks, he regularly took a late Friday afternoon plane to Stockholm for a weekend visit with his father, then in his late eighties.

iv

Four sons were born to Hjalmar and Agnes Hammarskjöld. Three of them continued the family tradition of public service.

The eldest, Bo, like his father, became Governor of one of the Provinces. He has been described as 'one of the ablest government officials in Sweden . . . the ideal official, able to prescribe ideal solutions to the toughest problems'. Now retired and living in the outskirts of Stockholm, he is still looked to as among his country's most distinguished Elder Statesmen and is frequently called into counsel on a wide range of public and philanthropic matters. Separated from his youngest brother by fourteen years and already away from home when the latter was growing into manhood, their associations were not frequent or intimate though fraternal affection was strong.

The second brother Ake, two years younger than Bo, was no less brilliant and outstanding in his all too brief career, cut short by a rheumatic ailment at the age of forty-four. He became Secretary-General of the International Court of Arbitration at The Hague to which he was appointed when only twenty-nine and of which his father was already a member and continued so for over forty years. Like his father, he was also a member of several conciliation commissions under the League of Nations.

There was an interval of seven years before the birth of the third Hammarskjöld son, Sten. Handicapped by illness through much of his life, he was a journalist and novelist as well as briefly a civil servant, but retired early in his career. Closest to Dag in age and

growing up together as schoolmates and playmates, he has given
many charming portraits and anecdotes of the family and his precocious younger brother.

v

Dag Hammarskjöld was born July 29, 1905, shortly before his father
left the Cabinet to assume the Swedish Ministry to Denmark for a
brief two-year period. Then came the latter's appointment as Governor of Uppland and the family settled in 1907 in the great Castle at
Uppsala. Although there was the interruption of his father's gover-
norship to serve as Prime Minister through the tense war years of
1914–1917, Uppsala was the Hammarskjöld habitat for almost a
quarter of a century. It was here that Dag passed his childhood,
youth and young manhood. The molding influence of the ancient
City and its massive Castle which furnished the physical environment
of those formative years remained with him. It is significant that
from the six crowded days between his notification of election as
Secretary-General of the United Nations and his departure from
Sweden to New York to be inducted into these new and overwhelming responsibilities, he set apart a day to return to Uppsala, doubtless
primarily to visit his mother's grave in the cemetery close by the
Castle, where today he lies buried with his parents, but probably also
to revisit the Castle where he had grown up. He likewise took time to
drop in, unannounced, at the Archiepiscopal Palace at the foot of the
hill just below the Castle, where he had moved in and out almost
daily through earlier years as playmate and intimate companion of
the son and daughters of Archbishop Nathan Söderblom; the Palace
was now occupied by one of those daughters and her husband,
Archbishop Anders Brilioth.

On a lofty hilltop overlooking and overshadowing the City of
Uppsala with wide views across the countryside in all directions
stands the Castle, one of Sweden's oldest and most historic, on
foundations laid under Gustavus Vasa in 1545. What has since been
rebuilt as the Hall of State was, during the Hammarskjölds' occu-
pancy, a children's ideal playroom. A great corner turret housed a
circular banqueting hall. Mysterious passages interlaced the massive
walls eight feet thick. 'In a separate part of the castle were dark
dungeons which whispered ghostly tales of violent times and royal

feuds into young ears.' Here the youthful Hammarskjölds entertained their friends on expeditions of exploration and discovery; and it is reported that, on occasions of dances, Dag delighted to lure companions from the dance floor, which held no attraction for him, on search parties among the Castle's labyrinthine passages.

Below the Castle to the rear is located the School where the Hammarskjöld sons and their boyfriends received the foundations of their education. Directly below the Castle on the far side stands the stately Lutheran Cathedral, the prime sanctuary of the national Church. And, across the street from it, the modest Palace of the Archbishop of Uppsala who is also Primate of the Church of Sweden.

In the year when Hjalmar Hammarskjöld was summoned to form a Cabinet as Prime Minister, 1914, there succeeded to the headship of the Church one of the most gifted and remarkable Protestant churchmen of this century, Archbishop Nathan Söderblom. Söderblom was a first-rate scholar, a man of immense energy and far-ranging vision whose acquaintanceship and whose influence extended far beyond Sweden. He was one of the original founders of the contemporary Ecumenical Movement for Christian Unity. Like many other sensitive churchmen, he was humiliated over the total ineffectiveness of the Churches in forestalling World War I and outraged that Christians should be embattled, in alliance with their Governments on opposite sides of the conflict, praying uncritically for victory and bringing down mutual imprecations upon each other. With the War's termination, he took the initiative in rallying church leaders from both sides and of all major affiliations (except the Church of Rome) to organize in order to bring a Christian judgment and effective action to bear upon the most pressing problems of the social, political and international orders. The outcome was the first great official church conclave of modern times, the Universal Christian Conference on Life and Work, summoned to meet in Stockholm in 1925 to which most Protestant and Orthodox Communions sent delegates, and over which Söderblom presided. Dag Hammarskjöld, then a university student of twenty, attended as a 'steward', or usher. From the Stockholm Conference came a permanent Council; and the Universal Christian Council on Life and Work became in turn one of the parents of the World Council of Churches. Uppsala, as the archiepiscopal seat, was the focus of this pioneering development. 'The church policy of Söderblom in this period made the city an international center', declared Dag Hammarskjöld in tracing his father's career in his Academy address. Many years later, when a staff member of the World Council of Churches introduced its General Secretary to Hammarskjöld in Geneva and suggested that he might tell him something of the Ecumenical Movement, the suggestion was playfully brushed aside: 'Oh, I know all about that! I was brought up under Söderblom.'

When Hjalmar Hammarskjöld returned to Uppsala as Governor in 1917, two of Sweden's most honorable families found themselves within stone's throw. The ties between the Hammarskjölds and the Söderbloms were of the utmost intimacy. Agnes Hammarskjöld and Nathan Söderblom were often referred to as 'the twins', for they had the same birthday. The parents were constantly and closely associated in public service to State and Church and in countless projects of private philanthropy and good works.

Their children, who were of much the same age, became nearest neighbors and playmates. There must have been a continual traffic up and down the hill between the Castle and the Palace, perhaps on sleds or toboggans in the long Swedish winters of deep snow, and they were often in each other's homes. Jon Olof Söderblom and Dag Hammarskjöld were school classmates and in university days also the youngest Söderblom daughter, Yvonne. When Dag translated a play from the French into Swedish for a student theatrical, she took the principal feminine part. He so far departed from his antipathy to social occasions as to take her as his partner to the student dance. There was some talk of an incipient romance which both pairs of parents would have welcomed. But it was to be otherwise. Shortly thereafter, Yvonne Söderblom married a Lutheran minister who was later to become Bishop Anderberg of Gottland. And young Hammarskjöld left Uppsala for Stockholm. But he continued an affectionate friendship with the Anderbergs, remembered their anniversaries with greetings, and visited them at Visby in 1952.

The influence of the Söderblom parents upon the youngest Hammarskjöld was not inconsiderable. When he protested to Mrs. Söderblom his dissatisfaction with his university studies in French Literature—'I had thought that I was going to learn about ideas and their travels through the ages and not waste time on the love affairs of authors'—she suggested that he read Pascal, who thereafter was one of his favorite authors. Jon Söderblom reports: 'When someone once mentioned in some connection or other that my father, Nathan Söderblom, was supposed to have meant a lot to Dag Hammarskjöld, a lot of people were most sceptical, but to me there is nothing puzzling there; in fact, I believe it to be true, for Dag once confided to me that at one period he had been attracted by the idea of studying theology.'

vi

From earliest youth, Dag Hammarskjöld was marked for a career of precocious achievement.

In his student days at Uppsala both in school and university, 'Dag was by far the most brilliant pupil'. Matriculating in Uppsala University at the age of seventeen, he completed his B.A. in two years—his father had taken the degree when eighteen—with major concentration in history of literature, philosophy, French and political economy.Thus was formed a mind which was later to be characterized by Hugh Gaitskell of Britain as 'razor-sharp' and by a close associate at the United Nations as 'very brilliant, orderly, pragmatic and subtle, capable of lightning speed in both comprehension and construction, yet strictly disciplined'.

Young Hammarskjöld's intellectual interests were in no sense limited to academic disciplines. A wide acquaintance with both classical and modern literature which was to broaden and deepen across the years had its foundation in student days. He read Joseph Conrad, Thomas Wolfe, Hermann Hesse and Thomas Mann, among others. And 'he tried to make his fellow students appreciate Emily Dickinson and Katherine Mansfield'. Meantime, his knowledge of the outside world was quickened through visits to the Castle by the future emperor of Ethiopia, Tagore, the Indian Christian mystic Sundar Singh, and many more.

While maintaining his residence at the Castle with his parents, Dag Hammarskjöld was an active participant in student affairs. Social life among Uppsala University undergraduates centered then as now in the 'nations', paralleling roughly American fraternities. Uppland was the oldest 'nation'. During Dag's student days, it celebrated its tricentenary with an elaborate festival. It is indicative of the admiration and regard in which he was held that he was chosen First

Curator and had responsibility for the major address—'his first public appearance in the grand style'.

A number of university contemporaries and friends have given us their recollections of their most brilliant college mate. Jon Söderblom describes him as 'not only the most gifted in his class, but a good comrade who remained unswervingly loyal to his friends all his life. As a boy, he was completely natural, an amusing playmate and an entertaining friend'. His brother Sten recalls: 'He was very good at straightening out problems and finding solutions in differences of opinion'—another early anticipation of one of the mature man's greatest gifts. 'However, he was not a "softie"! We could never impose our will on him.' On the contrary, physical toughness matched intellectual brilliance. 'He was a rather strong boy, outstanding in gymnastics, and while he didn't take part in our escapades we liked him', reports another school companion.

No picture of Dag Hammarskjöld's youth, however cursory, would be complete without emphasis upon life in the outdoors. We have cited Nature, along with Family and Fatherland, as the third most formative influence upon his mind and spirit. It was during his student days that love of the Swedish countryside and especially its mountains laid a hold upon his imagination which never slackened even in the years when public responsibilities anchored him far away and he managed to return to his homeland only on infrequent though cherished visits. Both his public and his private writing draw heavily upon not only observations but also lessons garnered from mountaineering.

Friends who joined him on hikes through the countryside and up into the mountains recall him as 'the best of comrades who "saw so many things" they would otherwise have missed. In the summer there was hiking and bicycling; in the winter, skiing. There was also mountain-climbing. . . . As a skier, Hammarskjöld's resources were power and endurance. He was better at going up the trail than down. His technique, while good enough to get him down the mountainside, was not superior, but, added a companion of those days: "In the evenings he could discourse on the art and technique of skiing much more beautifully than the rest of us." His sense of orientation in the mountains or countryside was uncanny. "We had a Sunday hiking club and he would map out the route so that through any wilderness, we got back to town", a friend reports. "When you were with Dag you did not need a guide", added another'*. Still another of his fellow students at Uppsala University who accompanied Hammarskjöld on camping trips to Lapland says: 'His sense of duty and industriousness did not weigh heavily upon him. . . . Amidst all his intellectualism, sense of responsibility, and idealistic enthusiasm, there was in the young Hammarskjöld something of the playful lad.'

Later, he proposed to the Swedish Tourist Association—the only organization other than the Swedish Academy in which he continued active membership after he left Sweden—the preparation of an anthology of Nature descriptions from Swedish poetry and prose which he coedited, in his own conception 'a book in which the cycle of seasons and the variety of scenery . . . wove together fragments of our literature into a picture of this country as it has been experienced by Swedes, separated in time, separated also by origin, philosophy and ambition, but joined in their ties to the soil out of which they have grown'. And, for the 75th Anniversary Meeting of the Swedish Tourist Association in 1960, he returned as its Vice-President to give the principal address entitled 'Know Yourself—Know Your World' which began with quotations from a Swedish poet expressing 'the deep roots he felt he had in his native soil and the openness towards the world beyond':

> ' ". . . I yearn for the ground,
>   I yearn for the stones where as a child I played." '**

In those youthful forays with friends, recreation and enrichment of mind were commingled. Fellow students at Uppsala, embroiled in passionate discussions over Freudianism, skepticism and other intellectual fashions of their day, report: 'Sometimes we went to fetch Hammarskjöld at the Castle to get his point of view, and in the marvelous spring evenings—as everyone knows spring evenings used to be marvelous in those days—we walked back and forth in the Odinslund Park solving problems.' Later, during the years of public service in Stockholm, a fellow economist recalls that on their hikes Hammarskjöld 'would always bring along a book, read it and then lie down for an hour to memorize and organize its contents into his mind'.

Thus there was formed a physique of great resilience and stamina

* Lash, *op. cit.*, pp. 24–25.
** *Servant of Peace*, p. 242.

which, even in the early years at the Finance Ministry, fortified him to 'work the night through' and later, at the United Nations, to carry an eighteen- to twenty-hour workday, seven days a week, weeks on end.

To Hammarskjöld, mountain climbing was far more than a source of pleasure or of physical well-being or even of intellectual comradeship. It was a shaper of character. We noted that when he landed in New York on his way to induction as Secretary-General of the United Nations and confronted the inescapable Press Conference, he fended off inquiries regarding his personal life but concluded his brief statement to the reporters with a reference to mountaineering as demanding the qualities most needed in public office.* In two papers in Swedish, he spelled out more fully the gifts of mountains to life:

'At some time all of us need tranquility and perspective. In the Swedish mountains one achieves solitude and distance, not by fleeing from reality, but by meeting a reality other than that of the workaday world.

'The mountain gives a new solitude . . . achieved in a camaraderie which it would be difficult to gain in other environments. . . .

'One gets a feeling of fear of the mountain as living nature. . . .

'The mountain gives us new, rich opportunities to know ourselves. It may expose weaknesses both of mind and body. But it can also give us proof of unexpected resources.'**

In only one major particular did Dag Hammarskjöld's life as a young man depart from the usual. While he had many women friends, 'he was not interested in girls or dancing. On Wednesday and Saturday evenings, when all the others were out dancing, "he only worked" '. Thus, there was already evident still another characteristic which remained with him and strengthened as time went on—indifference to conventional social life.

Perhaps closely related was a deeper, more inward quality which baffled some of his more sensitive and perceptive friends: 'He was already a little withdrawn, and willing to extend intimacy to no one outside his family.' 'He was a good fellow, but not one with whom to get intimate.' What even these friends appear not to have recognized

* See above, p. 6.
** *The Light and the Rock: The Vision of Dag Hammarskjöld*, edited by T. S. Settel (New York: E. P. Dutton & Co., Inc., 1966), pp. 66 and 62.

was that this inner solitariness was as much a problem to him as to them, a source of bafflement which was to haunt him throughout his life. They did not realize that, with all his facility in public, his great achievements, and his outgoing friendliness, Hammarskjöld harbored a gnawing loneliness, rooted in unconquerable shyness. In later retrospect, one of them rightly diagnosed: 'He carried an inner world within him, to whose echoes he listened eagerly, but about which he seldom found opportunity to speak.'

Thus, from Dag Hammarskjöld's early years emerges a young man of aristocratic lineage, reared from infancy in a family tradition on both sides for generations of service to Nation and Church and unquestioningly faithful to that heritage, gifted by nature with an intellect of exceptional power and developed through relentless discipline to its highest potential, with a physique toughened by exacting hardihood to sustain well-nigh unbelievable mental concentration and indomitable resolution, interests already reaching forth to embrace almost every facet of human culture across the ages and across the world, among his contemporaries a natural leader in both thought and action whose unassuming modesty somewhat masked strength of conviction and firmness of will, universally respected and, by some, revered, full partner in friends' recreations and pastimes save only their more frivolous diversions, yet withal the core of his being shielded by an impenetrable reserve from any who might presume a closer intimacy. Family and friends were well aware of the reserve; few if any had any inkling of its deeper and true cause.

III · 'ROAD MARKS'

Käre Leif,

Kanske du minns att jag än gång berättade för dig
att jag trots allt förde en sorts dagbok som jag ville att
du en gång skulle ta hand om. Här är den.

Den påbörjades utan tanke på att någon skulle få se den.
Med mina senare öden, med allt som skrivits och sagts om
mig har läget förändrats. Anteckningarna ger den enda riktiga
"profile" som kan tecknas. Och därför har jag under senare år
räknat med publicitet, ehuru jag fortsatt att skriva för mig
själv och icke för publik.

Om du finner dem förtjäna att tryckas har du rätt att göra
så - som en sorts "vitbok" rörande mina förhandlingar med
mig själv - och Gud.

D⌐

Dear Leif:

Perhaps you may remember I once told you that, in spite of everything, I kept a diary which I wanted you to take charge of someday.
Here it is.

It was begun without a thought of anybody else reading it. But,
what with my later history and all that has been said and written
about me, the situation has changed. These entries provide the only
true "profile" that can be drawn. That is why, during recent years,
I have reckoned with the possibility of publication, though I have
continued to write for myself, not for the public.

If you find them worth publishing, you have my permission to do
so—as a sort of white book concerning my negotiations with myself—
and with God.

Dag

THE FINDING of Dag Hammarskjöld's spiritual testament was in this fashion. Within a few days after his death, in fulfillment of a request which he had made during his lifetime, Per Lind who had accompanied Hammarskjöld as his Aide when he first came to the United Nations in 1953 flew across from Stockholm to New York, together with Hammarskjöld's legal adviser, to take charge of his personal effects and private papers. Most of these were in the spacious apartment on East 73d Street.

In due course, Lind and the attorney came to Hammarskjöld's bedroom. In the drawer of a small table next to his bed was a buff-colored clipfolder, discolored with age and much handling. Fastened to the top of the folder by a paperclip was a small envelope of United Nations Secretariat stationery on which was typed 'Leif Belfrage' and, in the lower lefthand corner, was written in Swedish 'Personligt', that is 'Personal'.

The folder with envelope affixed exactly as found was taken back to Sweden and handed to Dr. Leif Belfrage who had been Hammarskjöld's colleague in the Swedish Foreign Service and close friend for many years and was now in the post which Hammarskjöld had held a dozen years before as Permanent Under-Secretary for Foreign Affairs. The envelope contained a single sheet of blank paper on which had been typed in Swedish a twelve-line note; it was undated.*

Belfrage recalled that, several years earlier when Hammarskjöld had been staying with him in Stockholm, his guest had mentioned that he was keeping a sort of diary and that he wanted Belfrage to take charge of it someday. However, nothing was said of its character or contents.

Belfrage naturally assumed that the folder contained something in

* A facsimile and English translation are given on p. 30, opposite.

the nature of a political diary. It is not difficult to imagine his amazement when, on turning the cover of the folder, he saw that the first page was captioned 'Vägmärken' and that there followed about 175 pages of carefully typed 'entries' setting forth the author's private reflections over a period of more than thirty-six years.

Such were the circumstances of the 'discovery' of one of the most remarkable manuscripts of our day, if not of any day.

ii

Hammarskjöld's Vägmärken embrace just over six hundred individual 'notes' of varying length, from a single phrase to a page and a half, differing greatly in form and subject matter, mostly in stark prose, some in blank verse, toward the end a large number in the pattern of Japanese haiku* which had come to intrigue the author's imagination, the collection in its entirety treating of the whole gamut of themes which claimed his interest—from delight in natural beauty and excitement in hazardous sport to merciless scrutiny of interior motives, from caustic exposure of unreality and hypocrisy in others' conduct to unflinching confession of his own inconsistency and self-concern, from direct comment upon events of world import to a charming 'Elegy' on the death of a pet monkey. And yet, with all the wide sweep and variety of these meditations, they are held in unity by two dominant objectives: the achievement of absolute self-honesty and of a life-commanding faith.

Happily, Hammarskjöld has provided his own interpretation of the origin and intention of his writing. In a Christmas meditation he said:

'These notes?—They were signposts you began to set up after you had reached a point where you needed them, a fixed point that was on no account to be lost sight of.'**

The figure is from Hammarskjöld's experience in climbing. A not inappropriate translation of the Swedish title Vägmärken might be 'Trail Marks'. ' "Cairns"—the piles of stones that a climber leaves to mark his progress on an uncharted mountain', a reviewer who was an

* See below, p. 162 ff.
** Markings, p. 144.

associate of Hammarskjöld at the United Nations has aptly described them.* They were recorded to provide guidance for the author should he pass that way again. To be sure, with the passage of time, he began to play with the thought that someday these private reminders for his own memory might fall under the eyes of others. The 'marking' just quoted goes on to suggest that possibility:

> 'And so they have remained. But your life has changed, and now you reckon with possible readers, even, perhaps, hope for them.** Still, perhaps it may be of interest to somebody to learn about a path about which the traveler who was committed to it did not wish to speak while he was alive.'

And then, with the relentless compunction which never failed him, he adds:

> 'Perhaps—but only if what you write has an honesty with no trace of vanity or self-regard.'

Indeed, he had begun this entry not without misgiving:

> 'You ask yourself if these notes are not, after all, false to the very Way they are intended to mark.'

Nevertheless, there is no alteration of mood or manner, no evidence of sidelong glances in the direction of 'possible readers', no concession whatever to their interest or understanding, above all no shielding or suppression of what is uncomplimentary to himself.

iii

So much the printed text tells us of the nature and purpose of these 'Road Marks'. At once the question arises: does the original manuscript of Vägmärken yield any revealing and significant clues as to when and how its contents were recorded and the circumstances of their composition? The answer is affirmative.

In the first place, the entire manuscript was typed by Hammarskjöld himself, on an ancient machine which he had kept in his

---

* Brian Urquhart in The New Yorker, Oct. 31, 1964, p. 237.
** Hammarskjöld appears to have forgotten that, four years earlier, at a period of acute crisis in his life, he had contemplated that possibility: '. . . Why should you write down all this, for yourself, to be sure—perhaps, though, for others as well?' [87]

apartment for his own use over many years. So far as can be learned, no human eyes had seen a page of it. Indeed, no one was aware of its existence.

While the pages are of uniform size, they show varying degrees of discoloring by age and there are marked contrasts in the sharpness of the imprint.* Only careful scrutiny by an expert could establish conclusive proof, but the evidence is strong that the manuscript in its final version had been completed over a considerable period, probably at least several years.

Furthermore, it is clear that Hammarskjöld took his manuscript with great seriousness, as indeed he did all his writing. The methodical arrangement of the material, the careful dating of all entries by years and, after April 1953, of many by specific dates, the explicit provision for publication 'if you find them worth publishing', especially his description of 'these entries' as 'the only true "profile" that can be drawn'—all these are not only a faithful reflection of the man's mind; they furnish proof beyond challenge of the importance he himself attached to what he was recording.

Hammarskjöld was a poet by temperament and inclination and in his own right. Very early in his United Nations Secretary-Generalship, he confessed to his artist friend Bo Beskow in an intimate note: 'I dream of private writing down at Hagestad [his rural retreat near Malmo in southern Sweden] after the five year fight here. Then, if not before—!' Several years later, he reiterated the same hope: 'I think often of your stained glass windows and your work with the eternal problems of the space of the canvas. I hope to still have enough of patience, humility and stillness left when one day I am allowed to turn back to a life along these lines. Then perhaps I shall be able to say in the right way something of what should be said.' But, since public responsibilities pre-empted virtually every hour of every day, the only writing of the kind he longed to do was in these strictly private notes. That furnished the mood of their composition.

Presumably, most if not all of the individual entries were originally written in longhand, probably in the greenish-blue ink which has been rightly identified as Hammarskjöld's 'scriptorial trademark'. An

---

* For example, on the very first page, while the text of the 'markings' it records is very faded, the dates '1925–1930' are in strong black, indicating almost certainly that they had been added at a much later time. Again, the entries on the third page (page 7 of *Markings*) are in much bolder black than the pages which precede and follow, suggesting likewise that this single page was typed, or perhaps retyped, and inserted later.

Aide recalls noticing that Hammarskjöld was writing poetry while they were flying toward the Middle East, but was too diffident to speak of it.

All were carefully preserved in chronological sequence. At some point, perhaps many years later than the earlier entries, he began to transfer them to typescript. It is possible that the December 1956 date when he first 'reckoned with possible readers' may also mark the time both when he made mention of them so casually to Leif Belfrage, for he was on home leave in Sweden a few days thereafter, and when he began the typing. In any event, it seems likely that in this process, he may have discarded much, retaining only what he himself considered worthy and important for his own memory.*

One further bit of evidence of immense importance, the manuscript appears to yield. The suggestion has been advanced that Hammarskjöld had a premonition of a violent end; and the attempt has been made to justify this assumption on the basis of several 'markings' dated in the summer before his death. Were the assumption correct, it is almost unthinkable that Hammarskjöld would not have brought his writing to a consciously planned conclusion, certainly entering at the end what he would wish to leave as a last testament. On the contrary, the manuscript as found was obviously open-ended. It gave every indication of having been placed in its accustomed place in his bedside table, just as he was in the habit of leaving it on each of his many departures on journeys abroad. The last entry happens to bear a date just two weeks before he flew to the Congo; there is nothing distinctive or definitive about it. And alongside the folder was a pile of blank sheets of paper and pencils, as though anticipating a resumption of writing on his return.

iv

Almost casually, in contrast to the obvious care with which Hammarskjöld had prepared his manuscript across the years, the covering letter left decision as to its release to the public entirely to Leif

* W. H. Auden offers 'the most plausible guess' that Hammarskjöld may at the same time have rewritten many entries and added some entirely new ones under dates long past. In my judgment, the evidence from the manuscript appears to be against that assumption. I believe that 'the most plausible guess' is that, with possibly a few minor exceptions, the individual 'markings' which Hammarskjöld recorded in type are exactly as they had been composed, often many years earlier.

Belfrage's judgment: 'If you find them worth publishing, you have my permission to do so—. . . .'

It was not an easy decision. When, after consultation, publication seemed the only right course, there was the question of editing. Should some of the more intimate or more agonized self-disclosures be omitted or altered? It was Dr. Belfrage's firm resolve that the book should appear in its entirety exactly as the author had left it. There is even close approximation in the paging. The English edition, with a few relatively unimportant errors in transcription, likewise reproduces the original text with meticulous fidelity.

V

Much has been made of the fact that Hammarskjöld's 'Road Marks' contain 'not . . . a single direct reference to his career as an international civil servant, to the persons he met, or the historical events of his time. . . .*

Why should they? They were intended solely for the writer's own recollection and instruction; he knew well enough to what and to whom they referred. No 'direct reference', but countless allusions both to persons and to events, many of which can be confidently established.

Indeed, the book itself provides guideposts to those occasions. Through the first quarter century of writing, Hammarskjöld dated his 'markings' first by groups of years and later by individual years. Then, early in 1953 appears for the first time a specific date. There follows a period of almost two years when no precise indication of time of composition is given. But, near the end of 1954, Hammarskjöld again entered a definite date. Thenceforward until his death nearly seven years later, increasingly he placed specific dates over individual or groups of 'markings.' They number close to a hundred. To be sure, he prepared no calendar or index indicating what circumstance or encounter had stimulated his comments. Why should he? He knew what the dates represented.

However, through day-by-day comparison of his datings with his travel calendars, occasions of special significance in his public career, his published writings, and days of particular meaning in his private life, we are enabled to identify many of the occasions and settings

* W. H. Auden in the 'Foreword' to *Markings*, p. vii.

which prompted his reflections. Thereby they stand forth in revealing illumination.*

For example, dates and, in a particularly interesting section of the book, place-headings often indicate the locus of composition when he was absent from his New York headquarters—at his Swedish country home on his fiftieth birthday, on a plane between New York and London on New Year's Eve, in Rome on the third anniversary of his United Nations election, in Cairo near the crux of the Suez Crisis, at the Gaza Strip during a visit to United Nations troops at Christmastime, at 'Uppsala', along the 'Hudson Valley' in the spring.

Far more important, it thus becomes clear that many 'Road Marks' were staked down in direct reaction to specific events in Hammarskjöld's professional life; unquestionably, the explicit dates were entered to remind the author of the particular occasions.** The public career furnished the enveloping frame for the delineation of this 'profile'.

Indeed, beyond its astonishing intrinsic worth, just here lies the marvel of this work—that reflections on life and destiny, fate and faith, which would merit enduring recognition had they issued from monastic retreat and prolonged meditation, were, in fact, hammered out during the contemporary world's most urgent business. The result is, in Auden's words, 'an historical document of the first importance as an account—and I cannot myself recall another—of the attempt by a professional man to unite in one life the *via activa* and the *via contemplativa'*—two sides of a single self-consistent person. Hammarskjöld himself declares the secret: 'In our era, the road to holiness necessarily passes through the world of action.'† His life is the proof. His 'Road Marks' are the evidence.

vi

On October 18, 1964, and in the days and weeks immediately following, the front page of virtually every weekly Review of Books and the lead column on the Books page of almost every newspaper

---

* See 'Appendix: Correlation of Dag Hammarskjöld's *Markings* and Events of His Public and Private Life', pp. 223 ff.

** No less revealing are his recorded responses to anniversaries and other days of special meaning in his private life. See below, p. 223.

† *Markings*, p. 122, year-end, 1955.

and magazine in the United States were given over to this volume bearing the unpromising and somewhat mystifying title *Markings*. The reading public was not wholly unprepared for its appearance. The previous June, two American journals with large circulations had printed articles based upon the Swedish original of the book.* The first quoted at length from predominantly unfavorable Scandinavian reviews. The second, purporting to be based on personal acquaintance, gave vent to highly subjective, embittered exposures of the man. Neither was calculated to commend the book or encourage favorable expectations.

Clearly, neither reviewers nor reading public was prepared for its contents. *Markings* was instantly hailed as 'an extraordinary spirit-troubling document', 'a work so remarkable in its sheer unremarkableness, so fulfilled in its reticences and omissions that its value as self-portraiture is outstanding', 'an astonishing glimpse into the other-worldly aspirations of the man', 'a dramatic and fascinating account of one man's solitary effort to know himself and to order his life accordingly . . . a very private picture of a very public man', 'a kind of wisdom literature . . . a moving legacy of an extraordinary man's meditations in the "last dark hour of the night" ', 'the inner history of a religious quest', 'the remarkable record left us by this very remarkable man', 'one of the most unusual volumes in many a literary season', 'a truly remarkable document'.

No one, not even the publishers, was prepared for the book's reception. One of the weekly journals of widest distribution had declined the offer of magazine rights because the editors who read the manuscript 'concluded that the style and message were too subtle, if not actually obscure, for successful excerpting in a magazine article.' Yet, within a few months of publication, several popular magazines did print selections of excerpts.

The initial modest printing of 13,000 copies was exhausted within a few days of publication. For weeks thereafter, at the height of the Christmas buying season, in some localities it was virtually impossible to find a copy in most bookstores. Repeated reprintings were unable to overtake the demand. Two months after publishing date, it was in its tenth printing; yet *Time* reported: 'This disturbing book is so in

---

* 'Clues to the Hammarskjöld Riddle' by Oliver Clausen, *The New York Times Sunday Magazine*, June 28, 1964; 'The Secret Life of Dag Hammarskjöld' by John Linberg, *Look*, June 30, 1964.

demand that it is out of stock across most of the U.S.' By then, *Markings* had speedily climbed up all lists of 'Non-fiction Best-sellers' to the top position, and remained there through the next eight months—an impressive if not unparalleled record, certainly for a book of this type. In less than a year, its distribution exceeded 250,000 copies; ten months later, this figure was approaching half a million. Dr. Charles Malik of the Lebanon could report without exaggeration six months after the book's appearance: 'The publication of *Markings* was, in the world of the United Nations and in the general international world, an event of first importance. It turned out also to be quite a sensational event in the religious world and in the literary world of confessions and autobiographies.'*

How are we to account for this public response?

To be sure, one might have anticipated that *any* writing by so outstanding a public figure as Dag Hammarskjöld would claim a wide interest. When the character of *Markings'* contents became known, this may have provoked the curiosity of some potential readers, although it almost certainly alienated others. The spate of laudatory reviews undoubtedly had some influence in encouraging purchases. But none of these factors, nor all of them together, can adequately explain the phenomenal circulation. In the perspective of its first six months, an exceptionally discerning full-length conspectus of the volume and what it reveals of its author turned at the end to the mystery of its popularity: 'The public response has been as extraordinary as the book itself. Best-sellers attract all manner of readers, but unquestionably the number of people who have been stirred by this book must be very, very great.' Then, dismissing 'W. H. Auden's condescending, school-teacherish introduction', the writer concludes: 'Not Auden, not the reviews that present the reader with variations on his themes, have slowed the wide, ever-growing acceptance of this book.'**

Moreover, *Markings* presents almost every reader with baffling, for some insurmountable, obstacles. Many readers appear to have found themselves estopped by its early pages, or to have dipped into it here and there without better success, and to have laid it aside 'for later reading' which often never materializes. It is not one of the book's

* In *The Critic*, April–May, 1965, pp. 74–77.
** Max Ascoli, 'On Reading Hammarskjöld', *The Reporter*, May 20, 1965, pp. 37–40.

scornful critics but one of its most enthusiastic devotees who has hazarded the guess that 'Markings is probably the most widely purchased and little read volume in American homes today, except the Bible'!

It has been generally assumed that perplexities arise principally from obscurities in Hammarskjöld's thought or opaqueness in his writing. For the most part, this is not the case. Any reader, equipped with understanding of the person and purpose for which the book was intended and with knowledge of the circumstances of composition of the individual entries, should find most of them readily intelligible.

Again, some interpreters have sought to portray Dag Hammarskjöld as a dual personality, almost schizophrenic, and to suggest an impassable gulf between the man of the world, the man of affairs whose public image was familiar to all mankind, and the inner person, the man of faith who stands forth in this book self-disclosed.

Definitive disproof of such a split in the man is implicit in the circumstances of composition. When, where and how were these 'signposts' staked down? During the latter years of his United Nations service, the great bulk almost certainly were recorded in the silence of his office atop the United Nations Headquarters or in the seclusion of his New York apartment during early morning hours snatched after a typical eighteen- or twenty-hour working day.

One is driven to the conclusion that, despite the obstacles, thousands of readers have found in this unusual book something unexpected and profound which speaks in a unique way to their own interior life. It has been well said that it has proven 'all things to all people'. Nevertheless, perhaps hundreds of thousands who have heard of Markings have been led to possess a copy to have at hand, even though little read, in the hope that someday, somehow, they might be guided into a fuller understanding. The intention of this small volume is to attempt to lead toward that understanding.

vii

One further preliminary question, often asked: Why did Hammarskjöld wish to maintain such determined privacy regarding this writing and what it records, which has encouraged sensational references to his 'hidden' and even his 'secret' life?

The answer is to be found basically in the fact that, with all of his gifts not least for human comradeship, he was from earliest youth and continued to the end a painfully reserved person, his deepest and true self withdrawn within an unconquerable diffidence. He himself was fully alive to this. To a friend with whom he shared much spiritual kinship, he wrote: 'How frightful our poverty is when we try to give others something of ourselves. . . . Even in a non-egocentric sense there is . . . an inability to live in such a way that others may know what they can count upon in us. . . . To me the ineradicable shyness of this morning is a curse, and the conventional, awkward conversation a lie.'*

In the matter of his religious convictions and aspirations, this ingrained apartness was doubtless aggravated by the circumstance to which the same friend points: 'He was surrounded by companions who for the most part were spiritually and religiously unawakened, and to whom he had to speak in another language—a language foreign to his soul.'** Thus, habits of reticence regarding things of the spirit, formed early, were maintained. In his mature years of world eminence and responsibilities, he was continuously occupied with public matters involving controversy. Probably, he did not wish to expose himself to questioning and discussion on his most private concerns.

Moreover, as we shall see, once he had uttered what mattered to him most in a concise review of his soul's pilgrimage, and in the most public possible circumstances, on an American national radio program. There it was, for anyone to hear. Why need he say more?

* Sven Stolpe, *Dag Hammarskjöld: A Spiritual Portrait* (New York: Charles Scribner's Sons, 1966), pp. 46–47.
** *Ibid.*, p. 31. Cf. below, p. 61. In private talks with a score of Dag Hammarskjöld's Swedish friends, I was astounded to note how many of them opened our conversation, in the most casual and friendly fashion, with the statement: 'Of course, I'm an atheist.' or 'You realize that I am an atheist?' Probably, their religious attitude would be more often characterized in the Anglo-Saxon world as 'agnostic' or even 'humanist'. But 'atheist' was the word they unfailingly used. No wonder Hammarskjöld kept his religious interest and convictions strictly to himself.

IV · THE PILGRIMAGE

Introduction: Hammarskjöld's Credo

DAG HAMMARSKJÖLD UNDERSTOOD not only the wellsprings of his mature conviction but, no less, the logic of his own pilgrimage to that goal.

Once during his lifetime, Hammarskjöld had lifted the curtain which shrouded his private spiritual struggle and its outcome from even his most intimate associates—only once, to be sure, but on that occasion with such candor and clarity that he who runs might read.

As already reported, in late 1953, not long after he came to New York as United Nations Secretary-General, Hammarskjöld appeared on a radio program arranged by Edward R. Murrow. This talk, subsequently published in a volume entitled *This I Believe*, was reprinted most appropriately as a sort of 'Foreword' to Hammarskjöld's published speeches and statements.*

Hammarskjöld gave his statement the caption 'Old Creeds in a New World'. He took its preparation with even more than his customary seriousness; close colleagues at the United Nations recall that he submitted at least three preliminary drafts for their critical comment and suggestions. And, to Bo Beskow in Sweden, he wrote a year later: 'The pages of "This I Believe" that you happened to see are not polite statements but deeply engaged, partly in self-criticism.'

This brief affirmation is the most appropriate 'introduction' to the mind and soul and career of Dag Hammarskjöld. No more than a page and a half in length, it is beyond question one of the most

* *Servant of Peace*, pp. 23–24. It was also published in Great Britain in *The British Weekly* but, apparently, not in Sweden. However, it was widely known in Scandinavia. The *credo* is given in full on pp. 46–47.

OLD CREEDS IN A NEW WORLD

The world in which I grew up was dominated by principles and ideals of a time far from ours and, as it may seem, far removed from the problems facing a man of the middle of the twentieth century. However, my way has not meant a departure from those ideals. On the contrary, I have been led to an understanding of their validity also for our world of today. Thus, a never abandoned effort frankly and squarely to build up a personal belief in the light of experience and honest thinking has led me in a circle; I now recognize and endorse, unreservedly, those very beliefs which were once handed down to me.

From generations of soldiers and government officials on my father's side I inherited a belief that no life was more satisfactory than one of selfless service to your country—or humanity. This service required a sacrifice of all personal interests, but likewise the courage to stand up unflinchingly for your convictions.

From scholars and clergymen on my mother's side I inherited a belief that, in the very radical sense of the Gospels, all men were equals as children of God, and should be met and treated by us as our masters in God.

Faith is a state of the mind and the soul. In this sense we can understand the words of the Spanish mystic, St. John of the Cross: 'Faith is the union of God with the soul.' The language of religion is a set of formulas which register a basic spiritual experience. It must not be regarded as describing, in terms to be defined by philosophy, the reality which is accessible to our senses and which we can analyse with the tools of logic. I was late in understanding what this meant. When I finally reached that point, the beliefs in which I was once brought up and which, in fact, had given my life direction even while my intellect still challenged their validity, were recognized by me as mine in their own right and by my free choice. I feel that I can endorse those convictions without any compromise with the demands of that intellectual honesty which is the very key to maturity of mind.

The two ideals which dominated my childhood world met me fully harmonized and adjusted to the demands of our world of today in the ethics of Albert Schweitzer, where the ideal of service is supported by and supports the basic attitude to man set forth in the Gospels. In his work I also found a key for modern man to the world of the Gospels.

But the explanation of how man should live a life of active social service in full harmony with himself as a member of the community of the spirit, I found in the writings of those great medieval mystics for whom 'self-surrender' had been the way to self-realization, and who in 'singleness of mind' and 'inwardness' had found strength to say yes to every demand which the needs of their neighbors made them face, and to say yes also to every fate life had in store for them when they followed the call of duty, as they understood it. Love— that much misused and misinterpreted word—for them meant simply an overflowing of the strength with which they felt themselves filled when living in true self-oblivion. And this love found natural expressions in an unhesitant fulfillment of duty and in an unreserved acceptance of life, whatever it brought them personally of toil, suffering—or happiness.

I know that their discoveries about the laws of inner life and of action have not lost their significance.

notable personal confessions uttered in our day—humbling in its unashamed frankness, startling in the acuteness and accuracy of its self-knowledge, invaluable in its piercing illumination of the inmost thoughts and certitudes of this usually reticent person. Indeed, those who found themselves amazed at the depth and centrality of religious faith disclosed in his posthumous 'Road Marks'—and they include members of his own family, his closest colleagues and most intimate friends as well as the general public—were really without excuse in their surprise. It is all set forth, though to be sure in firmly compressed summary, in this talk. But, although it was widely heard and even more widely read on both sides of the Atlantic, almost no one appears to have taken it with the seriousness which its author attributed to it or to have recognized that *here* was laid bare the true Dag Hammarskjöld. It was, in effect, a *précis*, an anticipation of the full-length 'profile' in 'Road Marks'—the stark skeleton of belief clothed with flesh and blood in the book.

Hammarskjöld began his address by stressing the contrast between presuppositions prevailing during his youth and the outlook of the world of today:

'The world in which I grew up was dominated by principles and ideals of a time far from ours and, as it may see, far removed from the problems facing a man of the middle of the twentieth century. However, my way has not meant a departure from those ideals. On the contrary, I have been led to an understanding of their validity also for our world of today. Thus, a never abandoned effort frankly and squarely to build up a personal belief in the light of experience and honest thinking has led me in a circle; I now recognize and endorse, unreservedly, those very beliefs which were once handed down to me.'

He then pays filial tribute to his dual inheritance which we have already quoted in examining his debtorship to his parents.* These were the two controlling guidelines which determined Hammarskjöld's life and career: selfless service to the commonweal at whatever cost to personal interests and reverence for all men. His life and career were, in a very real sense, an incarnation of these two basic recognitions.

However, when Hammarskjöld declared that his thought had

* Cf. above, pp. 12, 18.

THE YOUTHFUL
DAG HAMMARSKJÖLD

Swimming with a friend; Dag on right, age
eleven. *Wide World Photos*

The four Hammarskjöld brothers, 1920: Bo, Dag (age fifteen), Åke and
Sten. *Wide World Photos*

FIRST MAJOR DIPLOMATIC MISSION
FOR THE UNITED NATIONS

Dag Hammarskjöld with Chou En-lai in Peking, January 1955. *United Nations*

MOUNTAINEERING

On Mt. Ruapehu in New Zealand, with George Ivan Smith, February 1956. *United Nations*

ON HOLIDAY

At Hammarskjöld's country home, Skånegard, southern Sweden. *Wide World Photos*

At left, Bill Ranallo, Hammarskjöld's bodyguard. *Svenska Turistföreningen*

THE LAST MISSION
THE CONGO

Welcomed by Moise Tshombe, Premier of Katanga Province, Elizabethville, August 1960. *Wide World Photos*

Guest of Honor at dinner given by Cyrille Adoula, Premier of the Central Government of the Congo, September 1961, four days before Hammarskjöld's death. *U.P.I. Photos*

come full circle, his self-interpretation was not strictly accurate. Its movement might more properly be likened to a spiral; his conviction returned to substantially the same basic certitudes, but at a higher level. In his final faith, there is hardly a discoverable trace either of the faith of his fathers, the rather rigid scholastic Swedish Lutheranism in which he had been reared and in which he must have been instructed before Confirmation into membership in the Church of Sweden, or of the evangelical piety of his mother which furnished the more intimate spiritual environment of his early years. As he himself confesses in later paragraphs of his *credo*, his principal tutor on the return path from sophisticated skepticism to an enlightened and mature Christian Faith was Albert Schweitzer:

'The two ideals which dominated my childhood world met me fully harmonized and adjusted to the demands of our world of today in the ethics of Albert Schweitzer, where the ideal of service is supported by and supports the basic attitude to man set forth in the Gospels. In his work I also found a key for modern man to the world of the Gospels.'

And his spirit was nourished in the enlargement and enrichment of that faith:

'. . . in the writings of those great medieval mystics for whom "self-surrender" had been the way to self-realization, and who in "singleness of mind" and "inwardness" had found strength to say *yes* to every demand which the needs of their neighbors made them face, and to say *yes* also to every fate life had in store for them when they followed the call of duty, as they understood it. Love—that much misused and misinterpreted word—for them meant simply an overflowing of the strength with which they felt themselves filled when living in true self-oblivion. And this love found natural expressions in an unhesitant fulfillment of duty and in an unreserved acceptance of life, whatever it brought them personally of toil, suffering —or happiness.

'I know that their discoveries about the laws of inner life and of action have not lost their significance.'

On this statement, he added a commentary in a private letter to Beskow:

'The last part says what I would say today: the counterpoint to this enormously exposed and public life is Eckhart and Jan van Ruysbroek. They really give me balance and—a more and more necessary sense of humor. My salvation here is "to take the job damned seriously but never the incumbent"—but it has its difficulties. The roads to a foundation that in the strongest sense is religious can be the most unexpected.'

In sum, the seedplot of the faith of the mature man he rightly identified as 'those very beliefs which were once handed down to me'. However, from that foundation there had slowly taken shape a far more sophisticated and far richer, a more subtle and more comprehensively classical Christian experience and certitude.

The heart of Hammarskjöld's *credo* is in its middle paragraph. After quoting the words of the Spanish mystic, St. John of the Cross: 'Faith is the union of God with the soul', he goes on:

'I was late in understanding what this meant. When I finally reached that point, the beliefs in which I was once brought up and which, in fact, had given my life direction even while my intellect still challenged their validity, were recognized by me as mine in their own right and by my free choice. I feel that I can endorse those convictions without any compromise with the demands of that intellectual honesty which is the very key to maturity of mind.'

This, then, marked the termination of Dag Hammarskjöld's spiritual pilgrimage. But the way thither was long and tortuous, marked by acute crises and agonizing inner struggle, in his own favorite figure climbing to heights of exhilarating vision and bracing exaltation but also passing through depths of debilitating darkness, depression and near-despair.

1. *The Starting Point:*
1925–1930

It was in 1925 that the phenomenally gifted Uppsala University student, having completed his bachelor's degree the previous year at the early age of nineteen and continuing on at once toward a *filialia* in economics and later a Bachelor of Laws, began the practice of noting down brief comments, some in free verse, others in prose, recording for his own future use his private inner reflections.

From his meditations during the five years of graduate study before he left Uppsala to settle with his parents in Stockholm, Hammarskjöld preserved only fifteen 'markings'. Over them, the author, probably much later, put the caption: *'Thus it was'*. To a striking degree, these earliest notes anticipated the main themes of what was to follow. They suggest the character of his 'Road Marks'. And they reveal the preoccupations of his thought and the state of his soul at the outset of his spiritual pilgrimage.

The very first entry established the mood for the whole:

> 'I am being driven forward
> Into an unknown land. . . .
>
> Shall I ever get there?
> There where life resounds,
> A clear pure note
> In the silence.' (5)

As one turns the page, the next two entries introduce themes which are to recur over and over again—'sacrifice' and 'death':

[51

'Smiling, sincere, incorruptible—
His body disciplined and limber.
A man who had become what he could,
And was what he was—
Ready at any moment to gather everything
Into one simple sacrifice.' [6]

*

'Tomorrow we shall meet,
Death and I—
And he shall thrust his sword
Into one who is wide awake.'

Typically, this self-accusation is added:

'But in the meantime how grievous the memory
Of hours frittered away.' [6]

To an Anglo-Saxon, certainly to an American mind, meditation upon death by a healthy and highly successful young man in his early twenties may appear morose, even morbid; yet this is only the first in a numerous sequence of comments on death. Such reaction is to forget the Nordic temperament, illustrated by the writings of Ibsen and Strindberg and, in our own day, by the films of Bergman. Few Scandinavians seem surprised or troubled by what some Western readers have called 'Hammarskjöld's preoccupation with death'. A spirited and gay young Swedish university graduate comments: 'Death is what we talked about all the time!'

Toward the end of these introductory 'Road Marks', two other persistent notes sound for the first time—'loneliness' and 'guilt':

'. . . Friendship needs no words—it is solitude delivered from the anguish of loneliness.' [8]

'We carry our nemesis within us: yesterday's self-admiration is the legitimate father of today's feeling of guilt.' [9]

It would be a mistake to suppose that such solemn themes are the only ones. There is also a delicate sensitivity to beauty, including bodily charm:

'Beauty: a note that set the heartstrings quivering as it flew by; the shimmer of the blood beneath a skin translucent in the sunlight.

Beauty: the wind which refreshed the traveler, not the stifling heat in dark adits where beggars grubbed for gold.'[7]

Also, lessons distilled from mountain climbing:

'Never measure the height of a mountain, until you have reached the top. Then you will see how low it was.' [7]

However, the major stress falls on the personal quest for authentic selfhood:

'What you have to attempt—to be yourself. What you have to pray for—to become a mirror in which, according to the degree of purity of heart you have attained, the greatness of life will be reflected.' [8]

'Life only demands from you the strength you possess. Only one feat is possible—not to have run away.' [8]

The reflections of those first five years conclude on the note of merciless self-scrutiny to ferret out unreality and hypocrisy:

'He bore failure without self-pity, and success without self-admiration. Provided he knew he had paid his uttermost farthing, what did it matter to him how others judged the result.

A Pharisee? Lord, thou knowest he has never been righteous in his own eyes.' [9]

Taken together, these few lines sketch a sharp profile of the youth on the threshold of manhood, but also a forecast of the mature person who is to take definitive shape across the years.

2. The Silent Decade:
1930–1940

Then there was silence for more than a decade.

In 1930, when Hammarskjöld, twenty-five, accompanied his parents to Stockholm, his private writing suddenly ceased; or, at least, we have no record of meditations composed during this period.

This change of locus came at an opportune time for him. He had decided to put aside work on a doctorate which he was subsequently to complete at the University of Stockholm.

Almost immediately, he was drafted into Government service as secretary of a Royal Commission on Unemployment, the first in a series of appointments which were to occupy him through the next twenty years. At once he found himself associated with a group of brilliant young economists known as the 'Stockholm School'; while not its originator, Dag Hammarskjöld has been credited with serving as its organizer and certainly a moving spirit. The 'School' derived much of its inspiration and controlling ideas from the British economist, John Maynard Keynes, whose epoch-making *A Treatise on Money* had recently appeared. During this period, Hammarskjöld spent some time at Cambridge and studied under Keynes.

His work for the Royal Commission accomplished a double purpose. His contribution to its Report served also as his doctoral dissertation, entitled 'The Spread of Boom and Depression'. Custom required a public defense of the thesis against two opponents, one selected by the Faculty, the other nominated by the candidate. In this instance, the debate continued to the maximum time limit of six hours. The faculty appointed Gunnar Myrdal, one of the most gifted among the 'Stockholm School's' rising young economists who had recently begun a teaching career at the university, and later was to become internationally famous for his studies of the American Negro, as Executive Secretary of the European Economic Commission of the United Nations, and in countless other capacities. Hammarskjöld chose Karin Kock, subsequently Sweden's first woman cabinet minister. Both 'adversaries' became friends and associates. Another friend, not an economist, who was present at the defense noted in his diary: 'It was the most subtle debate I ever heard . . . a brilliant performance.' But another auditor commented that Hammarskjöld argued 'with transparent opacity'. Hammarskjöld himself was apparently profoundly dissatisfied. To the friend who had been so impressed and wrote to congratulate him, he replied:

'I don't share your opinion of the debate; from an intellectual point of view it was just a circus, with a dialectical tight-rope act as the main item. The ritual seemed to me morally inferior. . . .
'I disagree with you even more strongly about the intellectual level of us economists. What may support your impression is the extroversion, the ease in public, which results from training in political discussion and administration and which gives economists the air of intellectual strength. I believe that as *scholars* the students of science are, generally speaking, of better material, though they lack the surface polish that would enable them to do themselves justice. But this view arises from my hostility to certain features of economics, and I am therefore rather suspicious of it.'

Surely, a remarkably candid and dispassionate comment from one just launched upon the career of an economist. In any event, Hammarskjöld's dissertation was marked *cum laude*, not the highest and expected distinction of *laudatur*. This must have been a disappointment to one accustomed to supreme academic achievement. In the view of some friends, this may have turned him away from a scholarly vocation. It appears more probable that his intentions were already committed to a career of public service in which he had made an impressive beginning.

The somewhat disparaging charge of 'opacity' in Hammarskjöld's public presentation needs to be corrected by the judgment of two senior colleagues. Ivar Rooth, head of the Bank of Sweden of which

Hammarskjöld now became secretary, said: 'It was only when he was talking pure theory that he could be a bit obscure; but his speeches in the Bank and to the Cabinet were if anything models of clarity.' Ernst Wigforss, under whom he was shortly to work in the Ministry of Finance, corroborated this appraisal: 'His ability to give clear and concise explanations of the essentials of a matter made it a pleasure to listen to him—provided you were alert and interested enough to follow his argument; but it was in some way analogous to the study of mathematical truths: if you had not undertood what came before, you got very little out of what followed.' And Erik Lundberg, an economist colleague, offered this explanation: 'He has a tremendous power of expressing himself orally in a way that people can't quite follow . . . he never tries to express himself in the easiest sort of way . . . he is not a man of simple statements.'

However opinions may have differed as to his powers of intellectual analysis and exposition, on the personality and character of the young Hammarskjöld there is no divergence of testimony. 'What first struck us about Dag Hammarskjöld', writes Myrdal, 'was his happy, cheerful approach to people. He never lost this and it made him seem especially open and natural, and I know of many people who never saw any deeper than this or went any further in their understanding of him.' However, Myrdal goes on: 'In actual fact, he was reserved and profoundly uncommunicative, solitary and excessively taut emotionally. His cheerful yet cool form of contact with the people he met was just one facet of the iron control that he had forced on himself as a matter of self-discipline.' Perhaps his closest friend and colleague through those early years in Stockholm, Henrik Klackenberg, today Lord Justice of the King's Supreme Administrative Court, gives a more sensitive and sympathetic interpretation which many who knew Hammarskjöld best consider perhaps the finest estimate of him yet written: 'I remember chiefly his moral stature and incorruptible justice, his integrity and whole-hearted commitment, and his never-failing sense of responsibility vis-à-vis the Task. Yet emphasis on these traits should not suggest an external, forbidding morality. On the contrary he had devastating charm. His colleagues readily became his personal friends. But least of all in the portrait of Dag Hammarskjöld should one lose sight of the gently considerate, somewhat diffident friendliness in this singularly live and richly-faceted personality.'

ii

Once launched upon a career in public service, Hammarskjöld's rise
to posts of ever higher and more demanding responsibility was steady
and rapid if not meteoric. His work on the Unemployment Commission brought him to the attention of the chief officers of both the
Finance Ministry and the Bank of Sweden. When barely thirty, he
was appointed Under-Secretary in the Ministry of Finance where he
continued for the next ten years as deputy of the Social Democratic
Minister, Ernst Wigforss. A year before, he had been drafted for
service in the Bank of Sweden as its secretary. A short six years later,
he was to become Chairman of this, the oldest bank of issue in the
world. He carried this dual assignment from 1941 to 1945, not
without some lifting of eyebrows by those who questioned the
propriety as well as the practicability of a single man discharging two
such exacting and intimately related offices.

These were the years when Sweden was being transformed into a
welfare state. Hammarskjöld is credited with having coined the
phrase 'planned economy'. His was a major role in writing the laws
which effected a gradual but far-reaching transformation in national
life.

Hammarskjöld's work schedule confounded his colleagues and
became a byword in official Stockholm. 'Dag Hammarskjöld worked
all his life with a sort of frenzy, a fact that many people will bear
out.' 'Though he worked so enormously, Hammarskjöld was always
clear and lucid no matter how heavy the agenda or hard the
negotiations. He could finish work at five o'clock in the morning and
start again at half past nine. Such intensity of labour makes most
people sour and fractious, but "he was always dignified and kindly in
his treatment of others and stimulated his colleagues to achieve what
otherwise they would scarcely have considered within their powers".'
It was well known in Stockholm that, as light after light was
extinguished in the great buildings where most of the Government
offices are located, a single lamp continued burning, in the Finance
Ministry or, later, in the Foreign Office. An official, returning to his
office at a late hour and inquiring of the porter if anyone was about,
would receive almost automatically the reply: 'Well, Mr. Hammarskjöld, of course.'

Beyond his primary technical tasks, Dag Hammarskjöld's greatest contribution sprang from an uncommon aptitude for reconciling opposed viewpoints and persons. Ernst Wigforss noted in his memoirs: 'He had a talent for winning people personally, straightening out differences and filling a leading role in a big organization.' In preparing the Government's budget, disputes with other departments inevitably arose; 'but these disputes never became personal. Hammarskjöld had a rare capacity for staying uninvolved personally. He fought hard for his point of view, but he managed to remain on good terms with his colleagues from other departments'.

These years, many of Hammarskjöld's friends consider to have been the happiest, certainly the gayest and most carefree of his adult life. Habits, attitudes and interests which had taken shape in youth continued virtually unmodified—the same well-nigh unbelievable regimen of work and mental concentration, the same exceptional skill in mediation and reconciliation, the same ever broadening preoccupation with general literature, drama, music and the arts, the same delight in the natural beauties of his Fatherland and relish in adventurous recreation, the same wide circle of companionships, qualified by the same abstention from the more conventional and artificial forms of social life. The Uppsala University student in his early twenties becomes the distinguished government official in his mid-thirties; indeed, continues substantially the same individual until his death. If there were significant changes, they were almost wholly in the interior self of whom friends and associates knew almost nothing.

This was also the period when a number of Dag Hammarskjöld's closest friends were marrying and establishing their own homes. Toward their wives, he was unfailingly gracious, indeed gallant, but he did not find it easy to accept the fact that the husbands were no longer so readily available for nocturnal walks and talks or climbing expeditions.

A colleague in the Finance Ministry with whom he often shared holidays married at the age of thirty-six. The following summer, they were together at a cottage near the sea where Hammarskjöld and the groom had been in the habit of vacationing. 'It was a little disconcerting', the wife recalls good-humoredly, 'to be expected to discuss French literature of the fifteenth century over porridge!' Almost a decade later, Hammarskjöld, returning from the leadership of the

Swedish delegation to the United Nations, was eager to explore the possibilities of the extreme north of Sweden for winter holidays and arranged to set off with his old friend on Christmas Day for a week's absence. However, the wife testifies that she never for one moment felt indignation or resentment at certain incursions into normal family life, but only profound admiration and affection toward the 'intruder'. The two qualities which she associates indelibly with her husband's longtime companion who became also her valued if somewhat distant friend are 'graciousness' and 'aloofness'.

Years later at the United Nations, Hammarskjöld seemed almost to resent the desire of some of his colleagues to steal part of the weekend for their families. Not untypical is this reminiscence: 'The desire for physical exercise would seize the Secretary-General at the oddest times. One snowbound Christmas morning, Heinz Wieschoff's telephone rang and he was heard to say, "Yes, Mr. Secretary-General, I'll pick you up right away." It was Hammarskjöld wanting a stroll. Wieschoff drove in to New York from Bronxville, picked him up at his apartment, and then brought him back to Bronxville where the two men strolled in one foot of snow along the Bronx River Parkway; eventually Hammarskjöld returned Wieschoff to the bosom of his family soaking wet and half alive.'*

This incident, like others in similar vein, may be more revealing of Hammarskjöld's solitariness and longing for human comradeship on Christmas Day than of inconsiderateness toward a family to which he was strongly attached. So resilient was his apparent self-reliance and buoyancy that even those closest to him were unaware of the inner 'loneliness' which afflicted him. As one friend after another deserted bachelorhood for marriage, their disappearance from the unconditional associations which they had enjoyed together deepened his inner 'aloneness'. On the other hand, this is an area in which Hammarskjöld appears to have been surprisingly insensitive. Without family obligations and enrichments in his own experience, he seems to have been unable to project his imagination into the realities of marital and parental responsibilities.

Inevitably, newly married friends attempted to interest Hammarskjöld in the possibility of marriage for himself, but without success. On one occasion, some of them thought they had found the perfect

* Emery Kelen, *Hammarskjöld* (New York: G. P. Putnam's Sons, 1966), p. 176.

choice, the daughter of a Swedish financier: 'she was pretty, charming, intellectual, a Doctor of Philosophy.' Dag's devastating comment
was: 'She didn't appreciate T. S. Eliot.' Another of his friends who
likewise had married at about this time reports a more acrid rejoinder: 'I have the impression that most married men devote 90 per
cent of their energies to coping with the neuroses of their wives; and
this can hardly produce good work. . . .' The real key is in the last
word: if ever there was a man completely wedded to his work, it was
Dag Hammarskjöld. In this whole matter, he was surprisingly self-
knowing. There is no reason whatever to qualify the explanation
which he himself gave many times: he had, across the years, created a
pattern of total dedication to his professional responsibilities which
provided no place for family obligations.

iii

Through this period of 'silence', there were no external signs of inner
strain or self-doubt. To be sure, we can hardly assume that there was
a sharp break at either its beginning or its close. Nevertheless, at this
time apparently Hammarskjöld felt no impulse to reflect and write.
Or, perhaps, in later perspective, he discarded the reflections then
recorded.

Almost the only light we have on what may have been transpiring
in Hammarskjöld's interior life during that decade comes from one
whom, then a budding novelist, he befriended and encouraged. Sven
Stolpe writes:

'I met Dag Hammarskjöld at the Sigtuna Foundation in 1930. . . .
I noted with amazement in my diary that Dag was the most remarkable student I had ever met in Sweden; he was *ratio pura,* I
wrote naïvely, and I predicted that he would become prime minister.
. . . The first person I met who was not only open and receptive
to the religious battle among the young elite of France but had good
knowledge of the whole *renouveau catholique* was Hammarskjöld.
. . . I listened in wonder to his remarks. He was unassuming: a
model of tact and delicacy. He understood everything. In the course
of many walks together we planned a defense of Christianity, a sort
of apologia against the so-called Hagerstrom school of philosophy,
which he had studied and thought out but did not fear. . . . When
in 1934 I published *The Christian Falange* he wrote to me: "You

have interpreted voices and lives which only a few of our generation in this country have known, and which none of us others have had the ability or strength to make accessible to all those whom in these days they must chiefly concern." '

Stolpe offers his own explanation of Hammarskjöld's reticence:

'At that time, in the early thirties, Dag Hammarskjöld kept this spiritual world of his concealed in all essentials. There were reasons for this. . . . Dag was his friends' friend and was careful to abstain from unnecessary criticism. . . . When he tried to touch on deeper themes, on religious and philosophical aspects of life, they completely failed to understand him. It was sometimes uncomfortable to observe how people to whom he had never even hinted at his inner world fondly believed themselves his intimates. Perhaps in this respect he was a little too skilful; if he had a use for people he let them imagine that they were his bosom friends. They never knew him.'

This is an overstatement of one half of the truth. Hammarskjöld's close associates and companions were 'his intimates' in those aspects of his many-sided nature which he chose to disclose to them, and they continued so until his death. But, with respect to the inner person, Stolpe does not exaggerate: 'Of Hammarskjöld's professional colleagues not one knew him. . . . I believe none of his friends had any idea of this side of him.'*

* Dag Hammarskjöld: A Spiritual Portrait, pp. 32–38, 66, 70.

3. 'The Middle Years':
1941–1950

IT WAS MIDWAY THROUGH THE DECADE which Hammarskjöld spent in Sweden's Ministry of Finance that he was elected to the added responsibility of Chairman of the Bank of Sweden.

In this same year, 1941, he resumed briefly the recording of his inmost thoughts. Why? We do not know. His mother to whom he had been so devoted had died in the preceding year; it is possible that her absence may have had some influence in turning his thoughts inward, or in making record of them. Hammarskjöld captioned his meditations for the single year 1941–1942 'The Middle Years' although at that time he was only in his mid-thirties. It is an appropriate heading for the whole period up to 1950 which was to mark a transition both in Hammarskjöld's public career when he moved to the Foreign Ministry and, no less, in his interior development.

Many of the themes of the earlier years recur—loneliness and death and, especially, self-judgment:

' "Upon my conditions". To live under that sign is to purchase knowledge about the Way at the price of loneliness.' [12]

'Praise nauseates you—but woe betide him who does not recognize your worth.' [14]

'The Strait Road—to live for others in order to save one's soul. The Broad—to live for others in order to save one's self-esteem.' [14]

However, there are also new notes which had been almost wholly absent in Hammarskjöld's more youthful reflections; two in particular, each of crucial significance both for understanding the man and for a right reading of his book.

Self-preoccupation is complemented by a sensitive and compassionate concern for others. It has sometimes been mistakenly charged that the latter quality was absent from Hammarskjöld's nature. On the contrary, far from his meditations being exclusively self-centered, throughout *Markings* few words recur more frequently than 'others'; it is one of the key words which sounds repeatedly, in nearly a fifth of the some six hundred entries. Sometimes, to be sure, he is comparing himself with those to whom he refers. But often, he is commenting understandingly upon one or another person who, though unidentified, claims his sympathy. And, not infrequently, there is a passionate but impotent longing to be of help to someone, perhaps to save him from himself:

'It makes one's heart ache when one sees that a man has staked his soul upon some end, the hopeless imperfection and futility of which is immediately obvious to everyone but himself.' (13)

This forecasts the solicitude for 'others' which appears most prominently in the next period.

The second new theme, however, is much the more significant and the more profound: God and the soul's right relation to Him:

'Your cravings as a human animal do not become a prayer just because it is God whom you ask to attend to them.'* (11)

In the next to last entry for 1941–1942, presumably toward year-end, the two dominant objectives of self-knowledge and faith are linked, and their right relationship defined:

'The road to self-knowledge does not pass through faith. But only through the self-knowledge we gain by pursuing the fleeting light in the depth of our being do we reach the point where we can grasp what faith is. . . .' (16)

ii

Again, an interval of silence intervened, this time of three years. Then in 1945, writing was resumed and continued without interruption until the end, sixteen years later.

* Cf. also *Markings*, pp. 12, 16. See below, pp. 176, 200.

Hammarskjöld was still only forty years of age. However, his reputation as distinguished economist and government servant was firmly established. The impression made upon his peers at first meeting was to be recorded in retrospect nearly twenty years later by the distinguished Danish diplomat, Eyvind Bartels, by then Denmark's 'highly articulate Ambassador in Paris': 'It was shortly after the war, at a meeting between the Danish Government and the Swedish, that I first saw Hammarskjöld. He was introduced by his friends in the Swedish Government as a prodigy and impressed us as such.' Bartels also cites Hammarskjöld's amazing foresight in anticipating the precise issue which overshadows Europe today, almost twenty years later.*

Toward the end of his term in the Ministry of Finance which coincided with the conclusion of World War II, Hammarskjöld was drawn more and more into foreign affairs. In 1946, he carried responsibility for renegotiating Sweden's Trade Agreement with the United States. The following year, he headed the Swedish Delegation in the discussions which led to the implementation of the Marshall Plan through the creation of the Organization for European Economic Cooperation, and served on its Executive Committee as its Vice-Chairman.

Much of the next three or four years were spent in Paris in connection with the OEEC, usually returning to Stockholm for the weekends. In Paris, his friendships broadened to embrace an international circle. With them he shared his avid intellectual and cultural and sporting interests. The head of the Norwegian delegation, Arne Skaug, reports that during long evening sessions of the Council 'Dag would read French poetry while I read Alice in Wonderland'. Dr. Karin Kock, who had been one of the examiners of his doctoral dissertation fifteen years earlier and was now a colleague in the Swedish delegation to the OEEC, recalls: 'We would have dinner; then Hammarskjöld wanted us to go to some highbrow play. Then afterwards we were supposed to resume our discussions and have as clear a mind as his.' Leif Belfrage likewise remembers late suppers at a small French restaurant where they would 'talk through half the night' and occasional respites when they would travel through France

---

* This tribute is the more noteworthy because it occurs in a scathing review of Markings quoted below, pp. 173–74. Bartels' appraisal appears in Auden's 'Foreword' to Markings, pp. x–xi.

with Hammarskjöld instructing his companions in French history
and culture. 'He knew all about the old churches and cathedrals.'

iii

This was the setting of intensive and demanding preoccupation with
a variety of assignments in behalf of his Government in its foreign
affairs in which the next group of 'Road Marks' were set down over a
period of five years, from 1945 to 1949. Hammarskjöld gave them the
title 'Towards new shores——?' The exact meaning of his sense of
novel direction, followed by a question mark, is not clear.

He begins on a note by now familiar—the unremitting quest for
self-identification—with one of the profoundest and most important
'markings' he ever wrote, notable for its recognition of what he terms
a 'congruence' between the self's choices and life's intention for it:

> 'At every moment you choose yourself. But do you choose your
> self? Body and soul contain a thousand possibilities out of which
> you can build many I's. But in only one of them is there a con-
> gruence of the elector and the elected. Only one—which you will
> never find until you have excluded all those superficial and fleeting
> possibilities of being and doing with which you toy, out of curi-
> osity or wonder or greed, and which hinder you from casting
> anchor in the experience of the mystery of life, and the conscious-
> ness of the talent entrusted to you which is your I.' [19]

Then follows a sequence of startling reflections on other persons,
all of them pathetic, some tragic in their self-deception and failure, at
least four enveloped in the stark realities of physical death, whether
accidental or self-imposed. With several of these tortured souls,
Hammarskjöld felt himself deeply involved, blamed by them and
accepting the blame for their unhappy state, yet unable to lead them
into the only true 'way out' through the fearless self-confrontation and
acceptance of fate which he was resolutely seeking for himself.

There is an unnamed wife: 'She knew that nothing would get
better, that it would never be any different. He had lost interest in
his work, and no longer did anything. . . .—And she knew more:
knew that there could never be a way out. . . .—And yet she sat
there praying.' [21]

There is an extended comment upon someone, probably a colleague or subordinate, whom Hammarskjöld had felt compelled to

'strip naked before his own eyes'—'He was impossible.'—and who reciprocated by casting on his exposer blame for failure to save him from himself. It is a peculiarly perceptive and pitiful portraiture of a self-defeated soul. Yet Hammarskjöld acknowledges spiritual responsibility: 'So, in the end, we were, in fact, to blame. . . . For it is always the stronger one who is to blame. . . . This is also the reason why, at times, it seems so much more difficult to live than to die.' (31-32)

At least twice, Hammarskjöld was witness to suicides, once by drowning and once through a shot in the temple.* Also, to another drowning which may have been accidental. And, another time, to a near-fatal motor accident. On each occasion, impotent to help, he is led to reflection on life and death. The incidents may have accentuated his concern with death; nearly a third of the 'markings' and half the pages in this five-year period comment upon 'death'. Contrariwise, an already deep interest may have led him to depict these occurrences in such vivid detail:

'Before it became clear to us what had happened, he was already too far out. We could do nothing. . . .
Just what was it we felt when, for the first time, we realized that he had gone too far out ever to be able to get back?' (22-23)

'Out in the main channel, a dark bundle turns slowly. A glimpse of a face, a cry. Of its own volition, again and again it thrusts the face under the surface. . . .
During their attempts at artificial respiration, they have laid bare the upper part of her body. As she lies stretched out on the riverbank—beyond all human nakedness in the inaccessible solitude of death—her white firm breasts are lifted to the sunlight—a heroic torso of marble-blonde stone in the soft grass.' (26-27)

'When the gun went off, he fell on his side beneath the maple trees. . . .
That eternal "Beyond"—where you are separated from us by a death chosen long before the bullet hit the temple.' (28)

'Descending into the valley, at the last curve he lost control of the car. As it toppled over the bank at the side of the road, his only thought was: "Well, at least my job's done."
His one, weary, happy thought. . . .' (30)

---

* Sweden has one of the highest suicide rates in the world.

These somewhat gruesome descriptions and somber interpretations are followed by a series of realistic observations of sea gulls:

'. . . Shameless amber eyes with no expression in them but that of naked voracity. . . . —ungainly gatherers of worms from those gaping wounds in the soil, their sides glistening oily and slippery in the wet. . . . —a well-nourished carrion bird who feels so much at home among us all.' (33-34)

However, as these five-year stark reflections draw toward a close, Hammarskjöld turns again to his professional career with scathing self-judgment which lays bare the contradiction between the public image and the real person as he knew himself:

'He seeks his own comfort—
and is rewarded with glimpses of satisfaction followed
   by a long period of emptiness and shame which
   sucks him dry.
He fights for his position—
all his talk about the necessary preconditions for doing
   something worthwhile prove an insecure barrier
   against self-disgust.
He devotes himself to his job—
but he is in doubt as to its importance and therefore,
   constantly looking for recognition. . . .' (36)

He concludes on the favorite themes of 'sacrifice' and 'the Way' as though in preparation for the even more soul-searching agony of spirit which a New Year is to prompt:

'You asked for burdens to carry—And howled when they were placed on your shoulders. . . .'

'O Caesarea Philippi: to accept condemnation of the Way as its fulfillment, its definition, to accept this both when it is chosen and when it is realized.' (36)

4. The Darkest Night:
1950—1952

With the termination of his responsibilities at the Organization for European Economic Cooperation in Paris, Dag Hammarskjöld returned to Stockholm and to service in the Ministry of Foreign Affairs, first as Secretary-General and then as Vice-Minister. In addition, he was appointed to the Swedish Cabinet as a non-party Minister without Portfolio. At the same time, he entered upon the most critical and crucial period for his interior life.

Hammarskjöld was now just forty-five. The years 1950–1952 found him at the pinnacle of civic office in Sweden. Public opinion and friends and colleagues alike regarded him as the epitome of the successful Man of Affairs, discharging with seemingly effortless ease and great distinction the highest and most honored role available to him. Those years also witnessed the depths of his inner despondency verging on despair. It was then that he experienced the most acute phase of self-questioning and self-accusation, of solitariness and dejection, a long twilight and black midnight, the 'Dark Night of the Soul', which continued until a wholly unforeseen and unexpected burst of dawn shortly before sudden elevation to climactic responsibilities at the United Nations transported him to a new world and a new life. Readers who find the early pages of Markings baffling or uncongenial would do well to turn to the entries for 1950–1953. Here we are admitted into the innermost privacies of a human soul struggling through almost total obscurity and, finally, emerging into light which, though not unshadowed, furnishes heretofore illusive illumination for the path he must tread.

Inevitably, we are led to inquire: why *at this particular time* should Hammarskjöld have been plunged to such depths? The most credible answer, as might be anticipated with so complex a personality, points to a convergence of factors, physiological and psychological, vocational and spiritual.

As is well known, many if not all men pass through a phase of transition near middle life which, while generally less traumatic than its more familiar feminine counterpart, may be severe and baffling. In Dag Hammarskjöld's case, there were reasons why it might have been expected to be more than usually acute. Basic was the fact that he was unmarried. In a man of at least normal sexuality but of exceptional spiritual sensitivity and moral rigor, it was but natural that the drives which often mount to heightened intensity at this time of life should have pressed hard upon the iron self-discipline which he had forged for their control, though he may have been wholly unaware of this. Undoubtedly, this factor was aggravated by the circumstance that virtually all of his friends were, by now, married. While this meant no termination of their friendship and they welcomed him as an honored guest in their homes, the altered relationship was quite different.

To these deeply personal and subjective factors was added perplexity regarding his professional future. Hammarskjöld now stood on the top rung of the ladder which he had chosen for his career. To a few close friends he disclosed, almost casually, that he could not discern the way ahead.

Some of them became aware of an inner disquiet. Clearly, he was restive and unhappy. Among themselves, they would speculate: 'Where does Dag go from here?' One offered to promote his candidacy as Chancellor of the Swedish Universities, but Hammarskjöld was not interested. The most important ambassadorships would doubtless have been open to him. After the example of his father and eldest brother Bo, he might have become Governor of a Province, but that likewise did not kindle his imagination. Gunnar Myrdal, with whom he had had associations since the memorable debate over his doctoral thesis, reports a revealing conversation: 'I remember once having lunch alone with Hammarskjöld a year or a year and a half before he left Stockholm. In his breezy, cordial, disciplined way he told me that he could not see what he could do in Sweden now. He mentioned various alternatives, but without any great enthusiasm. Being what I am, I naturally suggested that he ought to mount the ivory tower and write important books, but he just smiled deprecatingly and I know that he was thinking that that, unfortunately, was not for him.'

It would be no occasion for surprise if the inner unrest and vocational uncertainty had been accompanied by religious questioning, perhaps the doubt regarding inherited beliefs of which he spoke in his *credo*: 'my intellect challenged their validity'*. However, the evidence points to the opposite conclusion. Apparently, he had passed through that transition at an earlier stage, presumably during the period when his 'diary' is silent.

It was precisely during this time of agonizing tension that he found the needed reinforcement in his faith and that that faith deepened and strengthened under the stress.

The pivotal importance of these three years is revealed in both the quantity and the content of his meditations. It is clear that Hammarskjöld turned inward for solace and support whenever most deeply troubled. This is proof, if proof were needed beyond his own testimony, with what seriousness he regarded his 'Road Marks'. By now, he had been writing in his 'diary' for just a quarter of a century. But the entries for those twenty-five years account for less than a sixth of the book.

From 1950 onward, the 'markings' increase in number as well as deepen in desperation. The next three years record almost a fourth of the total for the entire thirty-six years. They are grouped year by year. However, in both mood and matter, the reflections of this three-year period are so much of a piece that they may appropriately be considered together.

In later years, as we shall discover, many 'Road Marks' were staked down in direct reaction to specific events in Hammarskjöld's public career and were often explicitly dated, doubtless to remind their author of the particular occasions. But close study of the book discloses that it was also his habit to turn to reflection on days of special significance in his private life—his own birthday (July 29), festivals of the Christian Year such as Christmas, Lent, Good Friday, Easter, and Whitsunday, and especially year-end and New Year. This first becomes evident on the opening page for '1950'.

* *Servant of Peace*, p. 23.

As though in premonition of the deep waters ahead, Hammar-skjöld begins the year 1950 with a new practice which he is to follow in six of the next eight years. The initial entry for the year is a brief comment upon a line from a familiar Swedish hymn which his mother, who had died ten years before, had been in the habit of reading aloud in the family circle each New Year's Eve. The hymn, written by Bishop Franz Mikael Franzén in 1814, bears the Swedish title 'Den korts stund jag vandrar här' which, in the hymnal of the American Swedish Lutheran Church, is translated 'The Little While I Linger Here'. Hammarskjöld quotes a line from the final stanza; he typed it in capitals, as a heading not simply for the comment which follows but for the entire year: SNART STUNDAR NATTEN—NIGHT APPROACHES NOW. W. H. Auden, seeking an equivalent which would be familiar and meaningful to English readers, has had recourse to a superficially parallel line from Baring-Gould's well-known evening hymn 'Now the day is over': 'Night is drawing nigh'. However, the two hymns are utterly different in character. Baring-Gould's is a simple evening song concluding on the hopeful note:

> 'When the morning wakens
> Then may I arise
> Pure and fresh and sinless
> In Thy holy eyes.'

The Swedish hymn is a meditation on the transience of life and its final verse declares an anticipation and grateful welcome of death:

> 'How vain the worldling's pomp and show,
> How brief his joys and pleasures!
> The night approaches now, and lo!
> We leave all earthly treasures.'

As the late President Evald Benjamin Lawson of Upsala College in East Orange, New Jersey, noted: 'The night referred to is that which comes at life's close, rather than the darkness falling after a single day.' Obviously, the Baring-Gould line in *Markings* conveys a wholly inadequate impression of this quotation which holds such a promi-nent place in Hammarksjöld's thought.

Year following year thereafter, he is to return at the outset of nearly every year to these words, steeped in nostalgic associations, to furnish stimulus for what he most wants to say to himself as he recalls the year just closed and readies himself for days ahead. There

could be no more convincing evidence of the grip upon him in
middle life of the traditions in which he had been reared and
especially of his mother's continuing influence. Indeed, to trace his
comments, usually just a line or two, upon this same text through the
beginnings of six of eight successive years is to have open before one
the movement of his spirit through this critical period of his life. On
the first occasion of its use in 1950, he simply paraphrases the
concluding lines of the verse he has taken as his text:

> 'Then, what are all things here below
> To Jesus' promise, "Where I go,
> I will receive you also." ' [37]

On the following New Year, 1951, his comment is: 'So! another year
it is. And if this day should be your last: . . . The pulley of time
drags us inexorably forward towards this last day. A relief to think of
this, to consider that there is a moment without a beyond. . . .'[61]
And in 1952: 'How long the road is. . . .'[81] But in 1953, to the
same text he will answer with an exultant affirmation*—evidence of a
decisive transition within his inner life. The altered mood continues
until he discontinues this practice four years later.

The initial meditation for 1950 upon the hymn verse is followed
immediately by a startling disclosure of turmoil within:

> 'In a whirling fire of annihilation,
> In the storm of destruction
> And deadly cold of the act of sacrifice,
> You would welcome death.
> But when it slowly grows within you,
> Day by day,
> You suffer anguish,
> Anguish under the unspoken judgment which hangs over your life,
> While leaves fall in the fool's paradise.' [37]

'Sacrifice' and 'death'—themes which had been with Hammarskjöld
from the beginning, but are now more persistent and pervasive. And,
closely related, 'loneliness' and frustration in personal relationships.
Also, a yearning for 'maturity'. Among the nearly 150 'markings' of
the three-year period, 1950–1952, these themes predominate. None is
new; but each now waxes with desperate intensity. All are intimately
interrelated.

* Below, p. 99.

ii

Much has been made of Dag Hammarskjöld's 'solitariness'. And justifiably. It is true; he was 'a very lonely man . . . even with his Swedish friends, there was always one part of him withheld. There was warmth and genuine affection but always some distance.'

All his life, Dag Hammarskjöld was plagued by an intense, harrowing inner 'loneliness'. It sounds like a persistent, melancholy minor obbligato through his interior reflections virtually from beginning to end. It is doubtful if any of those who knew him—members of his family, professional associates, his closest friends—had any realization of either the depth or the anguish of his aloneness.

'Loneliness' is the topic of two of the fifteen introductory 'Road Marks' of the postgraduate student at Uppsala University who, to youthful companions, 'seemed to have a happy nature. . . .' Through the next two decades, *Markings* contains no reference to the subject, though it can hardly be supposed that there was a cessation of the problem. Indeed, early in the 1930s, in felicitating a friend on his engagement, he wrote: 'There is an incurable loneliness of the soul.' And, a little later when still only twenty-eight: 'For all of us, no doubt, existence acquires an increasing chill as we grow older.' And yet, even this friend confesses: 'I must admit that until I read his book I had never dreamt that his isolation was so horrible a torment.'*

Very early in 1950, Hammarskjöld cries: 'The anguish of loneliness brings blasts from the storm center of death. . . .'[(38)] A little later, he confesses 'the same continual loneliness'[(49)]. And, near the close of the year, 'the loneliness which is the final lot of all'[(58)]. From then on, through the following three years, he returns to this plaint over and over and over again; just half of all his comments on 'loneliness' were recorded during these three years.

However, it is in the last of the three years, 1952, that he broods most frequently—one fourth of all the 'markings' in that year—and most disconsolately upon his solitariness. By now, as we have seen, he is established in his own home in Stockholm, surrounded by colleagues and friends who find him an exceptionally congenial and exciting if not convivial companion. His 'apartness' was doubtless attributed to natural reticence and inherent dignity. There was little

* Stolpe, *op. cit.*, pp. 46, 61, 114.

if anything in his outward behavior and relationships to suggest what his private confessions reveal: '. . . What makes loneliness an anguish is not that I have no one to share my burden, but this: I have only my own burden to bear.'[85] 'Pray that your loneliness may spur you into finding something to live for, great enough to die for.'[85]

At least once, in late 1952, he allows himself to toy with the possibility of suicide: 'Fatigue dulls the pain, but awakes enticing thoughts of death. So! *that* is the way in which you are tempted to overcome your loneliness—by making the ultimate escape from life.' But this possibility is firmly rejected: '—No! It may be that death is to be your ultimate gift to life: it must not be an act of treachery against it.' He turns to 'work' and 'others' as alternative sources of relief but, characteristically, with questioning of his motives: ' "Give yourself"—in your work, for others: by all means so long as you don't do this self-consciously (with, perhaps, even an expectation of being admired for it).'[86] This most somber year of Hammarskjöld's life concludes with two further comments upon the same theme: 'I dare not believe, I do not see how I shall ever be able to believe: that I am not alone.'[86] 'Loneliness is not the sickness unto death. No, but can it be cured except by death?. . .'[87]

With the early days of 1953 comes Hammarskjöld's summons to the United Nations Secretary-Generalship. There is only a slight slackening of private meditation. But it is highly significant that the topic of 'loneliness' which has loomed so large before is wholly absent through the first two years of his new life. To be sure, that does not mean that the harassment has been permanently banished. Later, he reports: '. . . once again you are aware of your loneliness—as it is and always has been . . . even when, at times, the friendship of others veiled its nakedness.'[116] However, he is given a profounder understanding: 'For him who has responded to the call of the Way of Possibility, loneliness may be obligatory. . . .'[120]

On his fifty-third birthday—and be it remembered, birthdays were often times of especially soul-searching meditation for Hammarskjöld —he writes his final and definitive interpretation of the solitariness which had dogged his spirit since youth and from time to time had threatened to plunge him into utter desolation, even perhaps self-destruction: 'Did'st Thou give me this inescapable loneliness so that it would be easier for me to give Thee all?'[166] *

* Cf. below, p. 160.

iii

Those who read Dag Hammarskjöld's interior solitude as aloofness or isolation from friendships completely misrepresent the man. On the contrary, all his life he cherished a host of appreciative acquaintances with whom he enjoyed mutually rewarding associations. Youthful companions on hikes and climbing expeditions, we noted, recall him as 'the best of comrades'. Colleagues in government work testify to the wide range of shared interests: 'They read the books of the Bloomsbury group, played Beethoven's last quartets, and followed the young proletarian authors.' We have mentioned the recollections of several associates in the Organization for European Economic Co-operation in Paris.

In fact, Dag Hammarskjöld possessed very special gifts in winning and holding the affection as well as the respect of others, which strengthened his public while at the same time enriching his private life. His father had declared: 'If I were as gifted as Dag and had his talent for dealing with people, I would have gone far.' (This from one who had held the highest offices in his nation's Government!)

Nevertheless, Hammarskjöld's life virtually its whole course through was marked by a sharp contrast not only between many diverse and enriching friendships on the one hand and intense inner loneliness on the other hand but also between these seemingly ready and rich comradeships and his own tethering sense of dissatisfaction and frustration in human relationships. Here was the double contradiction of the man's character and experience. Indeed, each was the obverse and also in some measure at once both the cause and the consequence of the other. Both were aggravated by his deeply ingrained distaste for conventional society.

Personal relations, always a baffling disappointment to Hammarskjöld, became, during this darkest period of 1950–1952, an aggravated vexation, paralleling his deepening loneliness. In earlier years, his thoughts about 'others' had focused upon *their* problems and his powerlessness to help. Now, it is his own inability to achieve satisfying rapport with 'others' which occupies him. These are the very years when 'others' are bearing witness to their delight in his stimulating and rewarding comradeship. Yet, Hammarskjöld records his private feelings: '. . . don't commit yourself to any one and, therefore, don't allow anyone to come close to you.' [43] 'Only tell others what is of importance to them. Only ask them what you need to know. . . .'[44] 'In spite of everything, your bitterness because others are enjoying what you are denied is always ready to flare up. . . .'[47] 'Do you really have "feelings" any longer for anybody or anything except yourself—or even that? . . .'[48]

For his unhappiness in personal friendships, Hammarskjöld blamed only himself. Of admissions of his own shortcomings and responsibility, there are dozens. Of accusations against others, not one.

At the close of 1950, he places two especially devastating notations of failure, possibly successive comments upon the same incident or, it may be, two different instances:

'How undisguised your thick-skinned self-satisfied loneliness appeared before his naked agony as he struggled to make a living contact. How difficult you found it to help, when confronted in another by your own problem—uncorrupted.'

*

'Suddenly I saw he was more real to himself than I am to myself, and that what was required of me was to experience this reality of his not as an object but as a subject—and *more* real than mine.' [59]

However, as with his agony of inner 'loneliness', his distress over his relations with 'others' had to wait for a satisfying resolution nearly another decade until he had been at the United Nations for more than five years. Likewise on his fifty-third birthday he wrote:'. . . Apart from any value it may have for others, my life is worse than death. Therefore, in my great loneliness, serve others. . . .'[166]*

iv

During this same period, disgust with the artificialities and futilities of social life, always a strong undercurrent in Hammarskjöld's feeling, bursts forth in contemptuous disdain: 'The overtones are lost, and what is left are conversations which, in their poverty, cannot hide the lack of real contact. We glide past each other. But why? Why—? We reach out towards the other. In vain—because we have never dared to give ourselves.'[40] 'Don't let small talk fill up the time and the silence except as a medium for bearing unexpressed messages between two people who are attuned to each other. . . .'[44] 'When the

* For the complete 'marking', see below, p. 160.

evening of being together was over, a feeling of emptiness bordering on guilt brought on the anguish which inevitably accompanies sloth and inadequacy. . . .'[59] 'To be "sociable"—to talk merely because convention forbids silence, to rub against one another in order to create the illusion of intimacy and contact. . . . Exhausting, naturally, like any improper use of our spiritual resources. . . .'[63] These 'markings' need to be read in their entirety to appreciate the full weight of their scorn.

In the midst of these confessions of distance from 'others' and strictures upon casual human relations, he inserts a definition of what he is seeking, especially revealing because it is directly autobiographical. He often refers to himself in the second or even the third person, as though standing over against himself in judgment: 'don't commit yourself to anyone', etc. Whenever, as now, he employs the first person singular, he is speaking straight from the depths of his soul: 'Hunger is my native place in the land of the passions. Hunger for fellowship, hunger for righteousness—for a fellowship founded on righteousness, and a righteousness attained in fellowship. . . .'[53] In the perspective of this ideal, it is not surprising that the associations which others found normal and which meant so much to them were profoundly unsatisfying to him.

The above 'markings' date from 1950 and early 1951 when Hammarskjöld was principally occupied with his OEEC assignment in Paris, the period which prompted the tributes to his sociability quoted earlier.

Five years later, in the third year of his United Nations Secretary-Generalship, Hammarskjöld recorded his definitive indictment of 'the organized rules for social behavior':

> 'While performing the part which is truly ours, how exhausting it is to be obliged to play a role which is not ours; the person you must really be in order to fulfill your task, you must not appear to others to be, in order to be allowed by them to fulfill it. How exhausting—but unavoidable, since mankind has laid down once and for all the organized rules for social behavior.' [112]

V

If Dag Hammarskjöld ever seriously considered marriage in his mature years, it may have been during this same period of intense inner turmoil and disheartenment, though the evidence is not conclusive. If the answer to that uncertainty should be affirmative—an answer which probably will never be confirmed—that factor would, of course, have heightened his solitariness and sense of estrangement from more conventional associations.

Much speculation has been expended on why he never married. Certainly, it was not for absence of opportunity. Inevitably, he was exceptionally attractive as well as interesting and engaging to women.

Nor were that interest and attraction unreciprocated. Hammarskjöld's frequent holiday companion, Henrik Klackenberg, writes: 'In our circle we sometimes joked about Dag's lack of interest in women as we often did about bachelors in general. But there is no doubt but that he was attracted by persons of the opposite sex. . . . On the surface he seemed to be rather shy and somewhat reserved when in the company of women, especially with respect to those who appeared to be "interested" in him. However, with the wives of his friends he was a gallant and popular conversationalist, perhaps inclined to be rather too "highbrow" sometimes. . . . His greatest interest lay at the cerebral level, and he much preferred to live with books and problems than to spend time socially talking nonsense and gossiping. . . . By no means insensitive to female charm, he appeared to enjoy most being together with more mature women with a greater experience of life. . . .'*

It was reported of him, as of many unmarried men of ability and eminence: 'He cannot bear ambitious, pretentious or aggressive women. . . . He is at ease with women only if the relationship is confined to the level of wit, intellect and chivalry.' Precisely the same might have been said of his attitude toward men.

On the other hand, Hammarskjöld was not immune to normal sexual feeling. Amidst a series of late poetic recollections of boyhood, he writes:

> 'He lowered his eyes,
> Lest he should see the body
> To lust after it.' (179)

And, somewhat later:

> 'Orgasms of bodies
> On hot nights, lit
> By flickers of summer lightning.' (187)

* For fuller statement by Judge Klackenberg, see NOTE below, pp. 221 f.

Nor was he insensitive to feminine grace. He writes of 'the aching beauty of a neckline'.[42]

The fact is that the body and its sensuous demands played a not inconsiderable part in his reflections. In a startlingly frank confession from this same critical period, he speaks both of his awareness of sexual desire and of how, for him, it was intimately linked with, perhaps sublimated in, communion with Nature: 'As a husband embraces his wife's body in faithful tenderness, so the bare ground and trees are embraced by the still, high, light of the morning. I feel an ache of longing to share in this embrace, to be united and absorbed. . . .'[77]

As we shall see, Hammarsköld sought, and found, solution for his loneliness in work and a deeper dedication. So, likewise, with sensuous desire. But this did not mean indifference to the imperiousness of the body. The latter continues a minor but recurrent theme; there is hardly a year which does not add some comment upon it. In one of his most important 'markings' from a later period to which we have already alluded, he declares: 'For him who has responded to the call of the Way of Possibility, loneliness may be obligatory.' Then he adds: 'Such loneliness, it is true, may lead to a communion closer and deeper than any achieved by the union of two bodies, but your body is not going to let itself be fobbed off by a bluff: whatever you deny it, in order to follow this call, it will claim back if you fail, and claim back in forms which it will no longer be in your power to select. . . .'[120] Later, he comments: 'the lust of the flesh gets its chance to reveal the loneliness of the soul.'[139] And, still later: '. . . Its lust can prepare a man to endure tribulation.'[161] All these anticipate his climactic declaration on this theme: 'The fire of the body burns away its dross. . . . The ultimate surrender to the creative act—it is the destiny of some to be brought to the threshold of this in the act of sacrifice rather than the sexual act; and they experience a thunderclap of the same dazzling power.'[166]

In speaking of Hammarsköld's university years at Uppsala, we mentioned his close friendship with a classmate who had been his near neighbor and playmate since childhood, which relatives and friends had expected to ripen into love. 'It is said that Dag Hammarsköld had a short romance with a girl of a well-known Uppsala family, while he was an undergraduate there. She was "witty, amusing and very charming" and he took her to Union balls and went sleighing with her, but it stopped there.'* Of another friendship, Sven Stolpe, whose wife had likewise been a fellow student, reports: 'The one woman for whom he felt tenderness and attachment he immediately renounced on discovering that one of his friends was also paying court to her. Afterwards he became one of that family's loyal friends; the renunciation seems to have been made without the slightest effort, though it could be observed that whenever he met the couple he always addressed his remarks to the husband, never to the wife.'**

Hammarskjöld's continuance in bachelorhood was not due to lack of concern of others for his marriage. During his professional years in Stockholm, we noted his friends had conspired to that end. To one of them, he acknowledged that 'it might have been better if he had married, but how could he invite a woman to share his kind of life when he was always at the Ministry until early hours of the morning'. 'He was always overburdened with work, with projects that had to be finished'; there was no time for romance or courtship.

Some years later, the Queen Mother of Sweden on a visit to New York inquired why he had never married. 'He explained that having watched his mother suffer so much from his father's absences on public business he did not feel that he wanted to subject a woman to such a life.' It was the same reason he had given to friends in younger years.

Judge Klackenberg confirms this interpretation: 'We occasionally spoke of marriage but more as a theoretical problem of how difficult it would be to combine the necessary consideration towards a wife with the kind of working life we pursued. The explanation he is said to have given the Queen Mother as to why he had not married appears to have the hallmark of probability and to contain a good portion of the truth. He knew that his mother had suffered from the fact that his father, owing to his super-human burden of work, had had so little time for her, and having in mind the great and demanding tasks with which he himself had been entrusted, he did not wish to cause such suffering to another woman.'

Nevertheless, Hammarskjöld was fully alive to the sacrifice which his choice demanded of him. In late 1955, disclosing to Bo Beskow how greatly he valued and leaned upon his few close friends, he

---

* Söderberg, op. cit., p. 38.
** Stolpe, op. cit., pp. 24–25.

added: 'When I see the other possibilities like yours, there can be a stab of missing something, but the final reaction is that what must be is right.' Almost certainly, the 'other possibilities' refers to marriage and family life. It suggests that, though Hammarskjöld had long since reconciled himself to bachelorhood as 'what must be', he was not without a continuing and acute awareness of the price.

It is to his 'Road Marks' that we must turn, however, for the most intimate and definitive disclosure of Hammarskjöld's thoughts on marriage. This is to be found in a sequence of confessions from these same years of 1950 to 1952, a sure indication that his spirit was much occupied with this theme during that troubled period. Some are enigmatic, others clear but of uncertain reference, one of decisive importance.

Early in 1950, he suggests tentatively: 'Perhaps a great love is never returned. Had it been given warmth and shelter by its counterpart in the Other, perhaps it would have been hindered from ever growing to maturity. . . .'[42] Who was 'the Other'? We do not know. Almost immediately follows a reflection on beauty in its many forms, including 'The language of . . . human bodies . . .'[42]. A little later, there appears a burning comment on human acquisitiveness, including physical desire: 'Our incurable instinct to *acquire*. . . . We press body against body—bringing to nought that human beauty which is only physical in that the surfaces of the body are animated by a spirit inaccessible to physical touch.'[45] And, toward the year's close, this reflection: 'Our love becomes impoverished if we lack the courage to sacrifice its object.'[56]

In the following year, 1951, Hammarskjöld returns to set forth more fully and explicitly the view of personal relationships to which he had been led:

'When you have reached the point where you no longer expect a response, you will at last be able to give in such a way that the other is able to receive, and be grateful. When Love has matured and, through a dissolution of the self into light, become a radiance, then shall the Lover be liberated from dependence upon the Beloved, and the Beloved also be made perfect by being liberated from the Lover.' [76]

Two entries beyond comes the confession cited above in which he voices a longing to share in the embrace of Nature which he likens to physical union in marriage.

In the summer of 1952, Hammarskjöld journeyed to Gottland and stayed at Visby with the friend of his childhood and youth, with whom his name had been linked as a possible fiancé, and her husband. Near the close of that year, between two of his most anguished cries of desolation stands far and away his most significant comment on marriage, both the most specific in contemplation of the possibility of a life partnership and also his final word on the subject:

'Incapable of being blinded by desire,
Feeling I have no right to intrude upon another,
Afraid of exposing my own nakedness,
Demanding complete accord as a condition for a life together:
How could things have gone otherwise?' (85)

There, in five lines of piercing self-understanding, the reasons for his abstention from marriage are summarized: refusal to yield to impulse, respect for others' privacy, an extreme physical modesty, above all an unattainable ideal of mutual understanding. Is he here speaking of a recent relationship, or is his memory reaching back into the past, perhaps far back to that time, twenty-five years earlier, when family and friends had expected an engagement with the woman whom he had recently been visiting? We shall never be certain of the answer.

Surely it is not without significance that this crucial 'marking' is followed almost immediately by the only explicit admission of temptation to suicide.

This sequence of 'Road Marks' across nearly a decade of Hammarskjöld's mature life reveals a man of exceptional sensuous sensitivity and strong passion, held within self-determined and self-imposed disciplines issuing in sublimations which heighten and augment both power and quality of creative achievement. In brief, he confirmed the experience of unnumbered bachelors across the centuries. Indeed a friend of his early professional years reports 'he once compared himself to a Catholic priest who renounces marriage in order to give his love to all'*.

Although henceforth there is silence concerning marriage, a year later, after the fateful transition of 1953, he writes of 'A human intimacy—free from the earth, but blessing the earth.'(93) And, again repeating phrases which he had used four years earlier: 'The Lover desires the perfection of the Beloved—which requires, among

* Stolpe, op. cit., p. 65.

other things, the liberation of the Beloved from the Lover.'[117] And still later, of 'Love, which is without an object, the outflowing of a power released by self-surrender . . . tamed by the yoke of human intimacy and warmed by its tenderness. . . .'[133]

However inconclusive this sequence of 'Road Marks' may be felt to be in determining Hammarskjöld's answer to the question of marriage for himself, they should set finally to rest the suggestions, insinuations, rumors, some of them vicious, of indifference to physical beauty, of misogyny, even of abnormality.

vi

In our sex-saturated culture, with its penchant for Freudian interpretation, it is, perhaps, inevitable that suggestions of sexual deviation should attach to a person of Hammarskjöld's prominence and obvious vitality who had deliberately chosen a solitary life in dedication to duty. There have even been whisperings of homosexuality. Sad to record, such rumors originated with a high officer of the United Nations who sought to block Hammarskjöld's election as Secretary-General, and seeped back from New York to Sweden. They were utterly without foundation. When a close colleague thought it only fair to warn Hammarskjöld of the rumors, he replied quite simply with an emphatic disclaimer: 'Before God, they are untrue.' Those who had been most continuously and closely associated with him, in Sweden, in Paris and in New York, scoff at such suggestions.

However, Hammarskjöld may have been not unaware of or insensitive to these insinuations. In one of his late poetic *haiku*, he wrote:

'Because it never found a mate,
Men called
The unicorn abnormal.' [193]

Judge Henrik Klackenberg, Dag Hammarskjöld's daily co-worker in the Finance Ministry with whom he spent much of their free time during the 1930s, has been at pains to respond at length to an inquiry on this delicate and unpleasant subject. He concludes: 'I can honestly and unhesitatingly bear witness to the fact that during the whole of our long and occasionally fairly intensive time together, I cannot recall any action or gesture or even any word of Dag's which could have indicated a sexual inversion. No thought of homosexuality ever occurred to me. . . . In Swedish public life there were some highly publicized cases of homosexuality on the part of prominent people concerning which we had lively and frank discussions. To me it is a completely absurd thought that I could have had these conversations with a person with homosexual leanings himself.'*

vii

Some commentators have placed far too much weight upon Hammarskjöld's occasional references to 'psychosis', 'masochism', 'narcissism', or to what they regard as evidence of psychological abnormality in his thought. He came to maturity when Freud's influence was in its ascendancy; we know that this was a favorite topic for discussion among his fellow students. Quite naturally, there are some echoes of reigning psychoanalytic vocabulary in his writing. But they are surprisingly few, no more than half a dozen.** Some are directed at others rather than at himself. Some are general reflections on human nature. Only three—one early, two quite late—are self-accusations: 'your unselfishness a thinly disguised masochism'[16] . . . 'Not to brood over my pettiness with masochistic self-disgust'[150] . . . 'the pleasure-tinged death wish (not, perhaps, without an element of narcissistic masochism). . . .'[159]†

Of the prevailing psychology and its practitioners, Hammarskjöld appears to have taken a very dim view. He concludes an especially sympathetic description of an unidentified person's 'concordant aspects of a single personality' with this scathing judgment: 'My friend, the Popular Psychologist, is certain of his diagnosis. And has understood nothing, nothing.'[73] A little later, he adds: 'How easy Psychology has made it for us to dismiss the perplexing mystery with a label which assigns it a place in the list of common aberrations.'[78]

viii

It was a distinctive characteristic of Dag Hammarskjöld's mental processes that his imagination tended to fasten upon certain words or phrases which became verbal symbols of his deepest perplexities and highest hopes. They emerge and recur time and again, weaving their way through his writing, sometimes from the very beginning to the

* Cf. NOTE, below, pp. 221 f.
** *Markings*, pp. 16, 23, 63, 73, 150, 159.
† Unfortunately, W. H. Auden has highlighted the last of these 'markings' as though it were representative. *Ibid.*, p. xvii.

end more than thirty-five years later, like a sequence of interlacing leitmotifs. Indeed, to trace one or another of these key terms through his book is to follow the course of his spirit's pilgrimage. We have already heard his reiteration of 'loneliness', 'sacrifice', 'death', and 'others'. Later, 'the frontier', 'the Way of Possibility', and others were added.

Near the beginning of the fateful three years, 1950–1952, appears for the first time, most unexpectedly, a word which is to haunt him thenceforward: 'maturity'. Unexpectedly, since Hammarskjöld is already in his mid-forties and at the summit of prominence and prestige. We have pointed to the contrast between his inner aloneness and apparent sociability, between his unhappiness over his relations with friends and their satisfaction in these associations. Even more striking is the contradiction that this man, regarded by all who had to do with him as a 'prodigy', a 'precocious genius', should be inwardly irked and depressed by what he felt to be immaturity in his own development. This is closely related to both his vexing solitariness and his dissatisfaction in personal relationships, and serves to round out our understanding of the 'inner person' at this stage of his pilgrimage.

In 1950, he admits: 'You find it hard to forgive those who, early in life, have come to enjoy the advantages which go with maturity. . . .'[41] Later in the same year, he protests: 'Is life so wretched? . . . You are the one who must grow up.'[55] And, again: '. . . Do we ever grow up?'[56]

Three years later, at the very outset of the year which was to mark the turning point in his private no less than in his public life, he returns to the subject, this time not in a questioning but in an affirmative mood—the first in a sequence of definitions which are scattered through his 'Road Marks' over several subsequent years: 'Maturity: among other things—not to hide one's strength out of fear and, consequently, live below one's best.'[89]

Hammarskjöld kept his solitariness and his social frustration strictly to himself, hidden even from those closest to him except for a very few incidental references in correspondence. In contrast, 'maturity' is a note which rings through all his utterances and writings, public no less than private. In his *credo*, 'This I Believe', it furnishes the climax of the pivotal sentence, midway through, upon which the entire confession turns: 'I feel that I can endorse those convictions [in which I was brought up] without any compromise with the demands of that intellectual honesty which is the very key to maturity of mind.' To his colleagues of the United Nations Secretariat, he declares: 'The weight we carry is based solely on trust in our impartiality, our experience and knowledge, our maturity of judgment.'* In his exposition of 'International Service' in connection with the tenth anniversary of the founding of the United Nations, he inserts a dictum which is not without its autobiographical undertones: 'Far from demanding that we abandon or desert ideals and interests basic to our personality, international service puts us under the obligation to let those ideals and interests reach maturity and fruition in a universal climate.' Then, he sets forth his fullest exposition of the phrase which recurs so often in his public speech, 'maturity of mind':

' " In the flourishing literature on the art of life there is much talk about that rare quality: maturity of mind. It is easy to circumscribe such maturity in negative terms. In positive terms it is difficult to define it, although we all recognize it when we have the privilege of seeing its fruits. It is reflected in an absence of fear, in recognition of the fact that fate is what we make it.** It finds expression in an absence of attempts to be anything more than we are, or different from what we are, in recognition of the fact that we are on solid ground only when we accept giving to our fellow men neither more nor less than what is really ours. . . . Maturity of mind seems to me to be the very basis for that attitude which I have described here as the essence of international service. . . . a mature individual, living under the rules of his conscience." 't

And in one of his most important late addresses, at Cambridge University on June 5, 1958, on 'The Walls of Distrust', he declares: 'There is a maturity of mind required of those who give up rights. There is a maturity of mind required of those who acquire new rights.'‡

Time and again, through the years of overwhelming responsibility for the world's peace, when foes and friends alike stood amazed at his capacity for instant and ripe decisions of utmost delicacy and gravity and risk, and while he was frequently extolling 'maturity' in his public addresses, Hammarskjöld returned in his private meditations

* *Servant of Peace*, p. 32.
** His radio *credo* had affirmed that 'fate is what we make it'.
† *Servant of Peace*, pp. 81, 84.
‡ *Ibid.*, p. 184.

to redefine this term which was so central for him. It was probably just after he had been notified of his nomination to the United Nations Secretary-Generalship that he wrote: 'Maturity: among other things, a new lack of self-consciousness—the kind you can only attain when you have become entirely indifferent to yourself through an absolute assent to your fate. . . .'(90) And, toward the close of his first year in his new post: 'Maturity: among other things, the unclouded happiness of the child at play. . . .'(93)

We might be tempted to assume that the 'maturity' which Hammarskjöld struggles to define and to make his own was *emotional* maturity. Nothing could be further from the fact. Dag Hammarskjöld acknowledged no such bifurcation or compartmentalization of human nature, in himself or in others. He seeks 'maturity' of the whole person; he speaks of 'the discipline by which a man can be educated to maturity—intellectual, emotional, and moral.'(112) In his public addresses, 'maturity of mind' embraces the total personality.

Hammarskjöld's final word on this theme which both disturbed and commanded him is from 1956. It brings to its close an extended meditation which gathers up much of what he had slowly come to believe about human relations. An earlier sentence was reported as his definitive reflection on 'love': '. . . tamed by the yoke of human intimacy and warmed by its tenderness'. Then he goes on: '. . . It is better for the health of the soul to make one man good than "to sacrifice oneself for mankind". For a mature man, these are not alternatives, but two aspects of self-realization, which mutually support each other, both being the outcome of one and the same choice.'(133)

Thus, we see that across more than half a dozen years, Hammarskjöld gradually worked his way through to a satisfying understanding and experience of this quality which so fascinated him. Here is evidence from study of this single key term of the transitional character of this period and of the advance achieved. But that is to anticipate our tale.

ix

How are we to account for the disparity between Dag Hammarskjöld as friends and colleagues knew him and the man as he knew himself, the seeming disjunction between the public figure and the person within, the interrelated contradictions between the world's portrait of him and what he himself insisted is 'the only true "profile" that can be drawn'?

Undoubtedly, there are a number of possible explanations, complementary rather than contradictory. But one factor appears to underlie all others, in some degree responsible for them.

For psychic aloneness and apartness so deep and so persistent, we should expect to find the substratum in childhood. And that expectation is not mistaken. The evidence lies just beneath the surface of Hammarskjöld's *Markings*, in a group of 'Road Marks' set down almost fifty years after the events they record.

In July 1959, Hammarskjöld had been on home leave in Sweden. Quite possibly, he had revisited the scenes of his youth at Uppsala.

On his fifty-fourth birthday, July 29, he had written a soul-searching meditation on 'humility'. Returning to New York, on August 4, he continued reflection on 'humility' with special stress upon 'the point of rest at the center of our being', another of his favorite and oft-repeated phrases.

On that same day, Hammarskjöld began the composition of the sequence of poems in the mode of Japanese *haiku* which had come to intrigue him. For the next three months, all of the 'Road Marks' are *haiku*, more than a hundred of them.* The first forty, apparently written over the weekend of August 7 and 9, are captioned 'From Uppsala'. They are retrievals of boyhood observations and experiences which had lain, vivid if dormant memories, across nearly half a century, doubtless brought to the surface of consciousness by his recent visit to his childhood home. He begins with re-creations of scenes from Nature, from life in the Castle, from incidents of youthful play. Then, suddenly, comes a succession of far more intimate and painful recollections:

> 'My home drove me
> Into the wilderness.
> Few look for me. Few hear me.'

Clearly, life in the family had not been as idyllic as has been supposed. We noted earlier that he recalls the opprobrium attaching to his father:

* *Markings*, pp. 175–95. See below, pp. 162 ff.

'A box on the ear taught the boy
That Father's name
Was odious to them.'

Then, three poems reveal peculiar sensitivity to playmates' cruel
judgment and the isolation of the youthful moralist:

'He fell when he tried to vault.
They all had their laugh
At such a sissy.'

And yet a classmate informed his biographer: 'Dag was never considered a sissy. It was never possible to push him around.'*

'His moral lecture
Blazed with hate.
What could have driven a child that far?'

'They laid the blame on him.
He didn't know what it was,
But he confessed it.'

Finally, three memories open windows into the youthful soul:

'He wasn't wanted.
When, nonetheless, he came,
He could only watch them play.'

'School was over. The yard was empty.
The ones he sought
Had found new friends.'

'Denied the Sought-After,
He longed to deserve
To be the Sought-After.' (180-181)

It is manifest that deep and aching 'solitariness' was not a development of mature years; rather, it was a direct legacy from boyhood's
wretchedness. The youth's sense of isolation from comrades, sunk
deep within the subconscious, had continuing power over the adult's
life. In the light of this disclosure, much which is otherwise puzzling
becomes understandable.

* Lash, *op. cit.*, p. 21.

Likewise, Dag Hammarskjöld's aversion to conventional social life dated, as we noted, from student days. Forty years later at the United Nations, it was well known that 'Hammarskjöld shuns formal "society", and avoids invitations in order not to acquire obligations'.

Again, Hammarskjöld's solitariness was, as his biographer suggests, in some part 'the price of leadership and responsibility.'* For this he had been prepared in his parental home. Despite the difficulties in his relations with his father, the son continued to be shadowed by the paternal example and by an inescapable sense of obligation to fulfill his father's expectations for him. In the same year 1950, in which so many of the 'markings' quoted in preceding pages were composed, he reminded himself: '. . . it is not for the egotistical satisfaction of perfection in your job, but for him that you work, that what he has a right to demand from you takes precedence over what you have a right to demand from him.'(49) In memorializing his father, the son declared: 'A mature man is his own judge. . . . The advice of others may be welcome and valuable, but it does not free him from responsibility. Therefore, he may become very lonely.' 'A man of firm convictions does not ask, and does not receive, understanding from those with whom he comes in conflict.'** This might have been spoken autobiographically. In the same memorial address, he drew a touching picture of his father, watching for 'those swarms of jackdaws which he had longed for more and more in his loneliness't.

True understanding of Dag Hammarskjöld's spiritual anguish must be sought, however, at a level deeper than a legacy fom childhood's isolation or a temperamental reticence or professional preoccupations or an overriding servitude to duty. His was the inner aloneness common to all men and women, or certainly to all persons who think and feel deeply about life and care passionately for inner integrity, more intense in Hammarskjöld's experience only in the measure of his greater spiritual sensitivity and moral resolution. For many, life is an unending quest for understanding by others, an understanding which is never complete, therefore a quest which is never satisfied. Surely, here is the profoundest and most disturbing disappointment in many marriages. Here is the perennial frustration in friendship,

* Lash, op. cit., p. 222.
** Servant of Peace, pp. 76, 64.
† Ibid., p. 64.

always seeking, always hoping, always expecting an intuitive and total mutuality of feeling, of conviction, of appreciation, of communion which is never fully realized. We reach and long and cry across the unbridgeable chasm which yawns between the depths of our being and the deep in one whom we revere and love. But we cannot attain. And, in consequence, we suffer disillusionment, sometimes despair.

Likewise, so far as Dag Hammarskjöld's sense of insufficiency and defeat was symbolized by his unsatisfied quest for a 'maturity' which he felt himself never fully to have achieved, he differed not in principle but only in degree from many and many a person whom the world hails as an outstanding 'success' but who falls so far short of the standard of his own inner ideal as to seem to himself a failure.

Indeed, the same is true of all the confounding surprises which his self-portrait reveals. Each is the mark not of a peculiar or immature person but just the reverse, of a man of superlative sensibility, uncommon self-awareness, and exceptionally high-pitched goal for human living. Dag Hammarskjöld, in his inner as in his public life, was not a 'sport', an eccentric. On the contrary, he was man as all of us, in the lesser measure of our slighter gifts and fumbling response, should aim to be.

For reasons which are not difficult to comprehend, these universal longings were, in Dag Hammarskjöld, more commanding, his yearning for their fulfillment more insistent and persistent, than with most. In a profound sense, the haunting, sometimes harrowing apartness which constitutes the leitmotif of a lifetime's meditation upon the meaning and destiny of human existence was the measure of the greatness of his soul. His was the inner solitariness of a person of brilliant intellect, tender spirit, and resolute integrity, burdened almost beyond sufferance by work and, in his latter years, by continual threat to the world's peace, a bachelor from duty who found conventional social life almost unendurably 'exhausting'.

By the same token, what he recorded as private 'Road Marks' for his own spiritual pilgrimage and has permitted to become a public possession speaks with unsurpassed truth and power to those in similar plight who are partners in his longing and have ears to hear, and will continue to speak with illumination, with reassurance, and with healing down the years. The most sensitive, the most earnest, the most honest will testify: 'He speaks to my condition', and will give thanks.

X

This surprising man whose inner suffering so belied the seemingly
exceptional stability, self-mastery, and success of both public performance and personal associations sought escape or at least relief
from his anguish through every channel and stratagem available in
his many-sided life—through Nature, through friendships, through
work, through service to others, through a firmer dedication to duty,
and, finally and climactically, through meditation upon the example
of Jesus. This sequence of resorts is both roughly chronological and
also at increasingly exacting levels.

Early in this period, he seeks solace in Nature, always a release and
refreshment for him: 'He is one of those who has had the wilderness
for a pillow, and called a star his brother. Alone. But loneliness can
be a communion.' (40) He cannot altogether surrender the hope that
human comradeship may ease his disquiet: '. . . only that can be
really yours which is another's. . . .' (38) But he can discover no
satisfying relief through that means. The failure of all external
sources of relief drives him deeper and deeper within:

'The longest journey
Is the journey inwards.
Of him who has chosen his destiny,
Who has started upon his quest
For the source of his being
(Is there a source?).' (58)

If friendship will not solve his problem, perhaps helpfulness to
others might do so: '. . . the nature of life is such that I can realize
my individuality by becoming a bridge for others. . . .' (53) Indeed,
while recognizing the multiple character of his distress and of possible resolutions of it, at one point he came to think that this might
be the only way out: 'That our pains and longings are thousandfold
and can be anesthetized in a thousand different ways is as commonplace a truth as that, in the end, they are all one, and can only be
overcome in one way. What you most need is to feel—or believe you
feel—that you are needed. . . .'(70) But in the same 'marking', he
goes on to define with relentless realism what then appeared to him

the two possibilities for the path ahead, and to anticipate a more demanding way of escape:

'Fated or chosen—in the end, the vista of future loneliness only allows a choice between two alternatives: either to despair in desolation, or to stake so high on the "possibility" that one acquires the right to life in a fellowship that transcends the individual.* But doesn't choosing the second call for the kind of faith which moves mountains?' (70)

To be sure, not all of Hammarskjöld's prolific reflections through these three years were occupied with the interrelated themes of loneliness, frustration in personal relationships and an unsatisfied quest for maturity. As in earlier years, he recorded poetic appreciations of Nature, acrid comments on human foibles, meditations on beauty, and many others.

It was through those same years that he brooded most often and deeply upon Nature and the analogues of human experience. There is also lyric delight in its glory:

'Time's flight. Our flight in time—flight from time.
Flying on strong wings—with time,
Never lingering, never anticipating:
A rest in the movement—our victory over movement.
Lightly, lightly—
Soaring above the dread of the waters. . . .' (52)

'Lean fare, austere forms,
Brief delight, few words.
Low down in cool space
One star—
The morning star. . . .' (72)

Moreover, these years of Hammarskjöld's 'Darkest Night' were not without very occasional shafts of light, promises of a fuller illumination soon to break. Early in 1952, midway through the triennium, he writes: ' "Thy will be done—" To let the inner take precedence over the

* *Markings* reads 'life in a transcendental co-inherence'. The English translators have used 'co-inherence' to render several different Swedish words and phrases. In most instances, a more literal translation of the Swedish has been substituted for this rather unfamiliar and somewhat obscure English word. Cf. pp. 135 and 178.

outer, the soul over the world—wherever this may lead you. . . .' [81]
Somewhat later in that year and shortly before his most despairing
outcries stands one of the most notable 'markings' in his book:

'. . . When the worries over your work loosen their grip, then this
experience of light, warmth, and power. From without—a sustain-
ing element, like air to the glider or water to the swimmer. . . .
through me there flashes this vision of a magnetic field in the soul,
created in a timeless present by unknown multitudes, living in
holy obedience, whose words and actions are a timeless prayer.
—"The Communion of Saints"—and—within it—an eternal
life.' [84]

The upshot is a reaching out for a more demanding dedication: 'Give
me something to die for—!' [85]

More significant, however, because prophetic of what lies ahead, is
the appearance of two wholly new themes. Though unrelated, indeed
contrasted, both point in new directions and anticipate the way forward which is also to be a way upward.

For one whose thought was so permeated by metaphors of climbing and exploration, it was but natural that the idea of 'frontier'
should hold a special fascination. He had spoken earlier of 'the frontier between life and death, as it has been drawn for all eternity' [44].
And an aphorism from T. S. Eliot, 'Old men ought to be explorers',
had prompted him to comment: 'Some have to be—because the
frontiers of the familiar are closed to them. . . .' [62]

Toward the end of the year 1951, there appears for the first time a
phrase which, in the fashion we have already discovered as characteristic of Hammarskjöld's mind, becomes a major motif to which he
returns no fewer than six times over the following four years. The
Swedish 'vid gränsen av det oerhörda' is rendered in the English
version of Markings 'the frontier of the unheard-of'. That is a correct literal translation. However, 'unheard-of' is not only bafflingly
opaque; it fails to convey the rich overtones of the Swedish 'det
oerhörda'. The latter are better suggested by such terms as 'ineffable',
'unfathomable', 'inapprehensible', 'inconceivable', 'hidden', 'latent',
'transcendental', 'the Beyond', or, perhaps best, by a word made
current coin in contemporary religious thought by Rudolf Otto who
was a favorite with Hammarskjöld: 'numinous'.

The keynote is struck in its first use:

'Now. When I have overcome my fears—of others, of myself, of
the underlying darkness:
    at the frontier of the unheard-of.
Here ends the known. But, from a source beyond it,
    something fills my being with its possibilities.
Here desire is purified and made lucid: each action is
    a preparation for, each choice an assent to the unknown. . . .
At the frontier—' [76]

In the last meditation for that same year, he repeats the phrase 'At
the frontier of the unheard-of' and then comments upon the closing
scene of Joseph Conrad's Lord Jim [80], in whose writings he appears
to have been steeped at that time.* Again, near the beginning of the
following year, he writes a long meditation on death and concludes
with the same phrase, with perhaps a suggestion of suicide. [82]

As with the other themes which most troubled Hammarskjöld in
this period, discovery of the deeper and truer meaning had to wait
until after the then-imminent turning point of his life. Early in 1954,
about a year after his assumption of United Nations leadership, he
writes: 'Then I saw that the wall had never been there, that the
"unheard-of" is here and this, not something and somewhere else,
that the . . . "surrendered" is what, in me, God gives of Himself to
Himself.' And he continues: 'Only he who at every moment is all he
is capable of being can hope for a furlough from the frontier before
he disappears into the darkness. . . .' [96] A little later, in the midst
of some of his most deeply religious reflections, following a moving
prayer for purity and humility of heart, come the final and decisive
definitions of this haunting phrase: 'The "unheard-of"—to be in the
hands of God. . . .' [100] 'So long as you abide in the Unheard-of,
you are beyond and above—to hold fast to this must be the First
Commandment in your spiritual discipline.' [101] In each use, if we
substitute for 'the unheard-of' one of the English words which more
nearly catches the inner meaning of the Swedish 'det oerhörda'—'the
Beyond' or 'the numinous' or one of the others—we begin to be
grasped by the character and development of Hammarskjöld's ap-

* The fact that the phrase is here placed in quotation marks has encouraged
the assumption that it is quoted from Conrad. But it appears that Hammarskjöld is quoting his own earlier use of the phrase.

prehension. Here, once more, to trace that single key phrase, so pregnant with meaning for him, through these four years is to follow the transition which was to transform his inner life.

The other new theme which appears for the first time during this period of extreme dejection is less mystifying but more surprising and also far more momentous for Hammarskjöld's spiritual biography.

Through the preceding twenty-five years of his recorded reflections, there had been not a single explicit mention of Jesus and very few glancing references to the Gospels.* Then, suddenly, just about midway in the three-year period, following several pages of relatively objective comment upon public office and just before a group of appreciations of Nature at springtide, there stands the longest sequence of connected entries in the entire book, running to two and a half pages. It is also among the half dozen most important, essential for the understanding of Hammarskjöld's pilgrimage. It is an extended meditation upon Jesus as he makes his way toward his death. This meditation anticipates thoughts which are to occupy Hammarskjöld more and more in later years and points toward the ultimate resolution of his soul's struggle for integrity, for self-identity, and for faith.** Is there light as to why this new theme appears at this time?

Holiday companions report that, on a climbing expedition three years earlier in 1948 when Hammarskjöld's attention was divided between intense self-examination and his sharpest observations upon the foibles and failures of 'others', they noticed that he had brought along for private reading a bulky leather-bound volume in which he was obviously absorbed. It was the original German edition of Albert Schweitzer's *The Quest of the Historical Jesus*. Almost casually, he suggested that it was a book which they should read. Apparently, he was just beginning a study which was to continue over a considerable time and which he later acknowledged in his radio *credo* as having been one of the decisive influences upon his life.† This passage seems to have been the first recorded precipitation from that study.

In later years there occurs further reflection on Jesus' life as it

---

* Pp. 15, 36, 44.

** For a fuller discussion of this pivotal passage and of Hammarskjöld's view of Jesus, see below, pp. 180, 184 f., 194, 195 ff. The passage is on pp. 68–70.

† 'In his work I found a key for modern man to the world of the Gospels.' *Servant of Peace*, p. 24. See below, p. 180.

moved inexorably toward its tragic end.* Nevertheless, at this time, the single meditation on Jesus stands alone. Hammarskjöld's quest continues unsatisfied. As we saw, the final entry for those three tortured years takes the form of the despairing query: 'Loneliness is not the sickness unto death. No, but can it be cured except by death? . . .' (87)

Then, the page is turned toward a New Year, that of 1953; and, all unforeseen, a new life.

---

5. The Turning Point:
1952–1953

N O ONE CAN FOLLOW with close attention Dag Hammarskjöld's interior reflections through the last dozen years of his life without becoming aware of a sharp change, a marked contrast between 'The Darkest Night' of 1950–1952 and from 1953 onward.

To be sure, there is no deliberate reversal, no avowed repudiation of what he had said to himself earlier. Many of the familiar themes—'loneliness', for example—recur, though less frequent and now muted; and they are pressed to climactic and positive conclusions. However, there is a deep and pervasive alteration of outlook, of temper, of dominant emphasis which is more readily sensed than identified. Relatively, there is less preoccupation with his own inner struggle, less confession of solitariness, less complaint over his relations with 'others'. On the other hand, there is far more comment obviously prompted by events in his public career. And there is markedly stronger positive religious affirmation.

The close of 1952 found Hammarskjöld at the peak of public achievement and at the nadir of private despondency. Near the end of the year, he had written: 'What I ask for is absurd: that life shall have a meaning. What I strive for is impossible: that my life shall acquire a meaning. . . .' [86] Also one of his bitterest yearnings for an intimacy which is denied him: 'How ridiculous, this need of yours to communicate! Why should it mean so much to you that at least *one* person has seen the inside of your life? . . .' [87] There were two anguished pleas for release: 'Give me something to die for—!'

'Pray that your loneliness may spur you into finding something to live for, great enough to die for.' [85] As we have seen, there was at least the thought of suicide. And the year ended on a union of the two dominant notes of 'loneliness' and 'death'.

The year 1953 is begun, presumably on New Year's Day, like each of the three preceding years with meditation on the familiar hymn line: '—night approaches now.' In the earlier years, his comments had been fully in the mood of the Swedish hymn—the transience of life and welcome to death.* But now there is a startling contrast. In 1953 Hammarskjöld responds to the same text exultantly:

> ' "—Night approaches now."
> For all that has been—Thanks!
> To all that shall be—Yes!' [89]

And, shortly thereafter: 'Not I, but God in me.' [90]

Clearly, between the despairing plaints of late 1952 and the positive and profoundly religious affirmations of early 1953, something had occurred within his interior self, of which he may not have been conscious then, but which reveals itself in his 'Road Marks'. Is it possible to locate that moment or event or period of transition more precisely?

It has been generally assumed that the event which effected such a radical alteration in outlook was Hammarskjöld's elevation to the United Nations Secretary-Generalship. Unquestionably, this was an important factor in consolidating the change. Hammarskjöld himself recognized this. From New York, he wrote to his old friend and former colleague, Ernst Wigforss: 'In this international work I have lost the sense of inner cleavage that I felt at home in Sweden.' Bo Beskow whose friendship with Hammarskjöld began shortly before the latter's United Nations election points to a more intimate factor: 'I watched him grow suddenly into full maturity—because of his great challenging responsibility, and because his father died. I lost my father at the same time; I know the change and, in a way, the freedom to be yourself.'

However, there is strong evidence which locates the 'turning point' at a different and earlier time. That evidence stands forth from the pages of *Markings*.

Fortunately, we are not left to guesswork or hypothesis in this

* Above, pp. 71–72.

matter. That somewhere along the way there was what Hammarskjöld considered a decisive moment of transition, he himself attests.
Looking back almost a decade after the event, in a passage dated
'Whitsunday [May 21] 1961', just four months before his death, he
put down what, for purposes of his spiritual biography, is the most
significant single entry in this amazing 'diary':

> 'I don't know Who—or what—put the question, I don't know
> when it was put. I don't even remember answering. But at some
> moment I did answer Yes to Someone—or Something—and from
> that hour I was certain that existence is meaningful and that, there-
> fore, my life, in self-surrender, had a goal.
>
> From that moment I have known what it means "not to look
> back," and "to take no thought for the morrow." . . .'* (205)

From this autobiographical recollection, three facts are clear:
Hammarskjöld recalled a quite definite event—'at some moment',
'from that hour', 'from that moment'—when the direction of his
inner struggle reversed and he faced in the opposite direction; he
interpreted this 'moment' as an act of affirmation when he was
moved to 'answer Yes to Someone—or Something'; at the time of
remembrance, he could not locate the precise 'moment'. Probably, he
had not recently reviewed his 'markings' of earlier years.** For he
himself had left strongly presumptive, if not absolutely conclusive,
indication of the 'when' within that earlier writing. It lies in the
single word 'Yes'—another of the half dozen words or phrases which
he came to use again and again and which serve as connecting
threads, tracing a development in his thought of which he may not
have been aware.

Up to the end of 1952, Hammarskjöld had used the word 'Yes'
rarely†, and then in quite different and trivial contexts. But, at New
Year 1953 he proclaims: 'To all that shall be—Yes!' 'Yes'—the first
occurrence of the affirmation which he is to repeat, often in italics,

* The echo of the phrases which had been used in the complaint near the end
of 1952 quoted above—'that life shall have a meaning', 'that my life shall acquire
a meaning'—is striking. The 'marking' for Whitsunday 1961 should be read in its
entirety, especially the concluding paragraph. It occupies the whole of p. 205. Cf.
also below, p. 199.
** Here is evidence that the manuscript of Markings was composed over a
considerable period of time.
† Pp. 21, 80, 81.

through the next several years with steadily enlarged and more precise meaning. 'Yes' rings like a refrain through the rest of his book. Three months later, he responds to his election as United Nations Secretary-General: 'To be free, to be able to stand up and leave *everything* behind—without looking back. To say *Yes*—'* (91) And two entries further on: 'To say Yes to life is at one and the same time to say Yes to oneself. Yes—even to that element in one which is most unwilling to let itself be transformed from a temptation into a strength.' (92) The following autumn, in his radio *credo*, he pays tribute to 'those great medieval mystics for whom "self-surrender" had been the way to self-realization, and who in "singleness of mind" and "inwardness" had found strength to say *yes* to every demand which the needs of their neighbors made them face, and to say *yes* also to every fate life had in store for them. . . .'** Early in 1955, he returns in his private meditations to the same keynote: 'To say Yes is never more difficult than when circumstances prevent you from rushing to the defense of someone whose purity of heart makes him defenseless before an attack.' (105) Later that year, in a series of 'Road Marks' following his fiftieth birthday and Peking's release, through his intervention, of American airmen sentenced as spies, he rebukes himself†: 'So you were "led into temptation," and lost that certainty of faith which makes saying Yes to fate a self-evident necessity. . . .' (109) The following year, 1956, he spells out the word's meaning more fully:

'You dare your Yes—and experience a meaning.
You repeat your Yes—and all things acquire a meaning.‡
When everything has a meaning, how can you live anything
    but a *Yes*.' (125)

More than a year after that, on October 6, 1957, a Sunday ten days after his re-election as Secretary-General, comes the climactic affirma-

* Again, note the anticipation of one of the key phrases in the Whitsunday 1961 passage: ' "not to look back" '! Italics in the original.
** *Servant of Peace*, p. 24. The italics are Hammarskjöld's. A recent interpreter of Meister Eckhart describes him as 'one of the world's great "Yes-sayers" '. (Raymond Bernard Blakney, *Meister Eckhart: A Modern Translation*. Harper Torchbooks, 1941, p. xiv.) This may explain Hammarskjöld's use of the key-word 'Yes'.
† The first part of this 'marking' appears on p. 133.
‡ Observe, once more, the recurrence of the earlier phrase: 'that life shall have a meaning . . . that my life shall acquire a meaning' and the anticipation of the same thought in the Whitsunday 1961 'marking': 'existence is meaningful'.

tion: 'Yes to God: yes to Fate: yes to yourself. . . .' (157) However, the word continues to indwell and illumine his mind. Indeed, shortly after the Whitsunday 1961 reminiscence, within a six-verse poem, Hammarskjöld makes his final declaration:

'Asked if I have courage
To go on to the end,
I answer Yes without
A second thought.' (206)

Toward the end of 1952 or in the first days of 1953, then, Dag Hammarskjöld's spirit passed through a crisis which he himself considered absolutely determinative for his life. This occurred, it should be noted, three months or more prior to his election to office at the United Nations. It constituted a preparation for what was to come which an older piety would have been inclined to describe as 'Providential'. Hammarskjöld himself, firm in his conviction of the formative Divine influence upon human life,* might likewise have so accounted for it. Interpret it how we will, it is sheer matter of fact that, in the months shortly preceding his election to supreme responsibility, his life was fortified in a quite new and crucial way for its demands.

NOTE

Dag Hammarskjöld spent the Christmas 1952–New Year 1953 period at Abisko in the northernmost part of Sweden in the company of Henrik Klackenberg. In response to a query whether he had noted 'any change in Hammarskjöld's basic attitude and spirit during this time together', Judge Klackenberg has replied:

'During the holiday week, the time I spent with D.H. passed in more or less the same way as during our usual trips to the mountains. . . . At that time, it seemed to me that in our contact there was nothing specially noticeable about D.H. Our conversations and discussions were concerned as usual with events, people and problems —literary, philosophical and political, i.e. most of the time he discoursed in his fluent and brilliant way and I just listened. At that time, it did not occur to me that this was a critical period in his life. However, I was slightly perplexed over the fact that he devoted some

* Cf. his interpretation of the resolution of the Suez Crisis four years later. Below, p. 140.

parts of the evenings to reading the Bible. [Apparently, this had not been Hammarskjöld's practice on previous trips together.] But nothing was said about this.'

However, Judge Klackenberg continues:

'I have tried to recall whether there was anything unusual in D.H.'s reactions which could indicate a difficult state in his personal affairs. Without wishing to attach any decisive importance to these memories, I can note observations which indicate a certain personal vulnerability, a tendency towards *noli me tangere* which I had not noticed earlier during the times we spent together.'

Then, citing a particular discussion, Judge Klackenberg adds:

'D.H. became silent and without being unfriendly withdrew into his shell.' [Previously, in similar discussions] 'either it used to be a lively argumentation, based on many viewpoints, designed to convince me of what was wrong in my objection, or else an open acceptance, "Yes, perhaps you are right." '

6. The Fulfillment:
1953–1958

I

DAG HAMMARSKJÖLD'S ACCOMPLISHMENTS at and through the United Nations are so well known and they have already been so well recorded as to preclude detailed retelling here.

Step by step over an eight-and-a-half-year period, the United Nations moved beyond the unhappy legacy of the League of Nations as a tribunal for conference and controversy to become an agency for action. This was largely the achievement of one man. Probably no other individual in history has effected so large a work of mediation and pacification among nations.

From that first bold 'Mission to Peking' in the early days of 1955 to seek the release of American airmen held captive by the Chinese Communist Government on through his intervention in the Suez Crisis in late 1956 and his mediation among the Arab States over Lebanon and Palestine in the summer of 1958 to the conflict within the Congo over Katanga which was to claim his life in September 1961, Hammarskjöld's attention and energies were almost continuously occupied by one 'crisis' after another which threatened to escalate into major war embroiling the Great Powers.

'Korea, China, Indonesia, Kashmir, Palestine, Hungary, North Africa. There are fires all around the horizon, and they are not fires announcing peace.' he declared in his address at Cambridge Univer-

sity in June 1958.* On New Year's Eve 1960, while the world turned
to festive celebration, it was Cuba, Laos and the Congo which held
the United Nations Staff at their posts long past midnight in conference with the Secretary-General, about to set off for Central Africa.
As crisis followed crisis, erupting on almost every continent, each in
turn was brought into the counsels of the United Nations; and after
debate, usually heated and often inconclusive, in the General Assembly or the Security Council, each was committed to the Secretary-
General for resolution. 'Give it to Dag' became a colloquial formula
to dispose of seemingly insoluble problems.

The record of that unique achievement has been set forth in an
admirable biography completed just before his death. It bears the
appropriate subtitle 'Custodian of the Brushfire Peace'.** That
achievement will continue to furnish subject matter for research and
writing through the coming years. It is beyond the scope of this
study. Our interest focuses upon those aspects of Dag Hammarskjöld's Secretary-Generalship which cast light upon the 'inner person' behind the 'public servant'.

ii

It was in the role which Hammarskjöld himself defined as 'international civil servant' that he won the respect of statesmen, the concur-
rence of Governments, and the grateful acclaim of their Peoples.

The role of the 'civil servant' had been much in Hammarskjöld's
reflection over many years. A year and a half before the wholly unforeseen call to the United Nations, he had published a singularly
self-revealing article in the Swedish Social-Democrat magazine *Tiden*
for September 1951, entitled 'The Civil Servant and Society'. Described as 'marginal reflections on a personal problem', it set forth his
conception of the obligations of the civil servant:

'The basic and obvious commandment in the code of the civil
servant is that he serves the community and not any group, party or
particular interests. This does not by any means mean that he ought

* 'The Walls of Distrust' in *Servant of Peace*, pp. 184–88.
** Joseph P. Lash, *Dag Hammarskjöld: Custodian of the Brushfire Peace* (New
York: Doubleday and Company, 1961). Richard I. Miller, *Dag Hammarskjöld
and Crisis Diplomacy* (New York: Oceana Publications, Inc., 1961), contains
much detailed material on the principal crises.

to be—or that it is proper that he should be—politically indifferent, but it does mean that, however deeply engaged politically he may be, as an *executive civil servant* he must not work for his political ideals, *because they are his.* Outside his official duties, on the other hand, he is fully entitled to work for his political ideals.*

'His private political judgment can never outweigh his duty as a civil servant unless he considers that his own view represents a communal interest about which, objectively, there can be no two opinions. . . .

'Finally the ethic exemplified by Schweitzer finds expression in the subordination of private interests to the whole: a moral obligation firstly to the community, in the sense of the nation; secondly to that larger community represented by internationalism. . . .

'To the superficial observer this blend of conservative, liberal, social-radical and internationalistic elements may appear eclectic in the extreme. If so, it is because he fails to see that these elements have not been dragged together from different directions, but have grown out of the same basic view which, so far from indicating any desire to have a finger in every pie, or an inability to choose, leads on the contrary to having no home in any political party, owing to the consistency with which the individual attitude to life is reflected in the political sphere.'

What more admirable *credo* for one who was shortly to be drafted to the most responsible, and possibly the most important, civil servant appointment in the world!

How persistently this theme continued central in Hammarskjöld's thought is suggested by the fact that 'The International Public Servant' was the topic he chose for his brief remarks to the Press Corps on his arrival in New York on April 9, 1953.** More than once, he seized appropriate opportunities to hold these ideals before the membership of the United Nations Staff, most explicitly as it happened in what was to prove his valedictory to them on Staff Day, September 8, 1961, just ten days before his death.†

In the final months of his service to the United Nations, the issue became acute because of violent and persistent attacks upon his administration by spokesmen for the Soviet Bloc. In response, when he was invited to give an address at Oxford University in connection

* The italics are Hammarskjöld's.
** *Servant of Peace*, pp. 27–28. Above, pp. 5–6.
† *Ibid.*, pp. 376–78.

with the conferral of an honorary degree on May 30, 1961, he took as his subject: 'The International Civil Servant in Law and in Fact.'* This was his last as it was unquestionably one of the most important public addresses he ever gave. Taking his start from a reported recent charge by Chairman Khrushchev that 'while there are neutral countries, there are no neutral men', Hammarskjöld reviewed in some detail the long development of the concept of an 'international civil servant' from before the creation of the League of Nations through the League's experience to the provisions in the United Nations Charter for its Secretariat. His conclusion was that ' "neutrality" means that the international civil servant, also in executive tasks with political implications, must remain wholly uninfluenced by national or group interests or ideologies . . . a dedicated professional service responsible only to the Organization'. This conception he redefined for the General Assembly in the Introduction to his Annual Report the following August with a phrase lifted from Article 100 of the United Nations Charter which he had reiterated many times: ' "the exclusively international character" of the Secretariat'.** The implications he spelled out quite explicitly to his Staff: 'The Secretariat is truly international, its individual members owing no allegiance to any national government.'†

The difficulties in fulfilling so demanding a neutrality were fully faced in the Oxford address in words which echo his article in *Tiden* just a decade before:

'The international civil servant must keep himself under the strictest observation. He is not requested to be a neuter in the sense that he has to have no sympathies or antipathies, that there are to be no interests which are close to him in his personal capacity or that he is to have no ideas or ideals that matter for him. However, he is requested to be fully aware of those human reactions and meticulously check himself so that they are not permitted to influence his actions. This is nothing unique. Is not every judge professionally under the same obligation?'

In direct rejoinder to Khrushchev's contention that 'there is not a single neutral person on this globe', Hammarskjöld drew this distinc-

* *Ibid.*, pp. 329–53.
** *Ibid.*, pp. 367 ff.
† *Ibid.*, p. 376.

tion in a Press Conference following the address at Oxford: 'I would say there is no neutral man, but there is, if you have integrity, neutral action by the right kind of man.'*

Responding to a query how anyone could be effective if 'cut off from his allegiance to any one country, in the first instance his native country', Hammarskjöld said: 'The reply is simply that to the extent that he, in truth and spirit, can eliminate all such allegiances and fall back on himself, he will find a new home country which is everywhere in the sense that he will find open doors wherever he goes.' He was not talking theory or merely propounding an ideal; he was speaking autobiographically. With all of his own rootage in and loyalty to his Fatherland, friends reported that, toward the end, he did not feel the same longing to return to Sweden. Dag Hammarskjöld, by the scrupulous practice of these principles, had become in fact, at the very core of his being, a citizen of the world as well as servant of all mankind.

In the discharge of his clearly defined role, Hammarskjöld's chief reliance was upon 'private diplomacy' rather than upon public debate, 'imbued by and inspired by a spirit of personal confidence'. 'It is diplomacy, not speeches or votes, that continues to have the last word in the process of peacemaking', a diplomacy of reconciliation rather than of recrimination. 'Private diplomacy' which Hammarskjöld sometimes referred to alternatively as 'quiet diplomacy' and which was, ideally, 'preventive diplomacy', if not his invention, was more fully and effectively employed by him than ever before and has become an instrument for international conciliation associated with his name.

In the spring of 1958, following the resolution of the Suez Crisis, Hammarskjöld went to Britain to receive the plaudits of the British Government and People; he seized an invitation to address Members of Parliament to speak on 'The Uses of Private Diplomacy'** and called attention to 'a three-stage operation: private diplomacy preceding public debate and then employed again to follow through'. Hammarskjöld insisted that 'private talks must remain private', and it was his scrupulous fidelity to this principle of confidence which justified Adlai Stevenson's tribute: 'Leaders who could not bring themselves to confide in each other were glad to confide in him.' As

* Ibid., p. 351.
** Ibid., pp. 170–74.

of the youth reconciling his university contemporaries and the young Finance Minister mediating fiscal battles between different departments in the Swedish Government, it could be said of the Secretary-General of the United Nations: 'Of all his talents, this, perhaps, was his greatest—a conciliatory spirit matched with a brilliant gift for evoking unanimity.' Behind an exceptional 'talent' and a superior 'gift' for reconciliation lay profounder qualities which gave them their opportunity and their effectiveness: what someone defined as 'moral magistracy', a 'reputation for probity', grounded in 'independence, impartiality and objectivity'. The full secret remained something of a mystery to those accustomed to and themselves embroiled in the familiar stratagems and deceptions and rationalizations of international negotiation. On his re-election to a second term as Secretary-General, the President of the General Assembly, in hailing him as 'surely our supreme international Civil Servant', spoke for them all.

That role could not be fulfilled merely through consultations on the '38th Floor' of the United Nations Headquarters Building in New York. It sent Hammarskjöld out across the earth, again and again, to every continent and more than eighty countries. In the eight and a half years, he left his headquarters seventy-six times on missions of shorter or longer duration—first to China, six times to the Near East, three times beyond the Iron Curtain to Moscow, Prague and other east European capitals, twice to southern and eastern Asia, once around the world via Australasia and the central Pacific Islands, twice to South America, in the last years six times to virtually every part of the African continent, not to speak of scores of visits to Geneva and other western European capitals and frequent short trips in Canada and the United States.

iii

When Hammarskjöld took over his post in April 1953, his initial concern was the reorganization and, above all, the restoration of confidence in a Staff sorely demoralized by Senator McCarthy's attacks and other disruptive factors.

Dr. Andrew Cordier, Hammarskjöld's deputy, reports that he suggested that it would strengthen Staff morale if the Secretary-General were to visit all Staff members in their offices, assuming that such visitation might require two or three months. 'In the next three weeks we had visited every one of the thirty-five hundred members of the staff in his or her own office in the forty-one stories of the Secretariat Building. His words of query, interest and encouragement are remembered by many staff members to this day.' In April 1958, when he was beginning his second term and the Staff tendered him a surprise party, Hammarskjöld expressed his great happiness and then recalled the similar occasion just five years earlier:

'I knew only one thing and that is that nobody can do more than is in his power, and I had only one intention and that was to do that much. . . . I knew that there is one thing nobody ever needs to lose, and that is his self-respect. And if I had any promise which I gave to myself five years ago, it was just this: Whatever happens, stick to your guns, so that you can feel satisfaction with what you have done, whatever the outcome. . . . I felt that the Staff problems should indeed have the first claim upon me. . . . I am both happy and proud to be one of you.'

Then he declared his intention to 'repeat a very fine and encouraging experience I had when I came here . . . to go around the house—all over it again—and met with you all again personally'. He concluded with a favorite verse from the Swedish poet Gunnar Ekelöf: ' "Will the day ever come when joy is great and sorrow small?" ' and added his own answer: 'On the day we feel we are living with a duty, well fulfilled and worth our while, on that day joy is great and we can look on sorrow as being small.' * When he had learned of his United Nations appointment, he had noted the same verse in his private 'diary' and had added this comment:

'It *did* come—the day when the grief became small. For what had befallen me and seemed so hard to bear became insignificant in the light of the demands which God was now making. But how difficult it is to feel that this was also, and for that very reason, the day when the joy became great.' (90)

iv

To gain an impression of how Dag Hammarskjöld the man actually functioned day by day in his United Nations role, we can hardly do

* *Servant of Peace*, pp. 166–69.

better than turn to those who were most closely associated with him, as one of them describes it: 'Day and night, often seven days a week, around the calendar . . . a normal working day of eleven hours but, during crises, often fourteen or eighteen or even twenty-four hours a day'—the men who saw him at close range under every imaginable circumstance, not only at United Nations Headquarters but as traveling companions on his frequent missions across the world.

Dr. Andrew Cordier had been with the United Nations since its inception and, as Deputy Secretary-General, it fell to him to inaugurate Hammarskjöld into his new post and then to be his nearest associate, with offices adjoining, as chief-of-staff. This is his report:

'To work with him was an easy task. . . . No information or his personal reactions to information was ever withheld. We always talked over with great thoroughness the developments of the day and took the necessary action to deal with them. . . . In my constant dialogue with him for eight and a half years, I never found him to be excessively complex and certainly not enigmatic.'

Dr. Ralph Bunche was with Hammarskjöld in the Near East during the Suez and Lebanon crises, was the United Nations chief representative in the Congo as the situation there moved toward conflict, when in New York was one of the small group of intimate advisers known as the 'Congo Club', and is felt by many to have had an especial spiritual affinity with his Chief. Commenting upon Hammarskjöld as his Staff colleagues knew him, Bunche says:

'His relations with his close collaborators were easy, friendly and informal, and always on a first-name basis. There was nothing formidable about him; he not only tolerated but seemed to relish views at odds with his own. His greatest weakness in administration was found precisely in the fact that he usually could not be hard when personal situations demanded it because of an underlying softheartedness. Dag was admired and respected by his associates, but he was not idolized by any of us and never gave the impression that he expected to be; quite the contrary, in fact.'

Bunche adds:

'He was a man of moods, and these could be mercurial. He could, and not infrequently did, display anger and outrage, but only after, and never during, some particularly bad meeting or conference.'

Both his delight in friendship and his genius for easy and intimate fellowship with colleagues, Hammarskjöld carried into his life at the United Nations. To his closest Staff associates, as Dr. Bunche indicates, he was always 'Dag'; and there was a ready and continual coming and going among their nearby offices at all hours of day or night. The strains and pressures of affairs were often lightened by levity. It was reported at the time:

'With a few friends and aides he engages in horseplay, exchanges highbrow jokes, makes up mischievous nicknames for the cast of characters that frequent the U. N. stage, and, says one of his friends, gives the impression "he's really giggling inside all the time".'

Dean Cordier recalls:

'He often involved Ralph Bunche, myself and several other members of the Secretariat in what amounted to a small informal reading circle on particular books or particular sections of books. John Steinbeck's *The Winter of Our Discontent* and James Baldwin's *Go Tell It on the Mountain* were among the books we so examined. A fascinating discussion regarding the meaning or meanings intended by the author inevitably followed.'

These, however, were refreshing interludes amidst the burdens of inexorable public tasks. There, what impressed his colleagues most was:

'his capacity for decisions which the hard, tough problems of world crises presented to him from day to day. In truth, he had a lightning capacity for the gathering and appraisal of facts, for the making and implementation of decisions. I never had the impression that he worried himself into decisions. One could see his brilliant mind at work picking out relevant facts, outlining alternative avenues of action, arriving quickly at a formulation of the policy or decision necessary to the problem. Nor did he worry about a decision after it was made. He frequently indulged in a reasoned self-confidence that the decision taken was a right one. . . . He combined sound, hard realism with an extraordinary imagination. When others saw no further possibility of progress, he devised a means and a pattern of further negotiation, for eventual break-throughs in touchy and baffling problems. His convincing and brilliant analysis of issues and his unique and effective techniques in carrying them to further stages of solution were combined with an energy which astounded collaborators and observers alike. . . . His unflinching courage rested upon his faith and his faith upon principles and ideals derived from a sturdy and valued heritage and an intellect alive with almost limitless appraisal of values with meaning for himself and humanity.'*

Another of his close associates on the United Nations Staff characterizes Hammarskjöld as 'that most rare of persons in human affairs —a man of true inner greatness in a position of high leadership. He was sustained and inspired by pure and firmly founded beliefs and ideals about life and human relationships to which he was true in word and act'.**

These testimonials from Staff colleagues may be complemented by the carefully considered appraisal of one whose relationships were somewhat more distant but also, for that very reason, more objective and who speaks in the perspective of a ranking representative of a Member Government. Dr. Charles Malik, Lebanon's chief delegate to the United Nations at the time of Hammarskjöld's election in 1953, as a member of the Security Council had voted for him, and served as President of the Thirteenth Session of the General Assembly in 1958–1959 which embraced the crisis over Lebanon. He writes:

'Here is the knight of peace, the selfless servant of the peoples of the world, the tragic hero who dared all, in absolute courage and utter self-disregard, and who, under the most ruthless calumnies and attacks, never flinched, even to the point of willingly making the ultimate sacrifice, in doing what he could to implement the decisions of the United Nations, to the end that international peace and security be maintained and the people of Africa, and especially at the time of his death the people of the Congo, acquire and enjoy a new measure of decency, dignity and national independence'.†

v

Burdened by responsibilities in mounting numbers and magnitude and harassed by problems of steadily aggravating gravity and intractability, it might have been expected that Hammarskjöld would hardly

* Andrew W. Cordier, 'Motivations and Methods of Dag Hammarskjöld', Dag Hammarskjöld Memorial Lecture, St. Louis, Mo., Oct. 21, 1965.
** Wilder Foote, 'Introduction' to Servant of Peace, pp. 13–14.
† The Critic, April–May 1965, p. 74.

have found time, or perhaps desire, for the cultural, artistic and personal interests which had so enriched and lent balance to his life through youth and early manhood. On the contrary, the stimulus of New York and the cosmopolitan associations of the United Nations greatly excited his interest and activity in all these areas.

His first specific undertaking almost immediately after arrival in New York was to initiate steps leading to the rehabilitation of Eugene O'Neill's reputation as a dramatist both in Europe and in America. In the early 1950s, O'Neill's standing had suffered almost total eclipse. His most recent play had been withdrawn before it reached Broadway. There was no longer interest in *Mourning Becomes Electra* and his other early successes. A recently published history of American drama notes the revival of O'Neill's popularity, but cannot explain it. Dag Hammarskjöld was in some measure responsible.

During those few hectic days in Stockholm in early April 1953 before Hammarskjöld flew to New York, his close friend and collaborator, Karl Ragnar Gierow, then Director of the Royal Dramatic Theater and now Director of the Swedish Academy, was surprised by a phone call from Hammarskjöld, explaining that he expected to be leaving Stockholm in a few days and might be gone for some time, and was fearful that he might miss a new production of one of Shakespeare's plays then running at the Royal Theater; could Gierow possibly secure a seat for him for that evening's performance? Gierow replied that of course he must join him in the Director's box. In conversation, Gierow asked if Hammarskjöld would undertake a commission on behalf of the Theater in New York. Eugene O'Neill's early plays had attained great popularity in Sweden and the playwright was known to be grateful. After O'Neill's death, Gierow had been in correspondence with his literary agents to inquire whether he had left any unpublished plays, and had received a negative reply. But Gierow was not satisfied. Would Hammarskjöld attempt to see O'Neill's widow and confirm the answer? The upshot was that Hammarskjöld searched out Mrs. O'Neill and learned that her husband had indeed left at least two new plays of which nothing was known by the public, moreover with the explicit request that, should they be produced, it should be at the Royal Theater in Stockholm. In due time, A *Long Day's Journey into Night* and A *Touch of the Poet* appeared first on the Stockholm stage and were later introduced on

Broadway, with the result that, within a few years, four or five of O'Neill's plays were appearing simultaneously in New York.

Hammarskjöld also discovered Djuna Barnes in semi-retirement in New York and persuaded her to allow him to translate her *Antiphon* into Swedish, a task in which Gierow was his collaborator and subsequently sponsor of its inaugural production in Stockholm.

Cordier relates that soon after Hammarskjöld's arrival in New York, they went together to the Museum of Modern Art to select pictures on loan to decorate the Secretary-General's office suite.* 'After about an hour of canvassing their collections, the Director of the Museum drew me aside and asked whether Mr. Hammarskjöld was the Director of the Swedish Royal Museum. I replied, "No, why?" His answer, "Well, we have never had anyone come to this museum who is so familiar with the lives and the contributions of the artists represented here, or who has made such perceptive comments on individual pictures." '

Some years later, in the very days when the situation in the Congo was deteriorating toward catastrophe and when Hammarskjöld's handling of the United Nations' role in the Congo was bringing down on his head bitter denunciation by the Russians with insistent demands for his resignation, Hammarskjöld was at work upon a translation into Swedish of the latest volume of poems by the French author Saint-John Perse, *Chronique*, in order that he might press Perse's candidacy for the Nobel Prize in poetry upon the Swedish Academy. Friends declare that nothing gave him more elated satisfaction than Perse's selection for this highest recognition in literature. He was also an original poet in his own right; a reviewer suggests that 'he might have achieved eminence in that calling as he did in others he chose to follow'. W. H. Auden pays this tribute:

'My own testimony is unimportant, but I want to give it. Brief and infrequent as our meetings were, I loved the man from the moment I saw him. His knowledge and understanding of poetry, the only field in which I was competent to judge the quality of his mind, were

* Dr. Alfred Barr, Director of Collections at the Museum of Modern Art, reports that Hammarskjöld's initial selection of paintings included Peter Blume's 'The Boat', Lyonel Feininger's 'Viaduct', Fritz Glarner's 'Relational Painting', Juan Gris' 'Guitar and Pipe', Henri Matisse's 'Gourds', Pablo Picasso's 'Still Life With a Cake', and Georges Rouault's 'Landscape With Figures'.

extraordinary, and, presumptuous as its sounds, I felt certain of a mutual sympathy between us, of an unexpressed dialogue beneath our casual conversation.'*

Hammarskjöld once confessed to a friend that, when the pressures of the world's affairs seemed almost insupportable, he found his only respite and relaxation in translating. In the last days of his life he was at work on a Swedish rendering of Martin Buber's great book, *I and Thou*.**

vi

Dag Hammarskjöld's preoccupation with literature went far beyond an intimate familiarity with its range and depth and variety across the ages and across the world, beyond personal friendships with authors of all types and schools and generations in his own day, beyond his own contributions in writing and translation. 'Perhaps less well known is the fact that Hammarskjöld also had very extensive interests as a bibliophile. . . . He was captivated by the refined problems of bibliophilism', is the testimony of his close friend and collaborator in this field, Dr. Uno Willers, Director of the Royal Library in Stockholm.†

Dr. Willers gives a fascinating account of this aspect of Hammarskjöld in some detail—his inveterate haunting of secondhand bookshops wherever he went in quest of rare volumes and first editions, the upbuilding of his own private library which, at the time of his death, numbered several thousand items located at four places in Sweden and New York, all arranged by Hammarskjöld personally 'according to a principle which was rather significant.' Dr. Willers cites a number of amusing but also revealing illustrations:

'He received [in New York] from several Stockholm firms catalogues which were, in most cases, dispatched on Friday by plane. It might therefore happen that when, on a Monday afternoon, one came to look for something one would receive the answer that a telegraphic order from the Secretary-General had already arrived; he often had

---

* 'Foreword' to *Markings*, p. xi.
** Cf. below, pp. 169, 187, 215 ff.
† Address at the Dedication of the Dag Hammarskjöld Library at the United Nations, Nov. 17, 1961, printed in the commemorative volume, pp. 50 ff.

recourse to a package of second-hand book catalogues as a diversion during the week-end.

'This interest increased with age, and manifested itself very obviously, among other things, in his genuine wish that his dearest books should be clothed in beautiful bindings. During his last years, nearly all these bindings were made by the head of the binding workshop of the Royal Library in Stockholm. Great packages of paper-bound books went across the Atlantic, and their owner sometimes showed himself impatient to see them again in their new state, as quickly as possible. When he ordered new bindings, he also gave very detailed indications as to the appearance he wished them to have—whether bound in cloth or calf-leather, in a particular colour, or with ornamentation in gold. For extremely rare books he bought protective cases so as to keep them intact in their original form.'

Somewhat trivial incidents open windows into the man's mind:

'One day, when Assistant Minister for Foreign Affairs, he was importuned by the representative of a great Stockholm newspaper who asked him a very difficult question: "If you were forced to live for some time completely isolated from the world, on an uninhabited island for example, with a single book, which book would you choose?" It happened that I was present, and I thought there would be no reply to the question. But, after some hesitation, he answered, briefly and concisely: "Cervantes' *Don Quixote*, if possible in an old French edition." '

It is not without significance that this incident occurred during the period, perhaps 1949 or 1950, when as we have seen Hammarskjöld was passing through acute interior turmoil.* Had the same question been put to him a decade later, it is doubtful whether it would have received the same reply. On his last mission to the Congo in September 1961, he did in fact carry a single book with him. It was a seventeenth-century edition of the *Imitatio Christi* in French.

In more serious vein, Dr. Willers comments:

'Let me stress that for Dag Hammarskjöld the literary content was the important thing. There were some authors that he esteemed in the highest degree, and there were others that had no value for him.

* During his time at the United Nations, when asked by an American journalist to name 'the three most indispensable books', he replied: 'The Bible, Shakespeare's collected works and *Don Quixote*'.

His compelling desire for integrity, which was always so pronounced, had the consequence that, in this matter as in so many others, he communicated his intentions and points of view only to his most intimate friends.'

There was a peculiar appropriateness in the fact that Hammarskjöld's last legacy to the United Nations was a scheme for a great Library, made possible by the generosity of the Ford Foundation. Hammarskjöld himself not only conceived the idea but personally supervised almost every detail of the planning, including the choice of topics and speakers for an impressive three-day Program of Dedication. In consequence, Dr. Andrew Cordier, in welcoming a distinguished company of librarians, scholars and others from all over the world who had come to participate, could say:

'We have, because of the tragic death of the late Secretary-General, modified the programme ever so slightly, but significantly, in order that we might pay tribute to him. I say ever so slightly because, as you know, this was his programme. And it has been changed only in two respects: one, the Library has been named in tribute to him; and, two, this morning we will have a special tribute paid to him by one of his oldest friends and closest associates.'*

As there was special appropriateness that Dag Hammarskjöld's final contribution to the United Nations should have been a Library, so it was no less fitting that the United Nations' principal memorial to him should have taken the form of the naming of the Library in his honor, and that its dedication should have been carried through in faithful accordance with his plans, two months almost to the day after he had given his last full measure of devotion in its service.

vii

Dag Hammarskjöld's interest spanned virtually the whole range of human culture—not only drama and literature, but also sculpture, painting and music.

In painting and sculpture, his taste focused upon the Moderns— Picasso, Braque, Gris, Matisse, Fernand Leger, Fritz Glarner, and Barbara Hepworth whose massive 'The Single Form' stands as a

* *Op. cit.,* p. 50. The address of tribute was that of Dr. Uno Willers, quoted above.

tribute to him in the United Nations Plaza. At the Inauguration of the 25th Anniversary of the Museum of Modern Art in New York on October 19, 1954, Hammarskjöld responded to an invitation to give an address with his own interpretation of Modern Art as an 'agnostic search, based on a re-evaluation of all values' which expresses 'the spiritual situation of our generation':

'Modern art has forged keys to a perfection which it has not itself reached. Shouldering courageously the problems of modern man, reflecting his situation in a world of conflicts born out of his own achievements, it has, thus, earned the recompense of being permitted also to illuminate the greatness of man in the high artistic achievements of the past.

'Art gives more to life than it takes from it. True art does not depend on the reality about which it tells. Its message lies in the new reality which it creates by the way in which it reflects experience. In our minds, we, all of us, sometimes chisel beauty out of the stone of matter. If we had the courage and perseverance to push these experiences of a few moments to their extreme point, we would share in the effort of the modern artist to isolate beauty from the impurity of life, even if it has to be at the cost of dissolving the very forms of life.'*

In music, however, Hammarskjöld's preference went, on the whole, to the great classic masters. In his apartment, he kept a carefully chosen collection of records. At times of exceptional tension, he turned for spiritual refreshment and recharging to Bach and Vivaldi 'again and again,' Mozart 'in smaller doses,' Brahms' later works, 'not the tumultuous Brahms', Mahler, César Franck, but also Stravinsky and 'of course Beethoven'. 'I must say that listening to Bach's *Sixth Brandenburg Concerto* is, in a way, like reading an extremely good book or poem.'

Shortly after coming to New York, Hammarskjöld took personally in hand the semiannual United Nations Concerts. 'In consultation with the conductor he selected the numbers for each concert and elaborated on the impact that each piece should make on its own, as well as in relation to other numbers on the program.'** At the annual observance of United Nations Day on October 24, the final choral movement of Beethoven's *Ninth Symphony* was often included. At the last such occasion when he was present, in 1960, on

* Part of the Address is reproduced in *Servant of Peace*, p. 62.
** Andrew Cordier, *op. cit.*

the fifteenth anniversary of the founding of the United Nations, the entire Symphony was given. Hammarskjöld prefaced the performance with a brief address, interpreting succinctly but in detail the *Ninth Symphony* as embodying the faith which should animate the United Nations: '. . . On his road from conflict and emotion to reconciliation in this final hymn of praise, Beethoven has given us a confession and a credo which we, who work within and for this Organization, may well make our own. . . . In that faith we strive to bring order and purity into chaos and anarchy . . . a reaffirmation of faith in the dignity and worth of the human person. And it ends with the promise to practice tolerance and live together in peace with one another as good neighbors and to unite our strength to maintain peace.'*

Eleven months later, at the memorial ceremony for Dag Hammarskjöld on September 28, 1961, the Philadelphia Orchestra returned to again render the *Ninth Symphony* in its entirety. Those who were planning the occasion, greatly daring, arranged to have this address reproduced from a record in Hammarskjöld's own voice. 'The audience soon sensed, and rightly so, that this was Hammarskjöld's last and deeply meaningful testament to mankind.'

viii

The interstices between official responsibilities and public cultural events of one kind or another were crowded, one would imagine overcrowded, with personal associations among an ever-widening circle of friends and acquaintances as varied in type and interests as the sweep of his own life.

Hammarskjöld delighted in the practice of hospitality in which he displayed exceptional charm as host. A 'normal' though certainly not usual working day at his office might conclude around eight o'clock. Unless obligations elsewhere prevented, he would make his way to his spacious apartment, furnished with meticulous taste with handmade Swedish and Danish furniture and handwoven rugs and draperies, to welcome a small group of guests for dinner and an evening of spirited talk. Carl Sandburg and the John Steinbecks from the world of

* *Servant of Peace*, pp. 379–80. Appropriately, this address is placed last among his collected speeches as a sort of 'Epilogue'; as his radio *credo* is placed first as the 'Prologue' to all the rest.

letters, the Pablo Casals, Fritz Kreislers and Leonard Bernsteins from the world of music, political analysts such as George Kennan, Barbara Ward and Walter Lippmann, from the stage and screen Lotte Lenya and Greta Garbo, suggest something of the diversity of the guest lists. Dozens of Scandinavian friends from both poles of Hammarskjöld's activity stayed with him in his apartment or in the hideaway retreat near Brewster, New York, to which he tried to escape over weekends. Andrew Cordier speaks of 'his complete social identification with like-minded people and inspiring conversation, often binding the group on elevated levels of understanding and inspiration on the topics of discussion. Guests always went away from his home delighted, inspired and enlightened'*. At the same time, the distaste for formal social occasions which had characterized him in youth deepened and his eminence conferred immunity from obligation; he simply refused to grace the unending sequence of cocktail parties and receptions where so much questionable diplomacy is reputed to be transacted.**

Even on his visits to statesmen overseas, discussion more often than not moved far beyond the business in hand to range literature and the arts. Hammarskjöld developed the practice of following up such visits not with the conventional 'bread-and-butter letter', but with the dispatch of a book which he might have discussed with his host or which he thought the latter ought to read. The titles of these gift remembrances suggest a lively and playful if sometimes pointed humor—to Krishna Menon, Dr. Zhivago; to Ben-Gurion, Teilhard de Chardin's The Phenomenon of Man; to an agnostic Swedish Foreign Office colleague, The Spiritual Espousals of the fourteenth-century Dutch mystic, Jan van Ruysbroek!

No picture of Dag Hammarskjöld at the United Nations is complete without inclusion of one other of his unfailing delights—hiking, climbing and varied contacts with Nature. While in the United States, these were limited largely to weekends at his tiny cottage fifty miles north of New York City. In Sweden, he acquired an old farmhouse immediately next to the home of his artist friend Bo Beskow overlooking the sea and moors near the south coast. When possible, he would spend a brief summer holiday there, often including his

---

* Op. cit.
** Adlai Stevenson shared Hammarskjöld's aversion. 'He defined UN social life as "protocol, alcohol and Geritol".' Francis T. F. Plimpton in As We Knew Adlai (New York: Harper & Row, 1966), p. 258.

own birthday, always accompanied by his omnipresent bodyguard and companion, Bill Ranallo. Most meals were taken with the Beskows. Ranallo and he alternated in responsibility for the modest housekeeping chores. Beskow recalls Ranallo's indignant protest when discovered sweeping up on his 'day off': 'Look at the S.G. over there, smelling the flowers!'

Among his companions of younger years with whom he delighted to reune on these rare returns to his homeland, 'he is completely at home and content. There is a palpable air of sadness about him when he is obliged to say his good-by at the airport'.

In addition to everything else, Hammarskjöld took time to maintain a lively private correspondence, particularly with family and friends in Sweden. Birthdays, wedding and other anniversaries were unfailingly remembered with a message of greeting.

Friends continued to press upon Hammarskjöld the possibility of marriage. To their solicitude, he responded with what had by now become his unfailing explanation: how could he possibly contemplate subjecting anyone to partnership in the kind of life he lived?

One of the few digressions from strict duty which Hammarskjöld permitted himself in the course of his frequent air journeys to various parts of the world was in March 1959 en route homeward from a mission of reconciliation between Cambodia and Thailand when he stopped off for three days in Nepal. The King placed his private plane and pilot at his disposal for a hedge-hopping flight among the highest Himalayas. Hammarskjöld, an avid photographer, took some magnificent pictures, subsequently published in the *National Geographic Magazine** with a brief descriptive interpretation captioned 'A New Look at Everest':

'The plane in which we were flying was a DC-3, non-pressurized and without oxygen. That naturally set an altitude limit of twelve to fifteen thousand feet. . . . The contrast between the sovereign quiet of the mountaintop and the wild ranges leading in toward it added to the other-worldliness, the feeling that we had penetrated into a world of cosmic purpose and character. . . . To someone who has learned to love the mountains and see in mountaineering one of the most satisfactory ways we can test our ability against nature—yet basically as a tribute to nature—it is somewhat shameful to approach the Himalayas by plane. My last words here should be a tribute to our

* Jan. 1961, pp. 87–93.

pilot, who did his job with the deep insight and love of the mountains that characterize the true mountaineer. He managed to convey, at least to this passenger, a bit of feeling of liberty, strength, and harmony we achieve when we fight a mountain and live with it, helped only by our body and our mind.'*

In the Staff dining room on the thirty-eighth floor of the United Nations Headquarters building in New York hung an enlargement of his photograph of Annapurna 'with a beauty of structure and a majesty far surpassing Everest or Gauri Sankar'.

ix

Inexorably exacting as were Dag Hammarskjöld's public obligations, many and diverse as were his cultural preoccupations, spanning all periods and schools which are often considered not merely antipodal but antithetic, at cross-purposes or even out of speaking distance from one another, cosmopolitan as were his personal associations, his life as the world and his friends knew it was marked by striking unity—or, more accurately, a nearly perfect bi-polarity.

It was a Swedish fellow economist who called attention to Hammarskjöld's 'strong feeling for consistency and continuity'. This 'feeling' was a projection of himself. The more one examines the man's practice, both official and personal, the more one is struck by these two characteristics, whether at any one period or its whole course through.

From the small boy, even in his first schooling achieving unprecedented grades and at the same time guiding playmates through the mysterious passages of the Uppsala Castle or reveling with them in the wilds of Nature and its recreations, to mankind's most responsible public servant, accomplishing prodigious feats of intellectual concentration and practical statesmanship and at the same time venturing to interpret contemporary art and classical music, prospecting Everest with a camera or guiding friends in discussion across the whole range of human affairs, the life is all of a piece.

His biographer, without benefit of Hammarskjöld's own self-disclosure and interpretation, lays his finger close to the secret:

* Other aspects of this memorable trip were later to be recorded in verse. *Markings*, p. 186. See below, p. 163.

'His interests are not compartmentalized. All flow from a single center at the core of which is a Schweitzerian reverence for life, where life is more than the antonym of matter. Spirit and matter are both manifestations of a central life force, or energy, which finds expression in painting, music, literature, friendships, nations and international society, and which . . . he believes is moving mankind by evolution toward new types and higher degrees of social organization.'*

Consistency and continuity—the two persistent traits of both the public servant and the private man. One would assume that the inner person where each of us lives alone with himself would likewise be dominated by the same two qualities. Such an assumption, however, is at far remove from the truth which his 'Road Marks' lay bare.

II

Through the year 1952, Dag Hammarskjöld had been in the habit of dating his 'markings' first by groups of years and later by individual years. Then, early among the entries for 1953 appears for the first time a specific date: 'April 7, 1953'. For almost two years thereafter, no precise indication of the time of composition is given.

'April 7, 1953.' It is surprising that so few reviewers and readers appear to have noticed this first precise identification, and to have asked the question, 'Why?' The answer is not far to seek.

On April 1, Hammarskjöld had received official notification that his election as Secretary-General of the United Nations awaited only his consent to accept. On April 8, he was to leave Stockholm for New York, to be inducted on the 10th. April 7 was his final day in Sweden before departure to assume his new responsibilities. Almost certainly the entries in his 'diary' which immediately preceded the April 7 date line were composed during the six days following word of his nomination. The two pages of 'markings' (90–91) may, therefore, be considered *en bloc* as a chain of comments on a single theme.

Those eight days were hectic with winding up his official obligations and private affairs in Sweden and hurried preparations for his departure, his resignation from his position in the Swedish Cabinet and its acceptance, an official visit and long talk with the King, farewells with his father and friends, a day's trip to the scenes of his childhood and youth in Uppsala, to his mother's grave and to the

* Lash, *op. cit.*, p. 214.

Archbishop's home. And yet it was during those days, or more likely in late night hours, that he found time to commune with himself, with his masters in the spiritual life, and with God, and to set down in his 'diary' the profoundest and also the most deeply religious reflections which he had thus far recorded.

Hammarskjöld begins: 'When in decisive moments—as now—God acts, it is with a stern purposefulness. . . . When the hour strikes, He takes what is His. What have *you* to say?—Your prayer has been answered, as you know. God has a use for you, even though what He asks doesn't happen to suit you at the moment. God, who "abases him whom He raises up." ' [89] '. . . what had befallen me and seemed so hard to bear became insignificant in the light of the demands which God was now making. . . .' 'Not I, but God in me.' '. . . He who has placed himself in God's hand stands free vis-à-vis men: he is entirely at his ease with them, because he has granted them the right to judge.' [90]

On April 7 itself, he turns to Thomas à Kempis, whom he had not previously quoted, as a tuning fork for his own thought. From a favorite French translation of The Imitation of Christ, he quotes sentences from Thomas' description of 'the Saints': ' "Their lives grounded in and sustained by God, they are incapable of any kind of pride. They attribute to God whatsoever good they have received, seek no glory from one another, but do all things to the glory of God alone" '*, and then adds his comment: 'I am the vessel. The draught is God's. And God is the thirsty one.' 'In the last analysis, what does the word "sacrifice" mean? Or even the word "gift"? He who has nothing can give nothing. The gift is God's—to God.' Then, anticipating the welcome to his new position which awaits him, his mind reflects on the life of Jesus: 'He who has surrendered himself to it knows that the Way ends on the Cross—even when it is leading him through the jubilation of Gennesaret or the triumphal entry into Jerusalem.' [91] 'Except in faith, nobody is humble. . . . To be, in faith, both humble and proud: that is, to *live*, to know that in God I am nothing, but that God is in me.' [92]

This is the extraordinary response of this remarkable man to what his predecessor, Trygve Lie, warned him was 'the most impossible job

---

* Bk. II, Chap. 10, 'Of Gratitude for the Grace of God'. The whole passage from The Imitation should be read. In the English translation of Markings, the quotation is mistakenly attributed to Thomas Aquinas.

in the world'. It is, likewise, definitive refutation to those who have sought to maintain that there was little or no relation between the 'public servant' and the 'inner person'.

ii

It would have been no surprise if, in Hammarskjöld's new role with its relentless and multiplying burdens, there would have been no time for interior reflections and their recording—and possibly no inclination.

On the contrary, through the first half of his United Nations Secretary-Generalship, entries in his 'diary' increase rather than diminish in quantity. Indeed, considerably more than half of the entire number of 'Road Marks' were composed during those last eight and a half years. They embrace some of the noblest, some of the most penetrating, some of the most delightful.

However, there is a discernible shift of mood, of emphasis, of perspective. Introspection is less prominent and less agonizing. Playfulness and humor are more apparent. He turns increasingly to the composition of poetry; from the latter part of this crowning period of his life comes the collection of *haiku*.

Nevertheless, the major emphasis continues upon the great themes of his vocation, of the dilemmas of public responsibility, and especially of God, of fate, of human meaning and destiny. Most striking, the religious note is more pervasive and more profound. Recourse to the Bible is far more frequent. Likewise, Hammarskjöld's immersion in the classical mystics is more evident. It is revelatory that he begins his dated comments on his new appointment with a peculiarly appropriate passage from the mid-section of à Kempis' *Imitation;* with the exception of a single earlier quotation from Meister Eckhart (in 1951), this is his first reference to one of the mystics. Of the nearly a hundred 'markings' centering upon God, all but seven occur in this same period. Statistics may seem an uncongenial index to spiritual realities, but there is good reason to believe that they do, in fact, accurately reflect the inner development.

At the same time, the intimate interweaving of public events and private meditation is more clearly manifest and now more often surely identifiable by virtue of the fact that many entries or groups of entries are explicitly dated.

In sum, throughout Hammarskjöld's service at the United Nations, his resort to inner reflection is more rather than less frequent, his 'markings' emerge more often and more directly from his professional tasks, and his private thoughts move increasingly at the deeper levels of religious faith.

iii

On his induction as Secretary-General on April 10, 1953, Hammarskjöld spoke to the United Nations General Assembly of the 'humility' with which he accepted election, 'a humility inspired as much by my knowledge of personal limitations as by my awareness of the extraordinary responsibility which you impose on me'. Pointing to 'the vital importance of loyalty, devotion and integrity' in a civil servant, he declared: 'I am here to serve you all. . . . It is for you to correct me if I fail.' Then he sounded two notes which must have surprised his hearers.

Recalling earlier servants of world peace, he declared that 'this Organization has been . . . "consecrated far above our poor power to add or detract"' and went on to quote further from Lincoln's Gettysburg Address: ' "The world will little note, nor long remember, what we say here, but it can never forget what they did. . . . It is for us, the living, rather to be dedicated here to the unfinished task which they have, thus far, so nobly advanced. It is rather for us to be here dedicated to the great task remaining before us." '

The other unexpected note should have struck sensitive ears as especially significant. In the days between his election and his induction, Good Friday and Easter had passed. 'In concluding', Hammarskjöld said, 'may I remind you of the great memory just celebrated by the Christian world, may I do so because of what that memory tells us of the redeeming power of true dedication to peace and good will toward men.' And he added: 'Common to us all . . . stands the truth once expressed by a Swedish poet*. . . . the greatest prayer of man does not ask for victory but for peace.'** Thus were publicly declared to those with ears to hear the new Secretary-General's underlying springs of action.

* Erik Axel Karlfeldt.
** *Servant of Peace*, pp. 28–30.

As Hammarskjöld began at the United Nations, he insisted: 'My first job is to run this House.' To the Press who had met him at the Airport, he said: 'I want to do a job, not to talk about it. . . .'

That 'job' commanded virtually his whole attention and energy for almost two years, until the last days of 1954. Except for a three day journey to Caracas and a few short trips to nearby American cities, he left his desk only for meetings at the United Nations offices in Geneva with occasional brief stopovers in London, Stockholm and Paris. The entire administrative machinery required drastic over-hauling. Fresh and abler personnel had to be enlisted for senior posts. The Secretariat had to be freed from harassment by investigators from Senator McCarthy's Un-American Activities Committee. FBI agents were forbidden access to the United Nations premises. 'You can't be here; whatever permission may have been given in the past is withdrawn', Hammarskjöld ruled. He considered such intrusion 'intolerable, absolutely intolerable'.

Since his 'markings' for this initial period at the United Nations are not dated, it is difficult to detect their particular occasions. There-fore, they seem to be enveloped in a private intimacy in contrast with many of later years; but that may be at least in part because we cannot identify their settings.

These were the years when many of Hammarskjöld's persistent themes are pressed to their conclusions:

Loneliness:
  'Thou who at this time art the one among us who suffereth the
    uttermost loneliness. . . .'[98]

Personal relationships:
  '. . . a need for human intimacy without conventional trap-
  pings. . . . The holiness of human life, before which we bow down
  in worship.'[99]

'*Maturity*: among other things, a new lack of self-consciousness. . . .'[90]

'*The "unheard-of"*—to be in the hands of God.'[100]

What was going on in Hammarskjöld's inmost thoughts as set down in his private meditations is supplemented by his personal correspondence. In a letter to Bo Beskow dated August 4, 1954, he reports: 'Here everything is as usual—which means great satisfaction in the work and much nostalgia for free Nature and free humans. I think of your musical practicing at Rytterskulle [Beskow's home]! Faulkner has published a book [A Fable] that is a monster but still the most important in American prose since Moby Dick. Partly unreadable, partly bewitching. All through terrific. What a strange genius and what a medium for human passion and suffering.'

In response to Beskow's reply, he wrote again six weeks later, on November 24: 'Your letter from the studio fell like rain on very thirsty ground. I am also hungry for letters, that is if they are alive as yours. I wonder if the period of change you are passing through may be a fruitful period—even if it seems dark at the moment—a time of accumulating force at the same time as you work yourself free. You have the curse of the artist to be your master, I that of the slave always being forced to solve given tasks! Tertium datur?' Then follow Hammarskjöld's comments on his radio address 'This I Believe' and on his Academy eulogy of his father, which we quoted earlier.

The year 1954 had begun with a return to the familiar hymn line:

' "Night approaches now—"
Let me finish what I have been permitted to begin.
Let me give all without any assurance of increase.' (95)

Near this year's end stands the fullest affirmation of his faith which Hammarskjöld has thus far declared. It indicates how greatly that faith had steadied and deepened amidst the demands of his new role:

'Thou who art over us,
Thou who art one of us,
Thou who art—
Also within us,
May all see Thee—in me also,
May I prepare the way for Thee,
May I thank Thee for all that shall fall to my lot,
May I also not forget the needs of others,
Keep me in Thy love
As Thou wouldest that all should be kept in mine.
May everything in this my being be directed to Thy glory
And may I never despair.
For I am under Thy hand,
And in Thee is all power and goodness.

Give me a pure heart—that I may see Thee,
A humble heart—that I may hear Thee,
A heart of love—that I may serve Thee,
A heart of faith—that I may abide in Thee.'[100]

Then, suddenly, appears another specific date—'12.10'—signaling the beginning of a new chapter for Hammarskjöld in both his public and his private life.

iv

In early December 1954, an issue erupted within the United Nations of the greatest difficulty and importance, both immediate and long-range. It was to test the capacity of the Organization—and of its Secretary-General—to act effectively in resolving an international confrontation of alarming potentialities.

Almost two years earlier, a dozen American airmen had been shot down in the Korean War and were being held captive by the Chinese Communists despite their obligation under the Korean Armistice Agreement to repatriate all prisoners. Now Peking suddenly announced that they had been tried and sentenced as 'spies'. Under the leadership of the United States, the sixteen nations which had joined forces in the Korean conflict introduced a resolution in the General Assembly, 'not knowing what else to do', requesting the Secretary-General to undertake 'continuing and unremitting efforts' to secure the release of the fliers 'by the means most appropriate in his judgment'. Neither Hammarskjöld nor his predecessor had ever been handed such a commission. Thus, the Assembly was unwittingly establishing a precedent to which the United Nations was to have recourse repeatedly and increasingly in subsequent years.

What 'means' would Hammarskjöld deem 'most appropriate' in discharge of this carte blanche authorization? Doubtless, what the Assembly had in mind was the forwarding of its resolution to Peking through conventional diplomatic channels. But China was excluded from membership in the United Nations and did not recognize its authority. Hammarskjöld knew that a formal and official representation would be received as an insult and rejected if not ignored. On the other hand, he suspected that the Peking Government, in hope of gaining admission to the United Nations, might wish to avoid a rebuff to the Secretary-General. The independence and boldness with which he already conceived his office is indicated in his disclosure to a diplomatic friend that, should the Assembly resolution be adopted, 'I'll go to Peking'. (He never did transmit the resolution to the Chinese Government.)

His inner response was set down in his 'diary' in the first dated entry since his election as Secretary-General:

'12.10
"God *spake once*, and twice I have also heard the same: that power belongeth unto God;
    and that thou, Lord, art merciful: for thou rewardest every man according to his work." (*Psalm 62:11, 12*)'[102] *

He had already cabled Premier Chou En-lai a request for a personal conference regarding the imprisoned airmen. This was the reply: 'In the interest of peace and relaxation of international tension, I am prepared to receive you in our capital, Peking, to discuss with you pertinent questions.' A week later, Hammarskjöld flew to Stockholm to be inducted as his father's successor in the Swedish Academy on December 20. He seized the three days in Stockholm to confer with the Chinese Ambassador to Sweden on details of his projected trip. Back in New York on Christmas Day he entered a six-word 'marking': 'To have faith—not to hesitate!' [102] And on New Year's Eve as he was flying to London on the first lap of his momentous mission to Peking:

' "If I take the wings of the morning and remain in the uttermost parts of the sea;
    even there also shall thy hand lead me." (*Psalm 139:8*)'[102]

A month after his return from Peking on February 12, 1955, a personal letter to Bo Beskow summarized his impressions of his trip:

'The China voyage was a fantastic experience. After that I am in a sense more grown up than before. Glorious and exciting, infinitely distant and still terribly real. That goes both for the country (the landscape), the atmosphere in Peking (this wonderful camp for nomadic rulers who have come down from the desert over the thin

* This is the first occasion on which he had quoted from the Psalter. Some twenty others appear in succeeding years. Psalm 62 was a favorite. Hammarskjöld always quoted Psalms in English from a 1762 edition of the Anglican *Book of Common Prayer*.

mountainedge—a camp with an infinitely repeated rhythm of burdened tentroofs), and Chou En-lai himself (with a brain of steel—
strong, self-disciplined and a very warm smile). The same goes for
the unreal voyage "around the globe in 7 days". Not to speak about
the human and political problem where one suddenly was alone holding the knife. Such a situation gets rid of the last traces of an "I",
that later tries its hardest to push forward again! My working team
was first class. Bill [Ranallo, Hammarskjöld's bodyguard] was great
and saved the morale in both my professors and the others when the
wind blew so sharp that only the most open simple human humor
and warmth could prevent frostbites.'

A distinguished American publisher with whom Hammarskjöld
had developed a friendship of unusual intimacy has recorded in a
private letter a conversation regarding the Peking mission:

'He described to me the obligations of the supreme international
civil servant, giving me some concrete instances of how he had done
his job and referring particularly to his mission to China. I said that
his job demanded a capacity for utter disembodiment. I pursued this
theme, and he reacted with that kind of intelligent warmth he always
showed me; I cannot help gasping whenever I hear or read of people
accusing him of having been cold.'

Not until the following summer did the outcome of Hammarskjöld's bold intervention with the Peking Government appear.
Three times the Chinese Embassy in Stockholm inquired the date of
Hammarskjöld's birthday and what he might appreciate as a remembrance. 'Most of all, release of the airmen', was the reply. On his
birthday, July 29, he was on holiday at his cottage in southern
Sweden. We have remarked that birthdays were always occasions of
special reflection and self-appraisal; this was his fiftieth. Again, he
turns to à Kempis' Imitation*: 'Why do you seek rest? You were
only created to labor.'[107], and adds his own commentary: 'Shame
mixed with gratitude. . . . God sometimes allows us to take the credit
—for His work.'[108] It is unsure whether he already had information or rumor of the forthcoming event. Two days later word
reached him that the American airmen would shortly be freed. He
repeats the phrase from Psalm 62 of the previous December: ' "God
spake. . . ." ', and then continues: '. . . "Not unto us, O Lord, but

* In Markings, the quotation is erroneously attributed to Thomas Aquinas.

unto thy name give the praise . . ." (*Psalm* 115:1)'. But he cannot stifle the self-rebuke: 'A troubled spirit? Isn't the cause obvious? As soon as, furtively, you sought honor for yourself, you could no longer transform your weakness into strength. . . .'* (109) Nevertheless, a practice had been established, radically altering the role of the Secretary-General in the United Nations.

Later in that same year 1955, he reflects upon that role: 'You are dedicated to this task—because of the Divine intention behind what is, in fact, only a sacrificial rite in a still barbarian cult: a feeble creation of men's hands—. . . .' (110) And then, presumably referring to his handling of the negotiations with Peking:

> 'He broke fresh ground—because, and only because, he had the courage to go ahead without asking whether others were following or even understood. He had no need for the divided responsibility in which others seek to be safe from ridicule, because he had been granted a faith which required no confirmation—a contact with reality, light and intense like the touch of a loved hand: a union in self-surrender without self-destruction, where his heart was lucid and his mind loving. . . .' (110)

However, a quite different vein of private thinking speaks in a personal letter to Beskow dated November 12:

'Where is the human warmth? Everywhere and nowhere. In my situation of life I suppose that is part of the price of an "insats" that you can give yourself *so* without reservation only if you don't steal even in the smallest way from somebody else: to really "die" in the evangelical sense, that is so frighteningly realistic as a description of man's situation—you can at certain times be forced to this paradoxical egoism. "Who is my mother and my brother, etc., etc.?" Instead I have the light easy warmth in contacts with such friends as Greta and you, or for example the Belfrages and Bill: a kind of comradeship under the same stars, where you ask for nothing and get so much.'

The letter concludes with the reference to 'other possibilities', that is marriage, which we quoted earlier (p. 81).

'The Belfrages and Bill'. Hammarskjöld had spoken with the warmest praise of the contribution Bill Ranallo had made to his Peking mission. Here, he links Ranallo with the Beskows and Leif

---

* The rest of this 'marking' was quoted on p. 101 above.

Belfrage and his wife as among those who supplied to his spirit the intimate companionship for which he had always passionately longed. An aristocrat by birth and instinct, Dag Hammarskjöld was without trace of snobbery. From his mother's practice as he accompanied her on her visits to persons of every social rank in Uppsala as well as from her teaching, he had absorbed into the core of his being her belief in the equality of all men.

As the year draws toward its close, his meditations over the Christmas season are unusually numerous and varied. On Christmas Day, he describes one of the many dreams which were a frequent undertone to his more rational reflections:

'In a dream I walked with God through the deep places of creation; past walls that receded and gates that opened, through hall after hall of silence, darkness and refreshment—the dwelling place of souls acquainted with light and warmth—until, around me, was an infinity into which we all flowed together and lived anew, like the rings made by raindrops falling upon wide expanses of calm dark waters.' [118]

The year concludes with the aphorism which might serve as a text for his whole book: 'In our era, the road to holiness necessarily passes through the world of action.' [122]

V

More than a year was to pass following his Peking mission before the next major testing of Hammarskjöld's wisdom and courage—and of the Organization and its ideals which he served.

All through the decade of the 1950s, the most ominous tinderbox for the world's peace lay in the Middle East, constantly threatening to ignite in a major Arab-Israel conflict, held under uneasy control by the Tripartite Declaration of the United States, Britain and France to repress any attempt to alter the status quo in Palestine by force or the threat of force.

Early in 1956 en route to southern Asia and Australasia, Hammarskjöld had stopped briefly in Egypt and Israel and had had exploratory talks with Nasser and Ben-Gurion. On his return, he counseled the Western Powers against formal United Nations action in favor of 'quiet diplomacy' by the Secretariat. Accordingly, he was prepared when the Security Council on March 20 unanimously instructed the Secretary-General to seek compliance with the Armistice Agreements which both sides were violating. The month of April was spent at the scene of conflict, moving back and forth between Beirut, Cairo, Gaza, Jerusalem, Amman and Damascus with stopovers in London, Rome and Paris. In Beirut on April 22, he wrote:

'To love life and men as God loves them—for the sake of their infinite possibilities,
to wait like Him,
to judge like Him
without passing judgment,
to obey the order when it is given
and never look back—
then He can use you—then, *perhaps*, He will use you.
And if He doesn't use you—what matter: in His hand, every moment has its purpose, its greatness, its glory, its peace, its meaning.*
From this perspective, to "believe in God" is to believe in yourself, as self-evident, as "illogical", and as impossible to explain: if I can be, then God *is*.' (127)

Back in New York at the beginning of May, Hammarskjöld presented a masterful report on his trip which evoked high praise from the Security Council. The French Ambassador voiced the prevailing sentiment: 'War has not broken out in Palestine. Mr. Hammarskjöld's stature has been increased by the test to which we subjected him, and the same applies to the prestige—which I know to be dearer to him than his own prestige—of his office.'

Hammarskjöld's mediation eased but did not dissolve tensions; it postponed but did not avert a militant confrontation. On July 26, Nasser nationalized the Suez Canal. Three days later, on his fifty-first birthday, Hammarskjöld records in his 'diary' a sequence of quotations, from Psalm 27, from Julien Gracques, from Sir Thomas Browne, and appends his response:

'Sayings resonant with significance—to one who is seeking the Kingdom of God, they contain the truth about *all* work.' (136)

Nasser's precipitate act initiated a sequence of developments extending over the following four months which history knows as 'the Suez Crisis'. A month after the nationalization of the Canal, on a

* *Markings* reads: 'its meaning, its greatness, its glory, its peace, its co-inherence'. Cf. above, p. 93 n.

Sunday, Hammarskjöld records an extended 'Road Mark', reappraising his role: 'It is an *idea* you are serving—an idea which must be victorious if a mankind worth the name is to survive. It is this idea which you must help towards victory with all your strength—not the work of human hands. . . .' (138) (Just a year before, he had characterized the United Nations as 'a sacrificial rite in a still barbarian cult: a feeble creation of men's hands' (110).) At the same time, he castigates himself for self-concern and ambition:

'Uneasy, uneasy, uneasy—
Why? . . .
Because—anxious for the good opinion of others, and jealous of the possibility that they may become "famous", you have lowered yourself to wondering what will happen in the end to what you have done and been. How dead can a man be behind a façade of great ability, loyalty—and ambition! Bless your uneasiness as a sign that there is still life in you.' (137)

In mid-September, another intimate letter to Bo Beskow discloses both his inner state, so contrasted with the seemingly imperturbable public appearance, and his never-suppressed longing for an existence far removed from that to which he felt himelf bound in duty:

'From my existence there is as usual so much to tell that nothing is told. It is an infinite struggle and taking of risks after the motto that Erik Lindegren has given: "Catch the Death!" In a sense without reward, "dangerous" at least in *that* sense that you so easily loose yourself in the wrong way, but still so very much worth while and stabilizing. You get, however, a strange impression of humanity and history. On the whole "true", I suppose, but not complete since simple human warmth is rated so low on the stock market of these "Men of Action". [At about the same time, Hammarskjöld was entering this comment in his private diary: 'The "men of the hour," the self-assured who strut about among us in the jingling harness of their success and importance, how can you let yourself be irritated by them. . . .'(139)]

'The world is a bit mad, and the more one is compelled to have to do with it, the more one longs for good, wise friends in some quiet nook, where you don't listen to the radio and are more interested in the migrating birds, that now, I suppose, have passed over Rytterskulle and, not minding Nasser, have gone back to the Nile and its frogs.'

A fortnight after this was written, on October 4, Hammarskjöld presented his Annual Report for 1955–1956. He spoke of 'three great challenges of our times', but the Middle East crisis was not mentioned among them. However, he did, somewhat tentatively, suggest the role which he hoped the United Nations might come to discharge amidst international tensions: 'We should, I believe, seek a development which would give greater emphasis to the United Nations as an instrument for negotiation of settlements, as distinct from the mere debate of issues.'* Some months earlier, in response to a Press Conference question: 'Would you mind telling us exactly what kind of preventive action the United Nations might be able to take in an area where war threatens or is right on the verge of breaking out?', Hammarskjöld had anticipated the present issue with a somewhat fuller delineation: 'If we take the acute situation in the Middle East. . . . I think that the preventive action is mainly what I might call midwifery. It is not a case of open mediation; I do not believe that the United Nations is a very good tool for open mediation in a situation such as this. . . . It is to be—you will excuse me for using the word—*quietly* helpful by being a third party with which the two conflicting parties can discuss matters and which may help them to bridge the gulf . . . by working out a maximum of understanding.'**

This was precisely the role which was now to be put to a crucial test. On the day following his Report, October 5, the Security Council began consideration of the Suez Crisis with all the principal Foreign Ministers in attendance. However, the significant discussions took place not within the Council sitting *in camera* as a Committee of the Whole but around a low coffee table in Hammarskjöld's office with Hammarskjöld serving as what he jokingly termed 'chaperon' but what has more accurately been characterized as 'catalyst', precipitating significant agreements.† As we have just seen, he himself had described the role as 'midwifery'.

As a result of this exercise in 'quiet diplomacy', all parties believed that they had been led to a solution. Then, on October 29, Israel invaded Sinai, and full-scale hostilities appeared inescapable. On the

* *Servant of Peace*, pp. 120, 122.
** *Ibid.*, p. 133.
† For a succinct account of the whole Suez Crisis and Hammarskjöld's part in it, see Lash, *op. cit.*, pp. 66–111. A more detailed record with documentation is in Richard I. Miller, *Dag Hammarskjöld and Crisis Diplomacy*, pp. 59 ff.

reconvening of the Security Council two days later, Hammarskjöld presented an epochal 'declaration' setting forth his conception of the nature of the United Nations and the responsibilities of its Secretary-General; this was both a summary of the policies distilled from his previous practices and, when unanimously accepted by the Great Powers, a mandate for his future course of action during the Suez Crisis and after:

'The principles of the Charter are, by far, greater than the Organization in which they are embodied, and the aims which they are to safeguard are holier than the policies of any single nation or people. As a servant of the Organization the Secretary-General has the duty to maintain his usefulness by avoiding public stands on conflicts between Member nations unless and until such an action might help to resolve the conflict. However, the discretion and impartiality thus imposed on the Secretary-General by the character of his immediate task, may not degenerate into a policy of expediency. He must be a servant of the principles of the Charter, and its aims must ultimately determine what for him is right and wrong. For that he must stand. A Secretary-General cannot serve on any other assumption than that —within the necessary limits of human frailty and honest differences of opinion—all Member nations honor their pledge to observe all articles of the Charter. He should also be able to assume that those organs which are charged with the task of upholding the Charter, will be in a position to fulfill their task.'

Then he added:

'Were the Members to consider that another view of the duties of the Secretary-General than the one here stated would better serve the interests of the Organization, it is their obvious right to act accordingly.'*

The next seven days, November 1 to 7, 1956, were the most critical for the life of the United Nations since its founding in 1945 and, indeed, the most threatening for the peace of the world since the conclusion of World War II.

The General Assembly, summoned into special emergency session by the Security Council, sat almost continuously, striving to stave off a widening of the conflict already involving Egypt on one side and Israel, Great Britain and France on the other, with the United States

* *Servant of Peace*, p. 124.

and the Soviet Union leading the smaller Nations in effort toward a peaceful resolution of the struggle. At the heart of the negotiations and in direction of the strategy of peace moved Dag Hammarskjöld, working ceaselessly by day and by night without respite. One day, he had occasion to phone Stockholm to confer with Leif Belfrage at the Foreign Ministry who inquired solicitously: 'Aren't you very tired?' 'Oh, no, no,' replied Hammarskjöld, 'I don't think I've slept more than two or three hours this past week, but I'm doing fine!' It was a feat of effective endurance which prompted President Eisenhower to the admiring tribute: 'He has a physical stamina unique in the world', a man 'who night after night has gone with one or two hours of sleep and worked all day intelligently and devotedly.'

One night, there was a brief break. Hammarskjöld's colleagues prevailed upon him to go to the bedroom adjoining his office for two or three hours' rest. When one of them went to call him, he found Hammarskjöld at his office desk, reading his Bible. From his 'diary', we now know what he was reading:

'11.1–7.56
' "I will lay me down in peace, and take my rest: for it is thou, Lord, only, that makest me dwell in safety." (*Psalm 4:9*)
' "Hold thee still in the Lord—fret not thyself, else shalt thou be moved to evil." (*Psalm 37:7, 8*)'(139)

Turning the page, we come unexpectedly upon the next entry:

> 'Every hour
> Eye to eye
> With this love
> Which sees all
> But overlooks
> In patience,
> Which is justice,
> But does not condemn
> If our glances
> Mirror its own
> In humility.'(140)

To Beskow, he described the negotiations over Suez in earthy, almost facetious words:

'Suez was my third child. Its parents arrived here in a state of great perplexity and some fury. God knows how it will go—but the baby isn't screaming so much now, and perhaps, with good help, I shall be able to teach it to walk. . . . Tragi-comedy in three acts. Act I: Secretary-General as Chaperone (that stage now over). Act II: Secretary-General shows inclination to appear as (an ever so respectable) Pimp (this act still unwritten). Act III: Secretary-General—if he's lucky—may try his hand at midwifery. . . .'*

When his efforts triumphed and a cease-fire had been achieved, Hammarskjöld writes:

'Without our being aware of it, our fingers are so guided that a pattern is created when the thread gets caught in the web.'(140)

And, a few days later:

'Somebody placed the shuttle in your hand: somebody who had already arranged the threads.'(141)

By Christmas, the Suez Crisis had been resolved. Hammarskjöld enters this Christmas Eve reflection:

'Your own efforts "did not bring it to pass," only God—but rejoice if God found a use for your efforts in His work.
    Rejoice if you feel that what you did was "necessary," but remember, even so, that you were simply the instrument by means of which He added one tiny grain to the Universe He has created for His own purposes.'

and then adds an extended comment from Meister Eckhart:

' "If, without any side glances, we have only God in view, it is He, indeed, who does what we do. . . . Such a man does not seek rest. . . . He must acquire an inner solitude . . . he must learn to pierce the veil of things and comprehend God *within them*." '(143)**

On the day following Christmas, he says: 'We act in faith—and miracles occur.' (145) But, on New Year's Eve: 'Your confidence was very slight. So much the more must you now abase yourself when, in spite of this, it has come to pass according to your faith.' (145) And,

---

* Quoted in Stolpe, *op. cit.*, pp. 82–83. On the Hungarian Crisis, which was coincidental with Suez, see NOTE, pp. 141 f.
    ** His meditation for Christmas Day, also based on Eckhart, appears on p. 183.

the last entry for this crisis-studded year 1956: 'Be grateful as your deeds become less and less associated with your name. . . .' [146]

At New Year's 1957, for the last time, Hammarskjöld again begins with the familiar hymn line: '*Night approaches now*—', then records his final comment upon it:

'Each day the first day: each day a life.
Each morning we must hold out the chalice of our being to receive, to carry, and give back. It must be held out empty. . . .'

and adds a petition from the General Collect in *The Book of Common Prayer:*

'. . . and those things which for our unworthiness we dare not, and for our blindness we cannot ask, vouchsafe to give us. . . .' [147]

A NOTE ON THE HUNGARIAN CRISIS

At the very moment of the United Nations' most intense preoccupation with Suez, the Soviet Union seized the opportunity to launch a full-scale assault on Budapest and establish a Communist regime in Hungary. The General Assembly convened in emergency session. On the crucial Sunday, November 4, Hammarskjöld was requested to present a plan 'within 48 hours' to establish the United Nations Emergency Force for the Middle East. *On the same day*, he was requested to 'investigate and report' on the Soviet invasion of Hungary, to send 'observers' to Budapest, to propose measures to halt Russian intervention, and to arrange for humanitarian relief! The response of the Communist leaders in both Hungary and Russia was an unequivocal and angry repudiation of the United Nations' 'interference' in what was held to be purely a domestic revolution. Observers were barred. Even Hammarskjöld's offer to make a personal visit to Budapest in the interest of humanitarian aid was rejected. Meantime, 'with the exception of one or two smaller powers, no one was prepared either inside the UN or outside to urge measures going further than moral pressure.'*

In retrospect, Hammarskjöld and the United Nations were criticized for giving priority to Suez over Hungary. Hammarskjöld replied by reviewing the chronological order of events in the two crises and then pointed out: 'If you disregard all other aspects and look at the

---

* Lash, *op. cit.*, pp. 87, 92–93, gives a brief summary of the incident. Cf. also Miller, *op. cit.*, pp. 126 ff.

time sequence, I think it is perfectly clear to you that Suez had a time priority on the thinking and on the policy-making of the main body in the UN. That was not their choice. It was history itself, so to say, which arranged it that way.' The United Nations had to be content merely to appoint a Special Committee which investigated and reported on the Hungarian issue.

vi

Armed hostilities in the Near East had been halted. A major war had been averted. But the uneasy peace was trailed by a plethora of 'mopping up' tasks: the recruitment and deployment of the United Nations Emergency Force (UNEF) drawn from neutral nations— 'something new in world history, a pioneering force symbolizing more a moral than a military compulsion'—the clearing from the Suez Canal of the nearly fifty craft scuttled in it by Egypt and its restoration to use, the withdrawal of troops by all the belligerents, the settlement of the particularly thorny issue of 'the Gaza strip', and others. Hammarskjöld likened the post-Suez period to 'convalescence', 'germination time', 'the lull after the sound and fury'. In May 1958, the 'lull' was to be rudely shattered by a new crisis in Lebanon, again involving the Great Powers, this time especially the United States and the Soviet Union, and threatening to escalate into armed conflict. These matters laid heavy claim upon Hammarskjöld's attention and energy through much of 1957 and 1958. Between his first stop in the Middle East early in 1956 and the end of 1958, he visited the scene of trouble no fewer than eleven times.

Early in 1957, Hammarskjöld fell under severe criticism in the United Nations General Assembly over his implementation of the Suez decisions. It is clear from his 'diary' that the taut self-control which lay just beneath the unruffled exterior was badly frayed. Instead of yielding to what must have been a strong temptation to vent in his private notes irritation and resentment upon those who provoked them, he turned a caustic criticism upon himself in a sequence of self-judgments as severe as any he ever recorded. He begins the year 1957 with a dispassionate exposure of the ethical ambiguity of public office: 'The most dangerous of all moral dilemmas: when we are obliged to conceal truth in order to help the truth to be victorious. . . .' [147] But two entries beyond, there is a much more intimate self-disclosure: 'Did the attack hurt you—in spite of its absurdity. . . .? —Not I, but God in me!' And a little later: 'Destruction! What fury in your attack . . . !' [148]

On February 22, Hammarskjöld made an especially important statement to the General Assembly on an impasse which had developed over the Gaza strip. Two days later, a Sunday, he reflects on ' . . . Original Sin, that dark counter-center of evil in our nature— that is to say, though it is not our nature, it is of it—that something within us which rejoices when disaster befalls the very cause we are trying to serve, or misfortune overtakes even those whom we love', and then is led on to this response: 'Life in God is not an escape from this, but the way to gain full insight concerning it. . . .' [149]*

What a contrast to this merciless self-condemnation was the judgment of those whom he served! As the longest and one of the most heated sessions the General Assembly had ever held was finally adjourned on March 8, its President declared: 'The General Assembly rapidly passed resolutions couched in general terms, and the Secretary-General has implemented them by delicate and arduous negotiations, supported therein by the force of world opinion.' Nevertheless, just a month later Hammarskjöld again takes himself severely to task, this time for the temptation toward morbidity: 'Not to brood over my pettiness with masochistic self-disgust, nor to take a pride in admitting it—. . . .' [150]** He asks himself: 'How am I to find the strength to live as a free man, detached from all that was unjust in my past and all that is petty in my present. . . .?' This is his answer: 'Life will judge me by the measure of the love I myself am capable of. . . .' [150]

Three days after these Spartan self-accusations, on April 10, 1957, Hammarskjöld, who had recently returned from a week's visit to Cairo and Beirut, addressed the Fiftieth Anniversary Dinner of the American Jewish Committee in New York. Speaking on 'Human Rights and the Work for Peace', he reminded his audience that it was the fourth anniversary of his induction into his present office 'to which I had been catapulted without any previous soundings, indeed,

---

* The concluding sentence of this 'marking' is on p. 213, below.
** Later this same year, he acknowledges 'the pleasure-tinged death wish (not, perhaps, without an element of narcissistic masochism)' [159]. Fifteen years before, he had confessed 'your unselfishness a thinly disguised masochism'. [16] See above, p. 84.

without any pre-warning'. Then, he took as his text a quotation by the distinguished Jewish scholar, Arthur Waley, from a Chinese historian's account of the philosopher Sung Tze and his followers in 350 B.C.:

' "Constantly rebuffed but never discouraged, they went round from State to State helping people to settle their differences, arguing against wanton attack and pleading for the suppression of arms, that the age in which they lived might be saved from its state of continual war. To this end they interviewed princes and lectured the common people, nowhere meeting with any great success, but obstinately persisting in their task, till kings and commoners alike grew weary of listening to them. Yet undeterred they continued to force themselves on people's attention." '

Hammarskjöld commented: 'To one who works in the United Nations, the quotation strikes a familiar note.' Later in his address, he argued a close relationship between the growth of human rights and 'the development of tolerance inspired . . . by ethical concepts of religious origin', concluded with a quotation from another Chinese sage: ' "Heaven arms with pity those whom it would not see destroyed" ', and added his own comment: 'Over the ages and over the continents, these words join with those of the Psalmist: "There is mercy with Thee; therefore shalt Thou be feared." '* This is one of the comparatively rare occasions when his public address echoes faintly the chords which were dominating his private meditations.

It was during this same year 1957 that the room which had been set aside for private meditation in the General Assembly Hall at the United Nations was transformed into 'A Room of Quiet'. Every detail was personally planned and supervised by Hammarskjöld. He composed the text for the leaflet which is given to the thousands who visit it each year:

'We all have within us a center of stillness surrounded by silence.

'This house, dedicated to work and debate in the service of peace, should have one room dedicated to silence in the outward sense and stillness in the inner sense . . . open to the infinite lands of thought and prayer.

'People of many faiths will meet here, and for that reason none of

* Servant of Peace, pp. 126–31.

the symbols to which we are accustomed in our meditation could be used. . . .'

Then, calling attention to the symbols employed, 'the shaft of light striking the shimmering surface of solid rock,' he explains that the light suggests 'how the light of the spirit gives life to matter' while 'the stone in the middle of the room' may be seen 'as an altar, empty not because there is no God, not because it is an altar to an unknown god, but because it is dedicated to the God whom man worships under many names and in many forms. . . . There are no other symbols, there is nothing to distract our attention or to break in on the stillness within ourselves. . . . It is for those who come here to fill the void with what they find in their center of stillness.'*

This statement obviously revolves on two words—'stillness' and 'silence'—which he had taken from Meister Eckhart.** These words sounded often through his meditations across the years: "To preserve the silence within—amid all the noise. . . .' (83) 'To . . . attend to that within us which *is* there in the darkness and the silence.' (97) '. . . that stillness which is born of silence. . . .'(122) An early letter to Beskow had voiced the hope that he might have some 'stillness' left when he retired from public office. In April 1956 while in Beirut on one of his most important visits, he had written:

> 'Understand—through the stillness,
> Act—out of the stillness.
> Conquer—in the stillness. . . .'(127)

A week after his fifty-fourth birthday in 1959, he was to speak of 'the point of rest at the center of our being' (174).†

In June 1957, he unburdened part of his inmost feelings in a letter to Beskow:

'. . . The pressure is slightly released but instead a certain fatigue is creeping out of the corners where it had hid over the winter. And any time something might break again. We live in a rather insane world and it is not growing wiser from the ruthless propaganda from known quarters. If people would only remember Fröding's simple

* *Servant of Peace,* pp. 160–61.
** See below, p. 183.
† Cf. below, p. 161.

words "that nobody is bad and nobody good", they would be able to be immunized against the simple propaganda about a world of villains and saintly martyrs. . . .

'. . . Well, let us hope for our spiritual self-cure. And let us keep ourselves healthy.

'But why speak about this—when the sun is shining over the coast ridges and the problems of form demand a solution, we will forget the distortions in the world we ourselves have made.'

At almost the same time, looking back over the tangled events of the preceding six months, he says to himself:

'For someone whose job so obviously mirrors man's extraordinary possibilities and responsibilities, there is no excuse if he loses his sense of "having been called." So long as he keeps that, everything he can do has a meaning, nothing a price. . . .' [154]

This comment prepares the way for the next major event of his life.

vii

Dag Hammarskjöld's five-year term as Secretary-General of the United Nations was to expire in April 1958. However, the election of a successor—or his reappointment—was to come before the Security Council and then the General Assembly the previous September.

As the time approached, his thoughts inevitably turned toward a reassessment of his role. In June 1957 he had commented on 'someone whose job so obviously mirrors man's extraordinary possibilities and responsibilities'. And, on his fifty-second birthday at his holiday home in southern Sweden, he writes: 'You are not the oil, you are not the air—merely the point of combustion, the flash-point where the light is born. You are merely the lens in the beam. You can only receive, give, and possess the light as a lens does. . . .' [155]

In his Introduction to the Annual Report for 1956–1957, dated August 22, 1957, Hammarskjöld seized the occasion for a comprehensive and dispassionate review of the most testing and telling year in the United Nations' history thus far. He reminded the Organization that, both in the establishment of the United Nations Emergency Force and in the clearance of the Suez Canal, responsibilities had been assumed 'previously untried by world organization'. 'The

United Nations Emergency Force is the first of its kind. . . . created in a few days under emergency conditions without benefit of precedents' while 'the international clearance operation' likewise 'was the first undertaken of its kind attempted by a world organization' through which 'the Canal was reopened to full traffic in a little more than three months'. And the Special Committee on the problem of Hungary was also 'a new departure' even though its recommendations won no compliance.

This retrospective appraisal prompted Hammarskjöld to the most precise definition which he had yet ventured to offer of 'The Role of the United Nations' as he had come to conceive it: 'an admittedly imperfect but indispensable instrument of nations in working for a peaceful evolution towards a more just and secure world order'. 'Nations and groups of nations will never again be able to live and to arrogate judgments unto themselves in international affairs in ways which once were a matter of course.' He recalled that as far back as the Korean conflict in 1950, 'In the "Uniting for Peace" resolution, the General Assembly adopted a plan under which it might make appropriate recommendations to Member States "for collective measures, including in the case of a breach of the peace or act of aggression the use of armed force when necessary".' He spoke of the 'increase in membership' reflecting 'the renaissance of Asia' and 'the awakening of Africa'. Then, he suggested that 'the primary value of the United Nations is to serve as an instrument for negotiation among governments and for concerting action by governments', stressing especially 'the quiet work of preparing the ground, of accommodation of interest and viewpoint, of conciliation and mediation, all that goes into the winning of consent to agreed solutions and common programmes'*.

On the eve of the Security Council meeting in early September, he again addresses himself: 'Your responsibility is indeed terrifying. If you fail, it is God, thanks to your having betrayed Him, who will fail mankind. You fancy you can be responsible to God; can you carry the responsibility for God?'[156]

It took the Security Council only a few minutes to agree unanimously to recommend to the General Assembly Hammarskjöld's reappointment for a second five-year term. On September 26, the

* *Servant of Peace*, pp. 138–47.

General Assembly confirmed his election, also with unanimity. Israel, whose representatives were absent because of the Jewish New Year, sent instructions to have its affirmative vote recorded. The President of the Assembly, in announcing the action, hailed him as 'surely our supreme international Civil Servant', a 'self-effacing' man of 'scrupulous objectivity'.

Hammarskjöld's public response to his re-election was a brief statement in which he set forth more frankly than he had previously done exactly how he conceived his role:

'Nobody, I think, can accept the position of Secretary-General of the United Nations, knowing what it means, except from a sense of duty. Nobody, however, can serve in that capacity without a sense of gratitude for a task as deeply rewarding as it is exacting, as perennially inspiring as, sometimes, it may seem discouraging. . . .

'The significance of what this Organization stands for, as a venture in progress towards an international community living in peace under the laws of justice, transforms work for its aims from a duty into a privilege. . . .'

Insisting that the Secretary-General should not be asked to act 'if no guidance for his action is to be found either in the Charter or in the decisions of the main organs of the United Nations', he went on to declare:

'Within the limits thus set, however, I believe it to be the Secretary-General's duty to use his office and, indeed, the machinery of the Organization to its utmost capacity and to the full extent permitted at each stage by practical circumstances.

'On the other hand, I believe it is in keeping with the philosophy of the Charter that the Secretary-General should be expected to act also without such guidance, should this appear to him necessary in order to help in filling any vacuum that may appear in the systems which the Charter and traditional diplomacy provide for the safeguarding of peace and security. . . .'

It may be doubted how many of his auditors recognized that Hammarskjöld was thus putting the Organization on notice that he intended to use his office with greater freedom than he had thus far employed or than its founders may have contemplated.

Hammarskjöld concluded his public statement on the occasion of his re-election on a characteristic note: 'May future generations never be entitled to say that we failed because we lacked faith or permitted narrow self-interest to distort our efforts.'*

Hammarskjöld's inner response to his re-election was in a very different vein. ' "The best and most wonderful thing that can happen to you in this life, is that you should be silent and let God work and speak.". . .' (156) Five days later, he is still preoccupied with his task: 'Do not look back. And do not dream about the future, either. . . . Your duty, your reward—your destiny—are *here* and *now*.'(157) After another five-day interval, a Sunday meditation gives his definitive comment upon the word which had sounded over and over again since his first election five years earlier: 'Yes to God: yes to Fate: yes to yourself. This reality can wound the soul, but has the power to heal her. . . .'(157)

However, his dissatisfaction with his response to his life's task is voiced in two 'markings'. The first *may* be retrospective, recalling his reaction to his first election five years before; the second is clearly 'existential'. Both reveal the sharpest contrast to the adulation which is being showered upon him:

'You told yourself you would accept the decision of fate. But you lost your nerve when you discovered what this would require of you: then you realized how attached you still were to the world which has made you what you were, but which you would now have to leave behind. It felt like an amputation, a "little death," and you even listened to those voices which insinuated that you were deceiving yourself out of ambition. You will have to give up everything. Why, then, weep at this little death? Take it to you— quickly—with a smile die this death, and become free to go further —one with your task, whole in your duty of the moment.

*

'You have not done enough, you have never done enough, so long as it is still possible that you have something of value to contribute. This is the answer when you are groaning under what you con- sider a burden and an uncertainty prolonged ad infinitum.'(158)

The year 1957, so rich with accomplishment and well-deserved recognition, concludes with another Christmas Eve meditation writ-

* *Servant of Peace*, pp. 148–50.

ten in Gaza where he was spending Christmas with the United Nations Forces:

'In Thy wind—in Thy light—
How insignificant is everything else, how small are we—and how happy in that which alone is great.'[161]

Although Hammarskjöld's re-election was voted in September 1957, his second term as Secretary-General actually began on April 10, 1958. He was guest at a United Nations Correspondents Association Luncheon on the 9th and at a surprise party tendered him by the U.N. Staff on the 10th. At each, he responded with brief extemporaneous remarks, affirming his confidence in the Organization: 'the belief and the faith that the future will be all right because there will always be enough people to fight for a decent future.'* Again, there was hardly a hint of what his interior thoughts were affirming on that momentous occasion:

'4.10.58
In the faith which is "God's marriage to the soul," you are *one* in God, and
    God is wholly in you,
    just as, for you, He is wholly in all you meet.
    With this faith, in prayer you descend into yourself to meet the Other,
    in the steadfastness and light of this union,
    see that all things stand, like yourself, alone before God,
    and that each of your acts is an act of creation, conscious, because you are a human being with human responsibilities, but governed, nevertheless, by the power beyond human consciousness which has created man.
    You are liberated from things, but you encounter in them an experience which has the purity and clarity of revelation.
    In the faith which is "God's marriage to the soul," *everything*, therefore, has a meaning.
    So live, then, that you may use what has been put into your hand. . . .'[165]

This meditation, one of the half dozen most important for an understanding of Dag Hammarskjöld, is at once a concise summary of the destination to which the pilgrimage of more than a quarter century

* *Servant of Peace*, pp. 165–69.

has brought him and the definitive 'Guide Post' for the all too brief final reach of that pilgrimage.

viii

The three years which began with his mission to Peking and concluded in the afterglow of his re-election as Secretary-General were the period of Hammarskjöld's most prolific writing.

We noted that 1950–1952 recorded the abyss of his desolation and despair, and that these three years were marked by an intensification of inner reflection. So, 1955–1957 witnessed the height of his public achievement. It was precisely during those three years of almost continuous absorption in one after another crisis of world import—Suez, Lebanon, Laos, Cambodia—and of superb accomplishment in their resolution that he again turned inward with unprecedented frequency. Almost a third of all his 'markings' date from this period. They set forth the quintessence of his seasoned conviction on most of the topics which had claimed his major attention throughout his life, and also the heart of his mature faith. The reader who wishes to focus attention upon the summit of Dag Hammarskjöld's pilgrimage will find it disclosed there. No radically new topics are introduced; rather, the by now familiar themes are orchestrated with deepened resonance and greater power. What was to follow through the short period of his life still before him is aftermath though not anticlimax.

7. The Terminus:
1958–1961

THE FINAL three and a half years were, in almost all respects, climactic for Dag Hammarskjöld's public career.

To be sure, they were years marked by intense strains within the United Nations as well as among the Member Nations. The Soviet Union's opposition to United Nations policies and condemnation of Hammarskjöld as their architect and executor mounted in an accelerating crescendo culminating in the demand on October 3, 1960, that 'the post of the Secretary-General who alone governs the staff and alone interprets and executes the decisions of the Security Council and sessions of the UN General Assembly should be abolished' and replaced by 'a collective body' of three, the 'Troika' proposal. The debate was punctuated by Khrushchev's famous desk-thumping demonstration of hostility. 'To avoid misinterpretation', the Soviet Premier shouted: 'I want to reaffirm that we do not trust Mr. Hammarskjöld and cannot trust him.' This outburst furnished the occasion for Hammarskjöld's most forthright and detailed apologia:

'In my view, the issue is not a question of a man but of an institution. The man does not count, the institution does. A weak or nonexistent executive would mean that the United Nations would no longer be able to serve as an effective instrument for active protection of the interests of those many Members who need such protection.'

Then, he stressed the smaller and newer Nations who had come to hold an ever larger place in his concern and confidence:

'It is not the Soviet Union or, indeed, any other big Powers who need the United Nations for their protection; it is all the others. In this sense the Organization is first of all *their* Organization, and I deeply believe in the wisdom with which they will be able to use it and guide it. I shall remain in my post during the term of my office as a servant of the Organization in the interests of all those other nations, as long as *they* wish me to do so.'*

In the outcome, Hammarskjöld was overwhelming vindicated.

An eminent American editor to whom Hammarskjöld talked often with exceptional frankness reports in a personal letter to his family:

'This was the character of my relationship with Dag: a close friendship based on some deep-seated elements of congeniality. . . . After Khrushchev had turned against him, proposed the troika, etc., I told him he had no reason to be surprised. . . . He belonged to the West, and at a certain moment the Russians had come to recognize it. He looked at me with those friendly eyes I will never forget, and said that we who have been shaped by the spirit of Pascal cannot help becoming intolerable to them.'

However, the violence of the Communist attack was an unintended testimony to the immense enlargement of Hammarskjöld's role and prestige during the years since his re-election. In his response on that occasion, he had warned the Organization that he intended to administer his responsibilities with greater initiative than he or his predecessor had previously exercised.

Probably few of those who heard this manifesto had any realization of its far-reaching potentialities or to what lengths it would be implemented in the years to follow through Hammarskjöld's increasingly frequent and ever bolder response both to inadequacies in United Nations procedures and to requests from individual Nations for his personal intervention. In the sequence of crises which commanded his major attention and time from 1958 onward, sometimes he was executing General Assembly or Security Council mandates. More often, he was acting in his personal capacity as Secretary-General. Many of his most original and effective actions were to be justified as 'filling a vacuum', for example in the summer of 1958 his strengthening of the United Nations Observation Group in the Lebanon and

* *Servant of Peace*, pp. 317–19.

creation of a United Nations Office in Jordan very much along lines which had been vetoed in the Security Council by the Soviet Union*; then his affirmative responses in 1959 to invitations from Cambodia and Thailand to send a mediator to help them resolve a border dispute, and from Laos for a personal representative in its confrontation with North Vietnam, and from Guinea for assistance with 'all the economic, social and administrative problems natural in the first phase of its new independence', as Hammarskjöld put it.** Twice in 1959, in March and again in November, he himself journeyed to southeast Asia for personal conferences with the rulers and leaders of the Nations which had sought his help. This Hammarskjöld himself called 'preventive diplomacy'. It was also 'private diplomacy'. He justified it in his Introductions to the Annual Reports for 1958–1959 and 1959–1960†. The sum of the matter was that Dag Hammarskjöld had created a role utterly new in international negotiation, that of a personal mediator-at-large available for service to any who might seek or need his good offices.

These projects of 'preventive diplomacy' were interspersed among Hammarskjöld's more official United Nations assignments. From the spring of 1958 onward, he was much occupied with the quest for disarmanent. Tension and incipient conflict in the Middle East continued endemic; between August 1958 and July 1959, he made three return visits to that troubled area. In April 1960, the Security Council took cognizance of the Sharpeville massacre in South Africa which had outraged the conscience of mankind, asked the Government of the Union 'to initiate measures aimed at bringing about racial harmony based on equality', and requested the Secretary-General to undertake consultations with the Union's authorities 'to make such arrangements as would adequately help in upholding the purposes and principles of the Charter in the Union of South Africa'. The South African Government deeply resented the Security Council resolution since the Charter itself explicitly forbids United Nations intervention in the domestic affairs of Member States, and rejected the propriety of its implementation by the Secretary-General. Ham-

---

* For a brief account of the Lebanon and Jordan crises and Hammarskjöld's part in them, see Lash, *op. cit.*, pp. 113–19. Cf. also Miller, *op. cit.*, Chaps. VI, VII and VIII. Also, *Servant of Peace*, pp. 190 f., 205, 299, 343.

** Cf. Lash, *op. cit.*, pp. 139 ff. Also, *Servant of Peace*, pp. 299, 303.

† *Servant of Peace*, pp. 220 ff., 293 ff.

marskjöld circumvented the difficulty by falling back on the formula he had successfully employed with the Peking Government five years before. He sought conferences with the South African officials 'on the basis of the authority of the Secretary-General under the Charter'. They acquiesced; and in August, Hammarskjöld visited Johannesburg. Thus, again and again during these years, the now familiar directive 'Give it to Dag' was invoked as problems requiring United Nations action multiplied with steadily aggravating tempo.

Not South Africa but Central Africa, however, moved to the focus of attention and precipitated Dag Hammarskjöld's last and most difficult assignment.

As far back as 1954, he had voiced a keen awareness of the newly awakening Continent and amazement that it was so little in the consciousness of the United Nations membership. The Introduction to the Annual Report for 1955–1956, submitted literally on the eve of the Suez Crisis, speaking of 'three great challenges of our times', had cited first 'the relationship of the peoples of Asia and Africa with the peoples of Western traditions'*. Four months earlier, he had set forth his conception of 'An International Administrative Service': 'a career service under international responsibility for qualified men and women of any nationality, who were prepared to devote a significant part of their lives to work in the less-developed countries of the world as public officials"**. The Annual Report for the following year had spoken of 'the renaissance of Asia' and 'the awakening of Africa't. In January 1959, he pointed to 'two major sets of conflicts which have shown possibilities of leading to a new global conflagration—the Cold War . . . and the manifold tensions between the historical West and the people of the Asian and African continents'.†† Later that same year, he must have surprised his audience at the University of Lund by his reading of the threadbare phrase 'the confrontation of East and West': 'No matter how overwhelming other world problems may appear to us because of their proximity, it is possible that the future will attach greater importance to the rebirth of Asia and Africa'‡.

* *Servant of Peace*, p. 120.
** *Ibid.*, p. 116.
† *Ibid.*, p. 146.
†† *Ibid.*, p. 196.
‡ *Ibid.*, p. 212.

On the last day of February 1959, Hammarskjöld enplaned on a month's wide-ranging flight mainly in southern Asia with stops in Karachi, Rangoon, Bangkok, Vientiane, Phnom Penh, Kuala Lumpur, the unforgettable days at Katmandu in Nepal*, and Srinagar, but with the last stop a visit of several days in Moscow. On his return, he reported to Beskow: 'The voyage went well and gave fantastic, partly encouraging, partly very frightening experiences. The high spot: a private evening with Khrushchev (with a very animated discussion about Pasternak)**, a flight in a small plane around the giants of the Eastern Himalaya† and a day in Arcadia by the upper Mekong in the ancient kingdom of Luang Probang. . . . A *great* experience. . . .'††

This journey had immense effect upon his statecraft and also, as we shall see, upon his most private meditations on Nature, life and fate.‡

The first weeks of 1960 were given to one of Hammarskjöld's longest and most exciting trips, visiting twenty-four African countries, most of those south of the Sahara. It made a deep and indelible impression upon him. Henceforth, in both his official statements and in public addresses, the significance and needs of African peoples loomed more and more frequently and prominently. His Introduction to the Annual Report for 1959–1960 took as its opening topic 'Africa and the United Nations'. He pointed out that, when he had first come to the UN, there were four Member Nations from Africa; now there were twenty-six. He then went on to a full-length examination of the Continent—its divisions, diversities and conflicts, the negative and positive factors—and lodged a strong appeal for 'African solidarity within the framework of the United Nations'. At the end, he returned to declare his conviction of the crucial role of Asia and Africa in the Organization:

'The United Nations has increasingly become the main platform— and the main protector of the interests—of those many nations who feel themselves strong as members of the international family but who are weak in isolation. . . . Who can deny that today the coun-

* See above, pp. 122 f.
** Cf. Lash, *op. cit.*, p. 215.
† Hammarskjöld's detailed description of this flight in an article in *The National Geographic Magazine* for Jan. 1961 has been quoted above, pp. 122 f.
†† A further extract from this letter appears on p. 176.
‡ Some months later, a sequence of *haiku* recorded in verse other recollections of this part of the trip. *Markings*, p. 186. See below, p. 163.

tries of Asia or the countries of Africa, acting in a common spirit, represent powerful elements in the international community, in their ways as important as any of the big Powers, although lacking in their military and economic potential?'

Hammarskjöld here hinted at his conception of the smaller and newer Nations as a 'Third Force' within the United Nations, holding the decisive balance between the two giant Power Blocs. King Hussein of Jordan had toasted the United Nations as 'the summit meeting of the small nations'.

However, Hammarskjöld concluded his Introduction with ominous foreboding: 'It is impossible for anyone to say where the international community is heading. . . . It may seem to point out a road full of risks and of difficulties.'* Crisis had already gripped the Congo. It was to put the United Nations and its Secretary-General to their most taxing test. It was to preoccupy Hammarskjöld through the following year. Thirteen months later, it was to take his life.

Writing of the state of the United Nations when the Kennedy Administration took office at the beginning of 1961, Arthur Schlesinger, Jr., has characterized Dag Hammarskjöld with acute perceptiveness:

'The single clear point in the confusion was the Secretary-General. Dag Hammarskjöld, especially after his re-election in 1957, disclosed a presidential conception of the Secretary-General's "duty to use his office and, indeed, the machinery of the Organization to its utmost capacity". . . . He charged this conception with the quasi-messianic passion of an extraordinary personality. Half international civil servant in the tradition of the League of Nations, half Scandinavian visionary in the tradition of Swedenborg and Kierkegaard,** he inscribed in his journal that "in our era, the road to holiness necessarily passes through the world of action". From his lofty eminence as . . . "secular Pope," the proceedings below sometimes seemed empty gabble:

> Words without import
> Are lobbed to and fro
> Between us.

* *Servant of Peace*, pp. 293–97, 312–13.
** *Markings* shows little if any direct evidence of the influence of either Swedenborg or Kierkegaard; neither is quoted. The 'Scandinavian visionary' in Hammarskjöld flowed from poets and such great national figures as Linnaeus.

Forgotten intrigues
With their spider's web
Snare our hands.[168]

But his sense of mission was invincible. . . . With the resourceful-
ness of a bureaucrat and the fervor of a saint, he sought to make the
UN the chosen instrument of mankind in its quest for salvation.'*
At the end of May 1961, he made a quick trip to England to
receive an honorary degree from Oxford University and to give his
notable address on 'The International Civil Servant in Law and in
Fact', restating definitively his conception of the role of himself and
his colleagues in the United Nations.** In July, still another crisis
threatened, over Bizerte, and Hammarskjöld made his last trip to
North Africa to forestall it.

On one of the August weekends, he took to Brewster his friend,
Sture Linner, whom he had first appointed to take charge of the
United Nations Civilian Operations in the Congo and later pro-
moted to be head of all United Nations activities there. Linner had
spent a week at Headquarters in New York to report on the Congo
situation in all its aspects and to assist the Secretary-General in
planning ahead. The weekend became a typical 'Hammarskjöld
respite'. There was time for long walks and talks until early morning
hours over a wide range of mutual interests in literature, the arts,
philosophy and religion.

Returning to New York by car on Sunday evening, Hammarskjöld
amused himself by turning the radio dial through several stations
broadcasting musical programs, and challenged Linner to a contest in
identifying the numbers. His guest soon gave up; 'Dag knew everything'.

Later the same evening in his New York apartment, they again
talked until long past midnight, Hammarskjöld, relaxed and cheerful,
discoursing on a number of matters in connection with his professional and, not least, his private life. When finally Linner left in the
small hours of the morning, Hammarskjöld insisted on accompanying
him to the street to find a taxi. In the course of their search in a
driving rainstorm, they walked up the long East Side block, the talk

* Arthur M. Schlesinger, Jr., *A Thousand Days: John F. Kennedy in the
White House* (Boston: Houghton Mifflin Company, 1965), p. 467.
** *Servant of Peace*, pp. 329–53. See above, pp. 107 f.

continuing at full pace until, when they finally parted, they laughingly discovered that both men were drenched to the skin.

This incident conveys an admirable impression of Hammarskjöld a few weeks before the end.

On August 17, he filed what was to be his last Introduction to an Annual Report. It was altogether appropriate that his final formal word to the Organization for which he was about to make the ultimate sacrifice should conclude with a reiteration of his dream for 'assistance' to Africa. There was tragic irony and yet also consonance that it was a mission in Africa for reconciliation among Africans which should demand his death just one month later.

ii

The final three and a half years were climactic, likewise, for Dag Hammarskjöld's interior life. But in a very different fashion.

Indeed, one of the most surprising facts about his 'Road Marks' is the sudden and sharp change which followed his reinduction as Secretary-General. Presumably this was not deliberate or even conscious. Rather, it was probably wholly spontaneous. Nevertheless, it is as though, at this milestone in his public career, he had determined on a radical alteration in his private meditations.

This is suggested, in the first place, by the number of entries. The period after April 1958 claims over half of his biography; it yields less than a quarter of his *Markings*. The three years 1955–1957 had been the most prolific in writing, almost a third of all his 'markings'. The years 1958–1961 are the most sparse: in the rest of 1958 a dozen, in 1960 only six, in 1961 up to the time of his death just over twenty.

Even more striking is the contrast in literary form. Of the some hundred and fifty entries in this last period, only fourteen are in prose, all the rest in verse. More and more, he is prompted to poetic expression, although the very few prose comments are of the highest importance.

More significant in the perspective of our major interest is the contrast in content. Although the practice of dating entries continues, few appear to have been prompted by specific events in his public life. On the contrary, almost all the prose 'markings' are dated on his birthdays or on festivals of the Christian year—Christmas,

Easter, Whitsunday. The poems are prevailingly composed on Saturdays and Sundays, in many instances when he was at his retreat near Brewster.

The overall impression is that Hammarskjöld no longer felt the necessity or even the inclination for interior reflection upon what was transpiring in either his professional work or his personal relationships. To be sure, some of the familiar themes which had occupied him from the beginning persist. A few come to definitive statement. But, prevailingly his spirit is free to play at will upon its own concerns, its memories of times long past, its delight in Nature, and to voice its response in verse. And this in spite of the fact that these were the most crowded and the most momentous days of his career. At the very time when the 'public servant' was bringing to culmination the most distinguished career ever achieved in the Community of Nations, in his inner thoughts the 'private man' takes over almost altogether. It is now that the Man of the World speaks with unrestrained feeling, and also eloquence.

Following the comments stimulated by the events of his reinduction, there is silence for more than three months. Then, on his fifty-third birthday, he is moved to set down his final reflections on 'loneliness', 'others', 'death', 'sacrifice.' Clearly, while these themes reappear only very occasionally during the last years, they continue strong undercurrents at the deeper levels of consciousness:

'7.29.58
Did'st Thou give me this inescapable loneliness so that it would be easier for me to give Thee all?

Still a few years more, and then? The only value of a life is its content—for *others*. Apart from any value it may have for others, my life is worse than death. Therefore, in my great loneliness, serve others. Therefore: how incredibly great is what I have been given, and how meaningless what I have to "sacrifice."

> Hallowed be Thy Name,
> Thy kingdom come,
> Thy will be done—' [166]

Toward the end of 1958, he begins to write in verse in a sequence of half a dozen poems composed on three successive October Sundays:

'Fading beeches, bright against
A dark storm-cloud.
Wind rips up the forest-pond's
Steel-gray water.
On the earth between bloodstains
The tracks of deer.

Silence shatters to pieces
The mind's armor,
Leaving it naked before
Autumn's clear eye.' (167)

*

'Day slowly bleeds to death
Through the wound made
When the sharp horizon's edge
Ripped through the sky.
Into its now empty veins
Seeps the darkness.
The corpse stiffens,
Embraced by the chill of night.

Over the dead one are lit
Some silent stars.' (169)

*

'Too tired for company,
You seek a solitude
You are too tired to fill.' (172)

On his fifty-fourth birthday, July 29, 1959, Hammarskjöld was vacationing at his beloved home in southern Sweden. He begins a meditation on 'humility' as he had sought to achieve it, which he completed a week later after his return to New York:

'To have humility is to experience reality, not *in relation to ourselves*, but in its sacred independence. It is to see, judge, and act from the point of rest in ourselves. . . . In the point of rest at the center of our being, we encounter a world where all things are at rest in the same way. Then a tree becomes a mystery, a cloud a revelation, each man a cosmos of whose riches we can only catch glimpses. The life of simplicity is simple, but it opens to us a book in which we never get beyond the first syllable.'[174]

On the same day, he enters in the upper corner of the next page these unexpected lines:

> *'Seventeen syllables*
> *Opened the door*
> *To memory, to meaning.'* [175]

And he is launched upon his most sustained spell of writing which is to absorb him through the next three months.

In that summer of 1959, he appears to have had more leisure, first on the brief holiday in Sweden and later over weekends in his cottage near the Hudson River. It was then that he composed, or put in final form, some 100 *haikus*—after the Japanese mode, each verse of seventeen syllables arranged in three lines.* W. H. Auden aptly comments: 'It makes me very happy to see that in the last three years of his life, he took to writing poems, for it is proof to me that he had at last acquired a serenity of mind for which he had long prayed. When a man can occupy himself with counting syllables, either he has not yet attempted any spiritual climb, or he is over the hump.'**

Filling twenty pages, these *haikus* range over the full gamut of Hammarskjöld's life and interests—reminiscences of Uppsala days thirty and more years before including the painful glimpses into his boyhood home and associations which we have already quoted†, descriptions of Nature in *'Summers'*, comments on events and reports of observations at many places *'Far Away'*, and finally a group of poems captioned *'Hudson Valley'*. Selection is difficult; the full sequence should be read consecutively and in its entirety. Here are random samples, the first prompted by recollection of someone's death:

---

* When and through whom Hammarskjöld's imagination was first captured by this verse form is uncertain. Four years earlier, on the return flight from his momentous mission to Peking, he had stopped in Tokyo for a few hours. His only other time in Japan was an overnight stop following his mediation efforts between Laos and Vietnam in November 1959; but that was just three weeks after he had written his final *haiku*. Who brought this distinctive mode of poetic expression to his attention—perhaps a Japanese colleague at the United Nations? We do not know.

** 'Foreword' to *Markings*, p. xx.

† Above, pp. 88 f.

'Red evenings in March. News of death.
Begin anew—
What has ended?'

.   .   .

'The trees pant. Silence.
An irresolute raindrop furrows
The dark pane.'

.   .   .

'Swollen brooks
Under Easter skies.
Night. On the table sweet violets.'

.   .   .

'The boy in the forest
Throws off his best Sunday suit
And plays naked.'

.   .   .

'Black shooting stars
The swallows utter shrill cries
As they mate in mid-air.'

.   .   .

'New leaves at sunset
After May showers. A look back
Repeats the Fall.'

Eight pages later, under the heading *'Far Away'*, come a group of
haiku inspired by his visit to southern Asia five months before:

'The brilliant notes of the flute
Are heard by the gods
In the Cave of Birth.'

'Himalayan ice cliffs
Beyond the hills
Of Vezelay at Easter.'

'Apes. The moon woke them—
Round the world's navel revolved
Prayer wheels of steps.'

'A place of rest. Charcoal fires.
Deep in the mirror
Vishnu is at peace.'

Two pages further on comes the heading 'Hudson Valley':

> 'April snow.
> The cardinal sought shelter
> In the white forsythia.'

There follows immediately this gruesome description of a motor accident which one of his Swedish friends recalls seeing while walking with Hammarskjöld near his Brewster home:

> 'The belly the car slit open
> Was silent
> When borne to the roadside.'

However, the more familiar themes of his prose writing are not absent.

> 'On Christmas Eve, Good Friday
> Was foretold them
> In a trumpet fanfare.'

> . . .

> 'May I be offered
> To that in the offering
> Which will be offered.'

> . . .

> 'God took the form of man
> In the victim
> Who chose to be sacrificed.'

> . . .

> 'Congenial to other people?
> It is with yourself
> That you must live.'

> . . .

> 'Alone in his secret growth,
> He found a kinship
> With all growing things.'

The collection ends, shortly after the submission of his Annual Report for 1958–1959 in which he recapitulated his conception of 'The Role of the United Nations' and just before he set off on his last journey to the Far East, on this note:

'For him who has faith,
The last miracle
Shall be greater than the first.' (175-195)

That was, also, his last 'marking' for the year 1959.

The year 1960 was almost barren of recorded 'Road Marks', only six, the fewest in any year since he had begun to write regularly a decade earlier. However, the first, dated 'Easter, 1960', is his profoundest comment upon 'forgiveness' and 'sacrifice' to which we shall return.* He goes on:

'When I think of those who have preceded me, I feel as if I were at a party in the dead hour which has to be got through after the Guests of Honor have left.
When I think of those who will come after—or survive me—I feel as if I were taking part in the preparations for a feast, the joys of which I shall not share.' (197)

Then, on the next page, an entry for 'Christmas Eve' which is chronologically misplaced, probably because it is linked to Easter (108). The final entry for 1960, written on December 3, is the only rhymed poem Hammarskjöld wrote which W. H. Auden has rendered:

'The road,
You shall follow it.

The fun,
You shall forget it.

The cup,
You shall empty it.

The pain,
You shall conceal it.

The truth,
You shall be told it.

The end,
You shall endure it.' (201)

* See below, p. 199.

In 1961, all but one of the twenty-two 'markings' are in verse. The exception, however, is the invaluable Whitsunday reminiscence, recording the decisive turning point in Hammarskjöld's life more than eight years before.*

Through the summer months of 1961 before he set off on his last and fatal trip to the Congo, on weekends and other occasional holidays a sequence of entries recapitulates in poetic form much of what has gone before, the major topics and conclusions which had occupied his interior reflections across the years, and the goal to which his spiritual pilgrimage had brought him. The nagging self-doubt:

> 'Sleepless questions
> In the small hours:
> Have I done right?
> Why did I act
> Just as I did?
> Over and over again
> The same steps,
> The same words:
> Never the answer.' (209)

The price of dedication:

> 'Tired
> And lonely
> So tired
> The heart aches.
> Meltwater trickles
> Down the rocks,
> The fingers are numb
> The knees tremble.
> It is now,
> Now, that you must not give in.
>
> On the path of the others
> Are resting places,
> Places in the sun
> Where they can meet.
> But this
> Is your path,
> And it is now,
> Now, that you must not fail.

* See above, p. 100.

Weep
If you can,
Weep,
But do not complain.
The way chose you—
And you must be thankful.'[213]

There are also two or three unusually opaque poems depicting a victim confronting execution [206, 210, 212] which have encouraged the suggestion that they express his own 'death wish' or premonition of death; but the references are too obscure to support such interpretations.

Near the end, two prayers declare his final faith.* The second and briefer of the two, written six weeks before his death, is preceded by three quotations from Psalms. Had Hammarskjöld arranged his book as a testament, this might well have been placed as his last 'Road Mark':

'Almighty . . .
Forgive
My doubt,
My anger,
My pride.
By Thy mercy
Abase me,
By Thy strictness
Raise me up.'[217]

iii

The United Nations General Assembly was to reconvene on September 20.

In mid-August, the Congo crisis appeared near enough to resolution to justify a qualifiedly hopeful diagnosis to Beskow in Sweden: 'My comments on the Congo come close to the somewhat disappointed statement of one of the more revolutionary members of the Advisory Committee: "This is excellent, if it is true; but is it not too simple?" We seem to be so geared to trouble here that when a problem solves itself—in accordance with our plans—we do not

---

* The first and longer appears on pp. 202 f. below.

believe in it more than you do in Stockholm when you see the sun in December.'

Hammarskjöld was determined to present a favorable report to the General Assembly, if at all possible. There seemed good reason to hope that acceptance of an invitation from Premier Adoula of the Congolese Government might offer an opportunity to meditate between the several factions as well as to firm up the United Nations' plans for technical assistance. An atmosphere of optimism enveloped his departure from New York on September 12. Andrew Cordier's parting word was: 'As far as Leo [Leopoldville] is concerned, this will be the most pleasant of your trips there.' Hammarskjöld, always noncommittal about the future, replied: 'Yes, I hope so.'

While he was crossing the Atlantic, the situation deteriorated in accordance with his forebodings. When his plane stopped at Accra to refuel, he was informed that fighting had erupted between Tshombe's secessionist forces in Katanga and United Nations troops. The objective of his mission shifted from planning measures for internal reconstruction to an attempt to effect a 'cease-fire'. After three days of preliminary negotiation from Leopoldville, in the afternoon of the 17th, against the judgment of some of his trusted advisers, he enplaned for Ndola in Northern Rhodesia where Tshombe had agreed to meet him for personal conference. Toward midnight, his plane crashed a few miles from its destination in circumstances shrouded in mystery which probably will never be dispelled.*

Hammarskjöld's last mission has been spoken of as a failure. In fact, the cease-fire which he was seeking was effected within two days after his death. All parties to the confrontation, stunned and sobered by the sudden tragedy, which, it was thought, might have been caused by sabotage or by the fire of a roving flier associated with the Katanga secessionists, quickly concurred in a cessation of hostilities.

Since youth, Hammarskjöld had meditated often on 'death' as a 'sacrifice' in furtherance of high purpose. We saw that two of the earliest 'Road Marks' of the Uppsala University student linked the two terms.** Later reflection on the example of Jesus strengthened

* Cf. Arthur L. Gavshon, The Mysterious Death of Dag Hammarskjöld (New York: Walker and Company, 1962).
** See above, pp. 51–52.

and deepened the conviction: 'the road of possibility might lead to the Cross'[68]. Just four months before sacrificial death abruptly terminated this final effort of mediation and reconciliation, in the crucial Whitsunday 1961 'marking', he had declared: '. . . I came to a time and place where I realized that the Way leads to a triumph which is a catastrophe, and to a catastrophe which is a triumph. . . .'[205]* However, there is no evidence whatever to support a widely circulated report that he went to the Congo with unusual foreboding or that a premonition warned him that the gift of life which he was prepared at any moment to make would be demanded of him at this time, even that he might have planned it.** While the fashion in which death claimed Dag Hammarskjöld appeared as a meaningless accident of fate, it is a fact that it accomplished his immediate objective which might not have yielded to uncertain negotiation.

His last night had been spent in the residency of Sture Linner, head of the United Nations mission to the Congo. He left there the copy of the German original of *Ich und Du* (*I and Thou*) presented to him by Martin Buber and the first dozen pages of his translation into Swedish. Almost his last word to Linner was that they must discuss it together on his return. Beside the bed was the cherished copy of Thomas à Kempis' *Imitation of Christ* which was always on the table in his New York apartment next to his bed where the manuscript of *Markings* was found; it was the only reading he had taken on this trip. As a bookmark facing a favorite and especially appropriate passage was a card on which was typed his oath of office:

'I, Dag Hammarskjöld, solemnly swear to exercise in all loyalty, discretion and conscience the functions entrusted to me as Secretary-General of the United Nations, to discharge these functions and regulate my conduct with the interests of the United Nations only in view, and not to seek or accept instructions in regard to the performance of my duties from any government or other authority external to the Organization.'

* See further below, p. 199.
** Something has been made of the fact that he had recently drafted instructions for the disposition of his papers and that his apartment was found in spotless order. But he always left it so; and the directive regarding his papers was actually prepared by his secretary and signed only in response to her insistent urging.

V·DAG HAMMARSKJÖLD'S FAITH

No ASPECT of the many-faceted person mirrored in *Markings* appears to be so baffling as that which is central and, therefore, crucial for all the rest: Dag Hammarskjöld's religious faith. None has been so misunderstood. None so grievously misinterpreted, doubtless in most instances unintentionally.

Sad to say, misinterpretation has been most flagrant precisely where sympathetic appreciation might have been most expected, in Scandinavia. In a long and disdainful article, the editor of Sweden's largest national newspaper, a militant anti-clericalist, declared: 'He identifies himself more and more with Jesus. . . . By 1957, Jesus is transformed in Hammarskjold's diary into a politician. . . . It was a happy thing that he died before his Christ dream had quite removed him from reality.' Even more scathing was the Ambassador of Denmark in Paris; in a Danish Christian paper, he dismissed Hammarskjöld as 'a pitiful, miserable aesthete. . . . a despairing Dag Hammarskjöld', guilty of 'blasphemy'. The writer charges Hammarskjöld with having rearranged the entries in his 'diary' to prove a case, indeed of having done such editing 'before his last journey to the Congo'—a supposition decisively disproved by the manuscript itself. He even suggests that 'one might wonder whether the book was written by him at all' and lends credence to the infamous suggestion that Hammarskjöld may have contrived his own death: 'One almost wonders whether he did not seek and bring about the death.'—a contemptible calumny implying not merely suicide but also murder, since several close associates and friends shared Hammarskjöld's tragic fate. These assumptions and insinuations are cited only to indicate the irresponsibility of even so distinguished a detractor whose principal gravamen is: 'What shocks one is Hammarskjöld's evident belief that, like Christ, he has been chosen by God to be the sacrificial lamb, and that by accepting this destiny he, like Christ, can save mankind. Other critics have already pointed out this blasphemy. . . . To Hammarskjöld Christ was not the Son of Man who died for our sins. Christ was Hammarskjöld's forerunner.' The writer appears to be unaware of Jesus' own injunction to any who would be a follower to 'take up his cross daily and follow' him.*

The underlying source of these malicious aspersions has been exposed by a fellow Scandinavian journalist: 'What Scandinavian rationalism—and, frankly, irreligiosity—finds so hard to countenance is that this utterly sane, cool and intellectual man should turn out to have been a God-obsessed mystic.'** As a distinguished Swedish novelist has put it: 'In a half de-Christianised country even the most elementary features of Christian discipleship are unknown, or regarded as presumptuousness or blasphemy.' †

Unfortunately, 'rationalism' and 'irreligiosity,' while especially prevalent and militant in Scandinavia, are not confined to those countries. Doubtless, many Anglo-Saxons have experienced something of the same bafflement in understanding Hammarskjöld. A few have expressed similar though less extreme misgivings. Some United Nations associates have even voiced regret that *Markings* was published. One puzzled reviewer reports that 'sincere, discerning and loyal friends . . . consider *Markings* with embarrassment, not knowing what to make of so gratuitous an example of discrepancy, unreason and excess, and the more they liked the man the more they wish it had never appeared'††. The fact is, as has been suggested, 'His inner life seems to have been almost entirely unsuspected by even his closest colleagues. . . . His friends did not know him.'‡ The self-drawn 'profile' brings shock and, in some cases, resentment that one whom they considered an intimate proves to have been, at the core of his being, utterly different than they had supposed, almost a total stranger to them and their view of reality. This reaction is not admirable. It is somewhat childish. But it is very human.

---

* Cf. below, p. 185.
** Oliver Clausen, *The New York Times Magazine*, June 28, 1964, p. 10.
† Sven Stolpe, *Dag Hammarskjöld: A Spiritual Portrait*, p. 103. Regrettably, this delightful and generally trustworthy interpretation is somewhat vitiated by exaggerated attention to the derogatory articles just quoted. On the irreligiosity of many of Hammarskjöld's friends, see above, p. 41 n.
†† Clifton Anderson in *The New Republic*, Nov. 14, 1964, p. 24.
‡ Stolpe, *op. cit.*, pp. 98, 99.

Those whose approach to Hammarskjöld is sympathetic, even admiring, discover in *Markings* very different and sometimes seemingly incompatible findings. His 'profile' shows many different faces. Or, more correctly, the single countenance reflects many different expressions, as would be expected in so many-sided a person. Speaking across a span of nearly forty years and in varied circumstances and moods, the voice utters sentiments on a wide range of subjects which inevitably may sound contrasted if not contradictory. Like the Apostle Paul, Dag Hammarskjöld was such a rich and cosmopolitan person that almost everyone can find in his meditations something of what he most wishes to discover there. Each of us approaches what Hammarskjöld has written with his own preconceptions, prejudices and interests. With antennae of attention attuned to the wave length of our desire, we tend to hear only what corresponds. This is very evident in the individual 'markings' which are selected by different reviewers or readers as illustrative of 'what Hammarskjöld said' on this or that. Of any such citation, it must be asked: *when* did he write that, at what stage of his pilgrimage? and *under what circumstances?* and, especially, *how representative* is it?

This is particularly true of interpretations of Hammarskjöld's faith. A recent biographer, professing to describe his thought of God, quotes a single statement as though it were typical: 'God was a "non-God, a non-Spirit, a non-Person, a non-Substance". He was simply the One, pure and absolute. He came close to Spinoza who thought God was everything: "All is God; all lives and moves in God." '* But in *Markings* the four negative terms are placed within quotation marks and, in the original, are in German; Hammarskjöld is quoting from an unidentified German author. The passage follows one of Hammarskjöld's most direct confessions of personal dependence upon God.** Among Hammarskjöld's more than ninety references to God,† this quotation stands alone; it is completely *un*representative.

A member of Hammarskjöld's personal staff, a devotee of Oriental religions who delighted to call his attention to their writings, has suggested that, in his last years, his spiritual interest focused more and more upon Eastern faiths and his own belief became increasingly 'universal', less distinctively Christian. It is true that his several brief

---

* Emery Kelen, *Hammarskjöld*, p. 108. Cf. *Markings*, p. 110.
** See below, p. 213.
† For illustrations, see below, pp. 200–203.

stops in Asia and his associations at the United Nations with adherents of Oriental faiths quickened his imagination and admiration. We quoted above a *haiku* prompted by a visit to a Buddhist shrine near Katmandu in early 1959 which voices this sympathy:

'A place of rest. Charcoal fires.
Deep in the mirror
Vishnu is at peace.' [186]

And, a private letter to Beskow pays high tribute*: 'How much more mature and fine the Asiatic art of living is than ours. Evidently, it is first when you have accepted the thought that everything is an illusion that you can master the art of playing over the whole scale of reality with ease, style, seriousness and happiness. What does it matter then if you are poor, politically ignorant or threatened.' Earlier, he had reminded himself that 'Even the Way of the Confucian world is a "Trinity".' [135] These insights into Eastern thought and life enlarged his spiritual horizons. But that they supplanted his personal fidelity to Christian faith is decisively refuted by *Markings*; several of his most unequivocal reaffirmations of that faith were recorded in the form of prayers in the last weeks of his life[214-15, 217] **.

Again, because the Whitsunday 1961 account of the pivotal turning point in his life declares 'at some moment I did answer *Yes* to Someone—or Something' [205], the Danish diplomat adds 'hardly, then, to a personal God'. But over and over and over again Hammarskjöld speaks of God as personal. Very early, he had declared: 'That God should have time for you, you seem to take as much for granted as that you cannot have time for Him.' [12] Midway through his book, he addresses: 'Thou who has created us free. . . . Thou—who art also in me. . . .' [98] † Near the very end, one of his last prayers concludes:

'Thou
Whom I do not know
But Whose I am.
Thou

* The earlier part of this letter appears above, p. 156.
** Cf. above, p. 167, and below, pp. 202 f.
† This prayer appears in full below, p. 202.

Whom I do not comprehend
But Who hast dedicated me
To my fate.
Thou—'(214)

From first to last, he addresses God as 'Thou', the most personal of
all pronouns. The God whom Hammarskjöld knew was the God of
the Psalmists and of Jesus Christ.

ii

The influences to which Dag Hammarskjöld's spirit responded and
which, in interaction with his own experiences and reflections,
molded his faith were principally four. Three of these—his parental
inheritance, the thought of Albert Schweitzer, the medieval mystics—he acknowledged in his *credo* 'This I Believe'. The fourth—the
Bible and especially the Psalmists—stands forth on the pages of his
'Road Marks'.

I

In his radio confession, he declared: 'Experience and honest thinking
has led me in a circle; I now recognize and endorse, unreservedly,
those very beliefs which were once handed down to me.'* We
ventured to suggest, however, that this self-interpretation was not
quite accurate. If a spatial figure were to be used, it would more
properly be a spiral rather than a circle. His conviction returned to
the same basic certitudes, but at a higher level.

His mature belief, as we have remarked, discloses almost no re-
semblance either to the theology of his classical Lutheran heritage or
to that of his mother. For example, although 'faith' is one of his
most frequently reiterated words, in his public addresses no less than
in his private meditations, he often uses it freely to describe human
character and human relationships without any specifically religious
reference. He speaks of '. . . the humility which comes from others
having faith in you' (93, 156), of '. . . faith in this harmony between human beings' (95), and rejoices that 'we can serve as the
foundation for somebody else's faith in himself'. (151) He some-

* *Servant of Peace*, pp. 23–24.

times uses 'faith' as a synonym for 'courage' and often links the two words: 'To have faith—not to hesitate!' [102, 132] '. . . Faith which is the perpetual ultimate sacrifice. . . .' [105] '. . . that unity born of a dying-unto-self, which is the definition of faith.' [106] '. . . In faith and courage. . . .' [123, 137] He affirms faith to be a powerful instrument of human accomplishment: ' "To take Captivity captive." [Psalm 68:18.] Above all, a question of faith.' [138] 'We act in faith— and miracles occur*. . . . Faith is, faith creates, faith carries.' [145] And, on New Year's Eve following the Suez Crisis: '. . . . it has come to pass according to your faith.' [145] Speaking to the Evanston Assembly of the World Council of Churches in 1954, he describes the United Nations as well as the World Council as 'An Instrument of Faith' **. From his first to his last day at the United Nations, he stresses the importance of faith†: 'the belief and the faith that the future will be all right because there will always be enough people to fight for a decent future.'†† He celebrates the faith of the great artists of the past‡. In introducing Beethoven's *Ninth Symphony*, he glories in 'this enormous confession of faith in the victorious human spirit and in human brotherhood, a confession valid for all times'. . . .‡‡ He concludes his response to his re-election: 'May future generations never be entitled to say that we failed because we lacked faith. . . .'§

When Hammarskjöld does speak of 'faith' in a definitely religious sense, it is with a meaning closely akin to the great mystics and at far remove from his religious upbringing: '. . . an untroubled faith springing from the unity of all things.'§§ [80] 'in faith, both humble and proud: that is, to *live*, to know that in God I am nothing, but that God is in me.' [92] His favorite guide is St. John of the Cross:

---

* Cf. his concluding *haiku*, above, p. 165:
      'For him who has faith,
      The last miracle
      Shall be greater than the first.' [195]
** *Servant of Peace*, pp. 56–61.
† *Ibid.*, pp. 32, 40, 61, 62, 166, 379.
†† *Ibid.*, p. 166.
‡ *Ibid.*, p. 62.
‡‡ *Ibid.*, p. 379.
§ *Ibid.*, p. 150. See above, pp. 148–49.
§§ *Markings* reads: 'an untroubled faith in the co-inherence of all things.'

' "Faith is the marriage of God and the soul." '[97]* And on the day
of his reinduction for a second term, he writes:

4.10.58
In the faith which is "God's marriage to the soul," you are *one*
in God, and
    God is wholly in you,
    just as, for you, He is wholly in all you meet. . . .'[165]**

In all of this, there is not the dimmest echo of the 'justification by
faith' which was the very heart of Martin Luther's proclamation, and
of the theology of the Churches which bear his name. Evidently, the
central teaching of the Christian tradition in which Hammarskjöld
had been reared left slight imprint upon his theological conviction.
His indebtedness to his parental inheritance was at two points very
distant from Lutheran scholasticism, as he himself recognized: from
his father, 'a belief that no life was more satisfactory than one of
selfless service to your country—or humanity', and from his mother,
'a belief that, in the very radical sense of the Gospels, all men were
equals as children of God, and should be met and treated by us as our
masters in God.'†
    The latter was direct preparation for the second formative influ-
ence upon his faith.

2

We do not know who or what first directed Dag Hammarskjöld's
attention to the thought of Albert Schweitzer, or precisely when he
began studying Schweitzer's writings.
    In Hammarskjöld's personal library now lodged in the Royal
Library at Stockholm, there is a short shelf of six or eight Schweitzer
titles, principally in the field of ethics and all but one in English
translations. There are two surprising absences—Schweitzer's major
work on *The Mysticism of Paul the Apostle* and his charming
Memoirs of Childhood and Youth.
    Of these books, only one shows evidence of thorough and frequent
reading—*Von Reimarus zu Wrede* ('From Reimarus to Wrede'),

* See below, p. 184.
** Cf. above, p. 150. 'Markings' which treat most explicitly and fully of 'faith'
are on *Markings* pp. 92, 106, 145, 151, 165.
† *Servant of Peace*, p. 23.

published in English under the title *The Quest of the Historical Jesus*. It is a work which had stirred the religious world more deeply than any since Darwin's *Origin of Species*. Critics maintained that if its conclusions were accepted it would destroy Christian Faith. As Professor Paul Ramsey of Princeton University has said, 'Almost single-handedly Schweitzer forced New Testament scholars to take an entirely new direction in the twentieth century.' We mentioned earlier the recollection of several holiday companions that on a climbing expedition in 1948 Hammarskjöld was absorbed in this volume and remarked that his friends ought to read it. It seems probable, therefore, that it was at about this time when Hammarskjöld was in his early forties and was mainly occupied with the Organization for European Economic Cooperation in Paris, that Schweitzer's influence began to take hold upon his thought. Several years passed, however, before Schweitzer's views penetrated his inner reflections. This was the period when Hammarskjöld recorded some of his most somber observations on suicides he had witnessed and several of his sharpest exposés of other persons.* There is no hint of his preoccupation with Schweitzer. Indeed, it is striking that no words of Schweitzer are quoted anywhere in *Markings*.

In his exceptionally important article in *Tiden* for September 1951, Hammarskjöld had spoken of 'the ethic exemplified by Schweitzer', the first explicit reference. It was likewise in 1951 that evidence of Schweitzer's influence first appears in one of the most remarkable and significant of Hammarskjöld's 'Road Marks', all the more noteworthy because it stands almost alone in the midst of his most gloomy and despairing cries. It is the extended meditation upon Jesus approaching his end: 'A young man, adamant in his committed life. . . . —an adamant young man, alone as he confronted his final destiny. . . .'(68)**

Some two years later, in his radio *credo*, Hammarskjöld defined quite precisely the character and extent of his indebtedness to 'the ethics of Albert Schweitzer, where the ideal of service is supported by and supports the basic attitude to man set forth in the Gospels. In his work I also found a key for modern man to the world of the Gospels.'†

* See above, pp. 65 ff.
** See above, pp. 96 f, and below, pp. 195 f.
† *Servant of Peace*, p. 24.

Schweitzer himself once summarized his view of Jesus in these words: 'Within the Messianic hopes which His hearers carry in their hearts, He kindles the fire of an ethical faith. Thus the Sermon on the Mount becomes the incontestable charter of liberal Christianity. The truth that the ethical is the essence of religion is firmly established on the authority of Jesus. Anyone who ventures to look the historical Jesus straight in the face and to listen to what he may have to teach him in His powerful sayings soon ceases to ask what this strange-seeming Jesus can still be to him. He learns to know Him as one who claims to have authority over him.'* Albert Schweitzer's life philosophy has rightly been defined as 'ethical mysticism'**. Hammarskjöld's attitude to Jesus closely follows that of Schweitzer.

In response to an inquiry† in July 1965 as to whether he and Hammarskjöld had ever met and which of his books he believed to have been especially influential upon Hammarskjöld, Dr. Schweitzer replied in a typical note in his own unmistakable handwriting. It must have been one of the last he wrote before his death a month later. He reported that he and Hammarskjöld had met once in Switzerland, that they shared a close kinship of mind especially in questions of ethics, and that Hammarskjöld had intended to visit his jungle hospital at Lambaréné on the trip to the Congo which took his life.‡

The appropriate starting point for the study of any man's thought is his biography, especially the formative factors in his youth. In the case of Albert Schweitzer, we are fortunate to have this in his own words, in an exceptionally self-knowing book of boyhood reminiscences, *Memoirs of Childhood and Youth*. It is all the more regrettable that Dag Hammarskjöld appears to have been unacquainted with this testament; it reveals deep kinship of spirit between the two men, both in youth and in maturity, especially in the matter of relations with others which was such a continuing and harassing bafflement to the younger. Schweitzer speaks often in words which might have been written by Hammarskjöld and which would have brought him considerable encouragement and also correction:

---

* Quoted in A. C. Bouquet, *The Christian Faith and Non-Christian Religions* (New York: Harper & Brothers, 1958), p. 12 n.
** Cf. Henry Clark, *The Ethical Mysticism of Albert Schweitzer* (Boston: Beacon Press, Inc., 1962).
† From H. P. V. D.
‡ This intention is confirmed by Sture Linner.

'How often do I inwardly rebel! How much I suffer from the way
we spend so much of our time uselessly instead of talking serious-
wise about serious things, and getting to know each other well as
hoping and believing, striving and suffering mortals!

'To the fact that we are each a secret to the other, we have to
reconcile ourselves. To know one another cannot mean to know
everything about each other. A man must not try to force his way
into the personality of another. . . . There is a modesty of the soul
which we must recognize, just as we do that of the body. The soul,
too, has its clothing of which we must not deprive it. . . . In this
matter giving is the only valuable process; it is only giving that stimu-
lates. Impart as much as you can of your spiritual being to those who
are on the road with you, and accept as something what comes back
to you from them.'*

Hammarskjöld could doubtless have made his own the famous concluding paragraph of Schweitzer's great *Quest of the Historical Jesus*:

'He comes to us as one unknown and nameless, just as on the
shore of the lake He approached those men who knew not who He
was. He speaks the same words: "Follow thou Me!" and He puts us
to the tasks which He has to carry out in our age. He commands.
And to those who obey Him, whether they be wise or simple, He will
reveal Himself in the toils, the conflicts, the sufferings which they
shall pass through in His fellowship, and, as an ineffable mystery,
they shall learn in their own experience Who He is.'**

3

In his radio *credo* of 1953, after acknowledging Albert Schweitzer's
determinative influence in leading him back to 'the beliefs in which I
was once brought up', Hammarskjöld goes on to declare: '. . . how
man should live a life of active social service in full harmony with
himself as a member of the community of the spirit, I found in the
writings of the great medieval mystics.'†

For the date and circumstances of Hammarskjöld's discovery of the

* *Memoirs of Childhood and Youth*, tr. Campion (New York: The Macmillan
Company, 1925), pp. 56, 69.
** New York: The Macmillan Company, n.d., p. 401.
† *Servant of Peace*, p. 24.

Christian mystics, as with his first acquaintance with Schweitzer's thought, we are largely dependent upon internal evidence from his 'Road Marks'. As we have just seen, he was studying Schweitzer in the late 1940s when he was just past forty years of age. It is probable that he began to read the medieval mystics intensively shortly thereafter.

Actually, he quotes from only five of them. Earliest and most frequent is Meister Eckhart. He begins the year 1951 with a repetition of the familiar hymn line 'Night Approaches Now', responds with the comment: 'So! another year it is. And if this day should be your last:' and then adds this query from Eckhart: ' "—How can we ever be the sold short or the cheated, we who for every service have long been overpaid?" ' (61) More than five years later on the third anniversary of his United Nations appointment while stopping briefly in Rome en route to the Middle East, he is prompted to enter without comment another passage from Eckhart on the contrast between 'a contingent and non-essential will' and 'providential and creative, an habitual will. . . .' (126) Later that same year, he returns to 'Eckhart's "habitual will" ' for extended comment: 'In us the creative instinct became will. In order to grow beautifully like a tree, we have to attain a peaceful self-unity in which the creative will is transformed into instinct.' (135) And at Christmastide, after disclaiming credit for his achievements in the Congo Crisis,* Eckhart again supplies the stimulus for his meditation: ' "Of the Eternal Birth"—to me, this now says everything there is to be said about what I have learned and have still to learn.' Then he continues the quotation from Eckhart: ' "The soul that would experience this birth must detach herself from all outward things: within herself completely at one with herself. . . . You must have an exalted mind and a *burning* heart in which, nevertheless, reign silence and stillness." '(143) Clearly, the last phrases were to provide the inspiration for the phrase 'a center of stillness surrounded by silence' with which he was to introduce his interpretation of 'A Room of Quiet: The United Nations Meditation Room', written the following year.** Meister Eckhart reappears once more and for the last time in a pre-Lenten meditation for 1958 (163-64).

* See above, p. 140.
** *Servant of Peace*, pp. 160–61. See above, pp. 144 f.

From St. John of the Cross, Hammarskjöld took the key phrase which, as we have seen, defines faith for him: ' "Faith is the marriage of God and the Soul." ' [97] He quotes it in his 'Road Marks' five times over a period of some four years*: first, apparently on Good Friday in 1954 [97], again about a year later [105], next in the midst of an especially tense debate in the Security Council in June 1956 with the comment: 'In that case, certainty of God's omnipotence *through* the soul: with God all things are possible, *because* faith can move mountains.' [132], and once more shortly before Christmas 1957: 'One result of "God's marriage to the Soul" is a union with other people which does not draw back before the ultimate surrender of the self.' [160] Finally, it provides the text for his climactic reflection on his own vocation, on the day of his reinduction as Secretary-General for a second term.[165]** Thus, this phrase is Hammarskjöld's most frequently repeated quotation from any source.

Hammarskjöld quotes once from Pascal[126] to whom he had been introduced in student days by Mrs. Nathan Söderblom, and once from Sir Thomas Browne's *Religio Medici*[136].

Among the mystics, his favorite, however, is undoubtedly Thomas à Kempis. Although there are only two direct quotations, they are on days of overwhelming meaning for him—his first election as Secretary-General[91] and his fiftieth birthday[107]†. Even more significant is the fact already noted that, in his latter years, a copy of *The Imitation of Christ* lay by his bedside in his New York apartment and that this was the only book he took with him on the final and fateful mission to the Congo; it was peculiarly appropriate that it should be found on the table next to the bed in Leopoldville where he had spent his last night.

His reflections were saturated with the sentiments which dominate *The Imitation*. Indeed, à Kempis' very first meditation might have been taken as his ruling Guide Post:

'He that follows Me shall not walk in darkness, says the Lord.
These are the words of Christ, by which we are urged to imitate

* Also, in his radio *credo*; see above, p. 46.
** See above, pp. 150, 179.
† See above, pp. 125 and 132. In *Markings*, both quotations from Thomas à Kempis are mistakenly attributed to Thomas Aquinas.

His life and virtues, if we wish to be truly enlightened and freed from all blindness of heart.

'Therefore, let it be our chief business to meditate upon the life of Jesus Christ. . . .

'If you would understand Christ's words fully and taste them truly, you must strive to form your whole life after His pattern.'*

À Kempis' admonition is, in turn, a paraphrase of Jesus' own most oft-repeated and indubitably authentic saying: 'If any man would come after me, let him take up his cross and follow me.'**

Contrary to a widely held assumption, Hammarskjöld can hardly be identified as a mystic, if we assume that mysticism implies complete union of the human and the divine, though his thought reverberates with mystical overtones and undertones.

Josiah Royce once pointed out that 'The higher religious consciousness has its origin in the human heart in two interests. One is the interest of the moral being in finding some authority that may guide him in the conduct of his life. The other is the interest of the baffled and disappointed soul in coming into the presence of some external truth, some reality that is perfect, that lacks our weakness, that is victorious even though we fail, that is good even though we are worthless.'† As illustrative of the second type, Royce cited Spinoza. As example of the first, he might have pointed to his strenuous colleague, William James.

These two interests give birth to two contradictory types of mysticism. While they hold in common a conviction of direct and immediate personal relationship to God, they are poles apart in their presuppositions regarding the nature of both God and man, in their 'Way' to fellowship with God, and in their goal. The second, despairing of the impotence and futility of life, seeks the negation of all that is human and passive absorption in the divine—'the flight of the alone to the Alone'. This goal it pursues by the *via negativa*. 'From eternity to eternity God has triumphed. His holiness I cannot create. Let me, if haply I may, worship it, enjoy it as wondering, contempla-

* *The Imitation of Christ*, Bk. I, Chap. 1.
** Matt. 10:38, Luke 14:27; Matt. 16:24, Mark 8:34, Luke 9:23; John 12:25.
† *The Spirit of Modern Philosophy* (Boston: Houghton Mifflin and Co., 1892), p. 46.

tive, adoring, helpless onlooker, consoled, if at all, by the knowledge that though I fail and am lost, he is from everlasting to everlasting.'* In contrast, the other type of mysticism is through and through active and ethical: 'I don't ask so much who the Lord is, as what his will is. . . . God wants me to work; he asks service of me, not comprehension. . . . My philosophy consists in clear thinking about my duty; my faith is an assurance that the right will somehow conquer; my love is for all who desire God's kingdom to come; my hope is for the victory that is near at hand, and for the word, "Well done, good and faithful servant!" '** However, Rufus Jones, the great Quaker authority on the mystics who developed the contrast between 'negative' and 'ethical' mysticism with reiterated insistence, pointed out that in ethical mysticism 'The individual soul feels invaded, vitalized with new energy, merged with an enfolding presence, liberated and exalted with a sense of having found what it has always sought, and flooded with joy.'† He says elsewhere: 'The *essentia* of Mysticism is the experience of direct communion with God.'†† This is what another has defined as 'practical mysticism in which sacrificial service prompted by love is the ruling characteristic.'‡

In his last years, Dag Hammarskjöld 'discovered' Martin Buber, the great Jewish philosopher-theologian then living in Jerusalem. Buber's thought came to have an influence upon him not unlike Schweitzer's at an earlier period.

On one of his later visits to the Near East, he took the initiative to call on Buber in his home and on his return reported their meeting at a Press Conference as 'one out-of-the-way tourism with a strong personal accent, and that was that I had the pleasure of paying a call on Professor Martin Buber, for whom I have a sincere admiration'.

In a brief account of his relations with Hammarskjöld, 'Erinnerung an Hammarskjöld', in his *Nachlese*, Buber speaks of a visit in his home in January 1959; this was Hammarskjöld's last time in Jeru-

* *Ibid.*, pp. 49–50.
** *Ibid.*, pp. 47–48.
† Rufus M. Jones, 'Mysticism', in Hastings *Encyclopedia of Religion and Ethics* (New York: Charles Scribner's Sons, 1955), Vol. IX, p. 84.
†† 'Mysticism', in *The Dictionary of Philosophy*, ed. by Dagobert D. Runes, p. 203.
‡ John Wright Buckham, 'Mysticism', in *An Encyclopedia of Religion*, ed. by Vergilius Ferm, pp. 513–14.

salem. On the latter's return to New York he told the Press: 'The moment I get time, I would like very much to translate some three or four essays from [Buber's] *Pointing the Way*. On very many points I see eye to eye with him; on other points, naturally, there must be nuances. But as to the basic reaction, I think that he has made a major contribution and I would like to make that more broadly known.' This intention was reaffirmed in a letter to Buber's English editor later that same year.* An extended quotation from one of these essays formed a considerable part of his address on 'The Walls of Distrust' at Cambridge University in June 1958, with this explanation: 'I excuse myself for having quoted at such length. . . . I have done so because out of the depths of his feelings Martin Buber has found expressions which it would be vain for me to try to improve.'** However, it was not this work of Buber's but his *I and Thou* which, as already reported, he was engaged in translating and took with him to the Congo. It is not unlikely that, had he revised his *credo* near the end, the name of Martin Buber might have appeared with that of Albert Schweitzer.†

Buber has often been identified as a 'mystic', and so he was in some of his earlier writings. But he himself disavowed the term 'for I still grant to reason a claim that the mystic must deny it' and explained that he had to pass through mysticism in the ordinary sense of the term into his final and fuller conception of the 'life of dialogue' between God and man. 'I lack the mystic's negation. I can negate convictions, but never the slightest actual thing. The mystic manages, truly or apparently, to annihilate the entire world, or what he so names—all that his senses present to him in perception and memory—in order, with new disembodied senses or a wholly super-

* Cf. 'Introduction' by Maurice S. Friedman to Martin Buber, *Pointing the Way*, Harper Torchbook edition, pp. vii–viii.
** *Servant of Peace*, pp. 186–87.
† However, in a private letter on the influence of Buber upon *Markings*, Dr. Maurice Friedman confirms my impression: 'I find *no* evidence in it of influence by Buber but I have marked a number of passages of interest where they converged or diverged. (Of course, Buber was also decisively influenced by Meister Eckhart, but Hammarskjöld seemed to remain Kierkegaardian just in the way that Buber did not, i.e. focussing on the I-Thou relationship with God somewhat at the expense of that with man.)' Had Hammarskjöld completed his translation of *I and Thou*, this onesidedness in his thought might have been corrected.
A somewhat fuller account of the relations of Hammarskjöld and Buber is given in a NOTE: 'Dag Hammarskjöld and Martin Buber,' below, pp. 215 ff.

sensory power, to press forward to his God. But I am enormously concerned with just this world, this painful and precious fullness of all that I see, hear, taste. I cannot wish away any part of its reality. I can only wish that I might heighten this reality.' Buber's authoritative interpreter rightly suggests that the mysticism which Buber espoused was: 'a realistic and active mysticism, i.e. a mysticism for which the world is not an illusion from which man must turn away in order to reach true being, but the reality between God and man in which reciprocity manifests itself, the subject of his answering service of creation, destined to be redeemed through the meeting of divine and human need . . . a mysticism that may be called such because it preserves the immediacy of the relation, guards the concreteness of the absolute and demands the involvement of the whole being. Its true English name is, perhaps: presentness.'*

This is the ethical mysticism of Albert Schweitzer and Dag Hammarskjöld. As a matter of fact, the latter, even before his personal meeting with Martin Buber, was suspicious of conventional mystic claims. Reporting 'a contact with reality, light and intense like the touch of a loved hand: a union in self-surrender without self-destruction',** he concludes: '—How different from what the knowing ones call Mysticism.'[110] And, later, he defines the character of experience which he would recognize as authentically mystical:

> 'The "mystical experience." Always *here* and *now*—in that freedom which is one with distance, in that stillness which is born of silence. But—this is a freedom in the midst of action, a stillness in the midst of other human beings. The mystery is a constant reality to him who, in this world, is free from self-concern, a reality that grows peaceful and mature before the receptive attention of assent.' [122]

Few have more correctly understood Hammarskjöld or more truly interpreted him than Max Ascoli†: 'The Auden book review ["Foreword" to *Markings*] has led a large number of people to consider as mysticism what is Christian ethics at its best. In our time anyone who cares about religion on weekdays too and is not a professional man of God is called a mystic.' Of Hammarskjöld's response to his

---

* Maurice S. Friedman, in 'Introduction' to *Pointing the Way*, pp. viii–ix.
** A fuller quotation of this 'marking' is on p. 133 above.
† 'On Reading Hammarskjöld', in *The Reporter*, May 20, 1965.

United Nations election—'Not I, but God in me.' [90] 'I am the vessel. The draught is God's. And God is the thirsty one.' [91]—Ascoli comments: 'There was a horrified outcry when these words became known. That man took himself for Christ, it was said. But is there any other way to be a Christian if not by reliving Christ?' Hammarskjöld's key phrase which he repeats elsewhere more than once, 'Not I, but God in me', is of course a variation on Paul's confession 'I live, yet not I, but Christ lives in me'*, although he nowhere indicates awareness that he has adapted it from Paul.

The definitive proof of how Hammarskjöld valued mysticism is, however, again in his *credo*'s tribute to those who had guided him: 'those great medieval mystics for whom "self-surrender" had been the way to self-realization, and who in "singleness of mind" and "inwardness" had found strength to say *yes* to every demand which the needs of their neighbors made them face, and to say *yes* also to every fate life had in store for them when they followed the call of duty, as they understood it.'**

Of Meister Eckhart, a contemporary interpreter has suggested: 'What makes Eckhart difficult is the moral demand he makes on one. . . . He asks of us, not only our minds, but our hearts as well. . . .' The same writer quotes 'one recent commentator': 'Truly, Eckhart makes it hard for us to penetrate the world of his thoughts, for he demands of us a devotion and a faith such as contemporary man does not possess.' 'Today the scientific mind, by definition, must be skeptical and perhaps exhaust its powers in justified "No" to this and that. Only the mystic knows something to which he can say "Yes!" ' † No wonder Hammarskjöld felt such strong kinship of spirit with Eckhart. More than that; what was here said of the medieval mystic might, without violence to truth, be transposed almost without modification to this Man of Affairs of our day, especially the first and last sentences: 'What makes Hammarskjöld difficult is the moral demands he makes on one. He asks of us, not only our minds, but our hearts as well.' And: 'Only the man of faith knows something to which he can say "Yes!" '

* Gal. 2:20.
** *Servant of Peace*, p. 24.
† Raymond Bernard Blakney, 'Introduction' to *Meister Eckhart: A Modern Translation*. Harper Torchbooks, pp. ix, xvii, xxv. The 'recent commentator' quoted is Alois Bernt in his introduction to *Meister Eckhart's Buch der Göttlichen Tröstung*.

4

In view of Hammarskjöld's acknowledgment of debtorship to the
mystics, it might be supposed and has, indeed, been widely assumed
that they were primarily responsible for molding his religious life.
That appears to have been true up to the time when his radio *credo*
was written in late 1953. Thereafter, however, it is clear from his
'Road Marks' that the Christian Scriptures, especially the Psalmists,
were far more influential.

Of the factors which formed his mature faith, the least noted is the
Bible. Possibly, this has been taken for granted. More probably, it is
due to the fact that one may peruse the first half of *Markings* without coming upon a single quotation from Scripture; there were only a
half dozen glancing references to events or phrases in the Gospels.*

It was a year and more after Hammarskjöld had assumed his post
at the United Nations and some months after he had delivered his
radio talk that passages from the Bible first appear. From the end of
1954, they supply the bases for more than a tenth of the individual
'markings', sometimes standing alone, sometimes as stimuli to comments. Forty Scriptural quotations compare with a dozen from the
mystics. Thus, it is manifest that through his last years Hammarskjöld's mind was more and more stimulated and his spirit increasingly fortified by Scripture.

This does not imply, of course, that previously he had been unfamiliar with the Bible. It does mean that it had not exerted a major
influence upon his meditations. Serious and sustained biblical study
appears to date from the decisive 'turning point' of late 1952 or early
1953. We mentioned Judge Klackenberg's surprise to observe Hammarskjöld reading the Bible on their expedition to the far north of
Sweden at just that time. This made a lasting impression on his
friend's memory for, in their countless holidays together over more
than a decade, this had never previously occurred. It seems probable
that it was at about this same time that Hammarskjöld began to read
the Psalmists in the Anglican *Book of Common Prayer*; the twenty-
two quotations from the Psalms which follow were all taken from
this source.

* Pp. 15, 36, 44, 89, 91, 97.

Passages from the Bible were drawn almost equally from the Gospels and the Psalter, with very infrequent references to other parts of the Old Testament. Hammarskjöld meditated often on the Lord's Prayer.* It provided both stimulus and model for a succession of prayers of his own composition.** Phrases from the teachings of Jesus are dotted through his meditations.† Occasionally, he turned to the Fourth Gospel.†† However, his reflection centered majorly upon the course of Jesus' life, especially its termination in Gethsemane and on Calvary.‡ And the Psalms held an ever larger place in his meditations and writing.‡‡ There is one striking lacuna; *Markings* contains not a single quotation from or reference to the Apostle Paul, no conscious echo of his thought. This is further presumptive evidence that Hammarskjöld's reading of Albert Schweitzer had not embraced his great *The Mysticism of Paul the Apostle.*

Even more revealing than the frequency of Scriptural references are the occasions which directed Hammarskjöld to the Bible. Notification of his United Nations election had prompted him to a quotation from Thomas à Kempis[91]§. But when the General Assembly committed to him his first major diplomatic mission, to Peking to seek the release of the American airmen, his response is two verses from Psalm 62. As he embarks on his long flight, he enters the familiar words of Psalm 139. Six months later, when he learns that his Peking intervention has succeeded, he celebrates the triumph again with Psalm 62[108] and adds Psalm 115[109]. And, on the Christmas Eve following, he begins his meditations with Psalm 63.[117] Not infrequently thereafter, especially important actions in the United Nations are marked by reference to one of the Psalms [125, 131, 138]. As we have discovered, in the few hours of respite in the midst of the eight crucial days over Suez, he turns to reading the Bible; he enters phrases from Psalms 4 and 37. The year 1959 is begun

* Pp. 15, 81, 125, 142, 166.
** Pp. 125, 142, 170, 214–15, 217.
† Pp. 44, 105, 109, 111, 112, 130, 132, 134.
†† Pp. 69, 128, 133.
‡ Pp. 55, 68–69, 91, 97, 126, 135, 151, 154, 157, 187, 190, 204, 205.
‡‡ Pp. 102, 108, 109, 116, 117, 125, 126, 131, 136, 138, 139, 142, 153, 173, 204, 217. Hammarskjöld's choice of Psalms is interesting and somewhat surprising. Apart from single references to Psalms 27, 51 and 139, the more familiar and 'favorite' Psalms are absent, e.g., Psalms 1, 8, 15, 23, 46, 84, 90, 91, 96, 103, 118, 121 and the Psalms of Praise culminating in Psalm 150.
§ See above, p. 125.

with a sentence from Psalm 51. And as the unforeseen end was approaching, almost the last page he was to write is filled with verses from three Psalms followed by a prayer of rededication of his own composing[127].

When the evidence is thus examined chronologically and in relation to events in his public life, its teaching is clear. As burdens multiplied and his physical and nervous reserves were taxed almost to the breaking point, Dag Hammarskjöld turned more and more to his Bible. He found there illumination on his vocation, restored balance, and reinforcement of spirit. Had he been redrafting his confession in his latter years, it seems more than probable that he would have added to his tributes to Albert Schweitzer and the medieval mystics mention not only of Martin Buber but also of another determinative cause of his return to faith—the Scriptures.

iii

To recapitulate: Dag Hammarskjöld's religious life evolved from a substructure laid deep and strong in years of boyhood and youth. Among the stones in that foundation, the most central and important upon which the final structure was later to be reared was not the formal theology of traditional Christian teaching in which he must have been instructed; that theology appears to have supplied no part of the undergirding of the man's mature faith. It was, rather, the practical devotion of his mother grounded upon the teaching of the Gospels and expressing itself through unwearying concern and kindness toward any in need. This active compassion quite naturally joined with and was supported by the sterner command of duty—'requiring a sacrifice of all personal interests'—which was the most basic and durable foundation stone from his paternal inheritance.

Following perhaps a dozen years of young manhood when his 'intellect challenged' the beliefs in which he had been brought up, years marked both by silence regarding religion and intense inner turmoil, the thought of Albert Schweitzer brought him to recognize the validity of Christian ethics and guided him back to the Gospels and, more particularly, to their central Figure.

Somewhat later, acquaintance with three or four of the classical mystical writers instructed him 'how man should live a life of active social service' and led him to an affirmation of life and destiny and faith—'to say *yes*'—and to the practice of love 'in an unhesitant fulfillment of duty and in an unreserved acceptance of life' whatever it might bring 'of toil, suffering—or happiness'*. In his late years, the influence of the mystics was complemented and corrected by that of Martin Buber.

Lastly, at about the same time or more probably shortly after the decisive turning point in his life symbolized by the reiterated affirmation '*yes*', he returned to the Gospels and the Psalmists. Through the period of his climactic public responsibility at the United Nations, it was Scripture which furnished day-by-day spiritual nurture and confirmation of faith.

What, more specifically, can be said regarding the *content* of that faith?

iv

It is not difficult to identify and define Dag Hammarskjöld's final faith. However, anyone anticipating something eccentric or esoteric, or even novel, is doomed to disappointment. Those who have so represented Hammarskjöld's faith have misrepresented it. It was 'original' because it issued directly from the depths of his own soul, but it was not novel.

That faith shows forth three principal elements: the intimate presence of the living God, the example of Jesus, the imperative of duty. These elements should be thought of not after the fashion of three points of a triangle but rather three successive points along a single line. The order just given—God, Jesus, duty—is, obviously, the logical order. Moreover, as we shall see, that became what might be called the 'operative order' in Hammarskjöld's maturity—from God through Jesus to duty. However, it is the exact obverse of the chronological order in which the three elements took command over him; he moved from duty through the discovery of Jesus to the encompassing reality of God. This, he himself rightly discerned and set forth clearly in the autobiographical radio confession to which we have so frequently referred.

Both the earliest and the most persistent element in his faith, with

---

* *Servant of Peace*, pp. 23–24. The last phrases may echo the concluding words of Schweitzer's *Quest*; see above, p. 182.

which he began and from which he never escaped, was the conviction
of obligation to a life of public responsibility which he attributed to
his father's influence. The first thirty years of his private reflections
are largely occupied with this theme of personal vocation. Over and
over, he comments upon it and he flays his conscience mercilessly
because of the inadequacy of his response: 'He seeks his own comfort. . . . He fights for his position. . . . He devotes himself to his
job—but he is in doubt as to its importance and, therefore, constantly looking for recognition. . . .[36]* 'You asked for burdens to
carry—And howled when they were placed on your shoulders. . . .' [36]
'Time goes by: reputation increases, ability declines.' [41] 'Never
let success hide its emptiness from you, achievement its noth-
ingness, toil its desolation. . . . Whither? That I don't know. That I
don't ask to know.' [55] '. . .—so that my whole being may become
an instrument for that which is greater than I.' [57] Note that all
these 'Road Marks' are staked down near the onset of his 'Darkest
Night' in late 1949 and 1950. Thus, Hammarskjöld had been wres-
tling persistently with the problem of duty, of moral obligation, of his
vocation in public service for a quarter of a century before he began
to come in sight of the second major element of his final faith.

Already forty-six years of age, near the summit of public achievement and recognition, yet at the same time still struggling in a slough
of unconquerable despondency, through the writings of Albert
Schweitzer he discovered 'A young man, adamant in his commitment, who walks the road of possibility to the end without self-pity
or demand for sympathy, fulfilling the destiny he has chosen. . . .' [69]

However, this discovery—or, more accurately rediscovery since the
figure of Jesus had been implanted in his consciousness many years
earlier by his mother's simple and practical dedication—does not
appear at once to have taken a ruling grip upon his life. For another
two years, he continues to grope a shadowed way through doubt and
desperation, with only occasional fleeting illuminations[84].

Then, suddenly, the determinative crisis. And, almost immediately
thereafter, his vocation is defined not by him but for him: 'God has a
use for you, even though what He asks doesn't happen to suit you at
the moment.' [89] There follows at once an outpouring of recognitions of God, without anticipation or warning: 'Not I, but God in

* Cf. the fuller quotation of this 'marking' on p. 67, above.

me.' 'I am the vessel. The draught is God's. And God is the thirsty one.' '. . . The gift is God's—to God.' (90, 91)*

Nothing is more surprising in this volume crowded with the unexpected than this outburst. We cannot suppose that these affirmations of God formed suddenly out of nothing in response to his election to the United Nations' highest office, even though his meditations show no overt preparation for them. Rather, we must assume that they had been slowly forming beneath the conscious surface of his mind for some time, probably largely as a result of immersion in writings of the mystics. And that they burst forth as though welling up from subterranean springs whose flow had been blocked by surface barriers of unbelief and despondency.

Once God is acknowledged, He takes command. Henceforth, Hammarskjöld's interior reflections are in considerable measure a 'meditation upon God'. The movement of thought reverses: from God, through occasional further recognitions of Jesus as exemplar and leader, to life and duty.

V

In comparison with almost a hundred references to God scattered through his 'Road Marks', in the latter half of his book virtually on every page, Hammarskjöld speaks directly of Jesus infrequently—a half dozen times in all. But these embrace some of his fullest and most determinative 'markings'; among them, the earliest and the last are the most important.

In our study of 'The Darkest Night', we called attention to the fact that, midway through the three tortured years of 1950–1952, there stands an entry of two full pages for which there is no forecast in what has preceded and from which there is no discoverable effect upon what follows. (68–69) It opens with a phrase which sets the keynote for the entire passage: 'A young man, adamant in his committed life.' He is meditating upon Jesus' final meal with his followers: '. . . on the last evening, he arose from supper, laid aside his garments, and washed the feet of his friends and disciples'—one of the most deeply moving episodes in Jesus' career, the perfect acting out of his vocation. Then he repeats: 'an adamant young man, alone

* See above, p. 125.

as he confronted his final destiny.' There follows extended reflection upon Jesus' sense of mission from 'when he returned from the desert' through his whole life's course. Next, upon his injunction to his companions to follow his example, based upon the account in the Gospel of John, chapters 13 and 14. This leads to the query in what sense Jesus may be understood to have fulfilled the role Christian theology has traditionally attributed to him of one 'that taketh away the sins of the world'. The major meditation concludes on the note with which it had begun: 'A young man, adamant in his commitment, who walks the road of possibility to the end without self-pity or demand for sympathy, fulfilling the destiny he has chosen—even sacrificing affection and fellowship when the others are unready to follow him—into a new fellowship.' There are three appended entries in the nature of postscripts or afterthoughts. And then, the writing returns to the mood which dominates this part of the book: 'A sunny day in March.' . . . 'He came with his little girl. . . .' [71]

This lengthy passage on Jesus requires, indeed permits, no commentary. Many have found in it one of the most gripping 'profiles' which they have known of the man Jesus as he goes to his self-determined end. However, five years pass before Jesus himself again appears.

Amidst the outpouring of acknowledgments of God, prompted by his United Nations election, there is a warning on 'the Way' ahead as he recalls Jesus' passage 'through the jubilation of Genneserat' and 'the triumphal entry into Jerusalem' [91]*.

As Holy Week and Easter approached, Hammarskjöld often focused his thoughts on the climactic events of the Christian year. It will be recalled that his summons to the United Nations had occurred over Easter weekend 1953 and that his response had been strongly colored by its associations.

On Good Friday 1956, just before he is to set off on one of his crucial missions to the Near East, a comment by Pascal prompts his own reflection:

'. . . at every moment, Jesus dies in someone who has followed the trail marks** of the inner road to the end:

---

* Quoted in full above, p. 125.
** Swedish, 'märkenas väg'.

love and patience,
righteousness and humility.
faith and courage,
stillness.'[126]

A year later, possibly again on Good Friday, Hammarskjöld declares: 'For the sacrificed—in the hour of sacrifice—only one thing counts: faith—alone among enemies and skeptics . . . faith which reality seems so thoroughly to refute.' And then comes this bold comment: 'Would the Crucifixion have had any sublimity or meaning if Jesus had seen Himself crowned with the halo of martyrdom? What we have later added was not there for Him. And we must forget all about it if we are to hear His commands.' [151] A rigid orthodoxy might brand this reading of Jesus' consciousness as he confronted his end heretical; it explicitly challenges the tradition that he foresaw a vindication in Resurrection and Exaltation. Can we doubt that Hammarskjöld gives the historically correct interpretation? Moreover, it perfectly reflects the fashion in which he had found in Jesus his Guide for life.

Six months later, in the immediate afterglow of his re-election to the Secretary-Generalship, there appears a most unexpected entry. The precise provocation is uncertain, possibly something he had recently read or a comment he had heard:

'Jesus' "lack of moral principles." He sat at meat with publicans and sinners, he consorted with harlots. Did he do this to obtain their votes? Or did he think that, perhaps, he could convert them by such "appeasement"? Or was his humanity rich and deep enough to make contact, even in them, with that in human nature which is common to all men, indestructible, and upon which the future has to be built?' [157]

On Maundy Thursday 1961, the last Holy Week six months before his death, he again meditates upon its meaning as suggested in a passage from Ibsen's *Brand*.[204]

Charles Malik, in a generally laudatory appreciation, has taken Hammarskjöld sharply to task for his testimony to Jesus: 'On the strictly religious plane. . . . I find his great weakness from which every other weakness stems is his being more or less ashamed of the Name of Jesus Christ. His power of *witnessing* to Jesus Christ is very weak. . . . I do not understand how a man who appears to be soaked in these things stammers at the Name of Jesus Christ, even in his personal diary.'* In the light of the passages just quoted, it is clear that Malik and Hammarskjöld did not differ in their discipleship to Jesus but rather in that aspect of Jesus Christ to which their major loyalty was given. Malik, doubtless, misses any overt recognition of the Eternal or Pre-existent or Cosmic Christ who looms so large in the theology of the Eastern Churches of Malik's allegiance. For Hammarskjöld, Jesus is always 'that adamant young man' who pursues the human destiny which he believes God has ordained for him to its bitter and seemingly disastrous end, and who enjoins all who would be his disciples to do likewise. Indeed, if a single verse of Scripture were to be inscribed over Hammarskjöld's life, it would be the injunction which, as we have mentioned, was Jesus' most frequently reiterated word: 'If any man would come after me, let him take up his cross and follow me.' This injunction, Hammarskjöld obeyed, with resolute and undeviating fidelity.

This does not mean that Hammarskjöld was unaware of, or indifferent to, traditional Christian theology's interpretations of Jesus, particularly as Savior from sin. In that same early and lengthy meditation on Jesus as he marches toward death, he asks the question: 'Is the hero of this immortal, brutally simple drama in truth "the Lamb of God that taketh away the sins of the world"?' This is his reply: '. . . Absolutely faithful to a divined possibility—in that sense the Son of God, in that sense the sacrificial Lamb, in that sense the Redeemer. . . .' [69] Hammarskjöld may have been innocent of what is technically known as 'the Doctrine of the Atonement'. But he is here advancing what theology calls a 'Moral Influence' explanation of Atonement. By his utter fidelity to God's Will for him, Jesus inspires his followers to a like fidelity to *their* divinely intended vocation as they understand it; he strengthens them for fulfillment of their destiny; thereby, he 'saves' them from sin into life.

Speaking of Hammarskjöld's dedication to his office, Max Ascoli has said: 'He had to give all of himself, with complete selflessness, to the limit of his capacities and beyond. Sometimes in complete exhaustion he would have to summon the energy that would be his tomorrow. Had not Christ done just this?'** And Sven Stolpe has rightly defined Hammarskjöld's sense of 'vocation': 'He is chosen in

* The Critic, April–May, 1965, p. 76.
** Op. cit., p. 40.

the same way as all Christians who have been "called" are chosen; there is no more to it than that. . . . He must renounce all idea of personal happiness, and be content to sacrifice his private life for the sake of his task. All of this is a normal, Christian attitude.'*

However, a very late 'Road Mark' dated '*Easter, 1960*' deals with the more inward and mysterious meaning of Jesus' death stressed in classic explanations of 'Christ's work':

'Forgiveness breaks the chain of causality because he who "forgives" you—out of love—takes upon himself the consequences of what *you* have done. Forgiveness, therefore, always entails a sacrifice. . . .'[197]

Unexpectedly, the next dating is more than eight months later on '*Christmas Eve, 1960*', one of the very rare instances where Hammarskjöld departs from a strict chronological sequence in the ordering of his 'markings'. Obviously, this is because, in his thought, the birth and death of Jesus stand as the initiation and termination of a single event; this suggestion occurs elsewhere in his writing.

'How proper it is that Christmas should follow Advent.—For him who looks towards the future, the Manger is situated on Golgotha, and the Cross has already been raised in Bethlehem. . . .'[198]

There are other occasional references to Jesus in *Markings*.** And there are numerous quotations of phrases from the Gospels. The last mention of Jesus is, most appropriately, in the Whitsunday 1961 meditation which we have seen to be, in other ways, climactic. The concluding paragraph of that 'Road Mark' gathers up in final statement Jesus' meaning for the life and faith of Dag Hammarskjöld:

'As I continued along the Way, I learned, step by step, word by word, that behind every saying in the Gospels stands *one* man and *one* man's experience. Also behind the prayer that the cup might pass from him and his promise to drink it. Also behind each of the words from the Cross.'[205]

Hammarskjöld who felt special kinship with the thought of T. S. Eliot may well have cherished Eliot's lines:

* *Op. cit.*, pp. 115–16.
** Pp. 97, 126, 133, 135, 187, 190.

200]   DAG HAMMARSKJÖLD

'Remember the faith that took men from home
At the call of a wandering preacher.
Our age is an age of moderate virtue
And of moderate vice
When men will not lay down the Cross
Because they will never assume it.
Yet nothing is impossible, nothing
To men of faith and conviction.
Let us therefore make perfect our will.
O God, help us.'*

vi

Among the approximately six hundred 'Road Marks' staked down
along the 'Way' of Dag Hammarskjöld's pilgrimage, almost exactly a
hundred are concerned in greater or less measure with God.

In the first nearly thirty years of his writing, however, while more
than a third of all his 'markings' are recorded, there are only seven
references to God.** Few though they are, they suggest that God was
in the background of his mind, even if not a regnant factor in his life.
Some of the more striking of these references, revealing how Hammarskjöld thought of Deity in his early and middle years, have
already been noted. For example, the young man of thirty-five protests:

'Your cravings as a human animal do not become a prayer just
because it is God whom you ask to attend to them.'[11]

'. . . That God should have time for you, you seem to take as
much for granted as that you cannot have time for Him.'[12]

And he recognizes how little God counts in his own as well as others'
lives:

'On the bookshelf of life, God is a useful work of reference, always
at hand but seldom consulted. . . . But when we are compelled to
look ourselves in the face—then He rises above us in terrifying
reality, beyond all argument and "feeling". . . .'[16]

He is also 'the Examiner':

* *The Rock.* Used by permission of Harcourt, Brace & World, Inc.
** Pp. 11, 12, 16, 56, 77, 82, 83.

'. . . You pray for strength to meet the test—but also for leniency on the part of the Examiner.'[82]

And, near the close of this period of preparation, Hammarskjöld affirms:

'. . . A vision in which God *is*.'[83]

Then comes the gushing outflow of recognitions of God which dominate Hammarskjöld's response to his United Nations appointment when 'God acts' and establishes the 'demands' for his compliance but is also an inner presence:

'Not I, but God in me.'[90]

Thenceforth to the end, these two notes are closely interrelated and predominant—God as the determiner and empowerer of his vocation and God as an intimate reality of his inner life:

'. . . The chaos you become whenever God's hand does not rest upon your head.
He who has once been under God's hand. . . . how strong he is, with the strength of God who is within him because he is in God. . . .'[104]

'Forgiveness is the answer to the child's dream of a miracle by which what is broken is made whole again, what is soiled is again made clean. The dream explains why we need to be forgiven, and why we must forgive. In the presence of God, nothing stands between Him and us—we *are* forgiven. But we *cannot* feel His presence if anything is allowed to stand between ourselves and others.'[124]

A corollary is the strong and sure sense of God's agency in all worthy accomplishment:

'Your own efforts "did not bring it to pass," only God. . . .'[143]

'If you fail, it is God, thanks to your having betrayed Him, who will fail mankind. . . .'[156]

To this experience and this conviction, Hammarskjöld's response is a series of prayers, some half dozen in all.* Any man's living faith speaks most truly through his private prayers. So with this man. Here,

* Pp. 98, 100, 125, 142, 214–15, 217.

we are admitted into the inmost chamber of his 'negotiations . . .— with God'*. Again, two may be taken as representative—the earliest and the next to last. Early in 1954, perhaps in Holy Week, when he has been in his United Nations office for about a year, Hammarskjöld writes:

'Thou who has created us free, Who seest all that happens—yet art confident of victory,
Thou who at this time art the one among us who suffereth the uttermost loneliness,
Thou—who art also in me,
May I bear Thy burden, when my hour comes,
May I—'(98)

We have noted that in mid-summer 1961, less than two months before his death, Hammarskjöld composed two prayers; the second and briefer was quoted as what might well have been his final word if he had arranged these closing pages for publication.** Its companion, written just a fortnight earlier, is the longest and fullest declaration of Hammarskjöld's faith:

'July 19, 1961
        Have mercy
        Upon us.
        Have mercy
        Upon our efforts,
        That we
        Before Thee,
        In love and in faith,
        Righteousness and humility,
        May follow Thee,
        With self-denial, steadfastness, and courage,
        And meet Thee
        In the silence.

        Give us
        A pure heart
        That we may see Thee,
        A humble heart
        That we may hear Thee,

* *Markings*, p. v.
** Above, p. 167.

A heart of love
That we may serve Thee,
A heart of faith
That we may live Thee.

Thou
Whom I do not know
But Whose I am.

Thou
Whom I do not comprehend
But Who hast dedicated me
To my fate.
Thou—' (214-15)

vii

In the content of Dag Hammarskjöld's faith, there is one puzzling gap and two surprising lacunae.

It would be an oversimplification to say that it is God who, he believes, has committed to him his vocation—he uses the traditional Christian term 'calling'—who sustains and empowers him throughout and who rewards him with such sense of accomplishment as he permits himself to recognize; but, that in carrying out that vocation, Jesus is his guide. Yet, on the whole, these appear to have been the realities of his life. Strange to observe, there seems to have been little if any direct connection between these two elements within his faith. In his several meditations upon Jesus across more than a decade, there is no mention of Jesus' dependence on God. He is always the 'adamant young man, *alone* as he confronted his final destiny'. To be sure, he is fulfilling a Divine imperative: 'If God required anything of him, he would not fail.' (68) However, there is no hint of Divine support or comradeship on 'the Way'. It is always 'one man and one man's experience' (205). Again, among his references to God, save when he is quoting Jesus directly and twice when he speaks of the Trinity(123, 135), Hammarskjöld never addresses God or speaks of Him by the one word which was Jesus' unfailing term: 'Father'. Apparently, despite the controlling role of Jesus in the determination of Hammarskjöld's career, he never learned from Jesus the sure confidence of a son in his Divine Father.

The unexpected lacunae in Hammarskjöld's faith are the Holy Spirit and the Church.

The word 'Spirit' occurs only two or three times in *Markings*. He speaks a number of times about 'spirit' in man [81, 109]; 'A landscape can sing about God, a body about Spirit.' [93] But only twice clearly of Divine 'Spirit', in both instances in verses which seek to express something of the Trinity:

> '*Before* Thee, Father,
>   In righteousness and humility,
> *With* Thee, Brother,
>   In faith and courage,
> *In* Thee, Spirit,
>   In stillness.' [123]

In a somewhat parallel passage he is really expounding Confucian belief.*

In other words, Hammarskjöld's faith lacked the enrichment and reassurance, the sense of Divine intimacy and potency which are the unfailing gifts of the Holy Spirit. In one sense, this is not surprising. 'The Holy Spirit has always been the neglected stepchild of Christian theology.' It has been a lacuna in the experience and belief of Christians generally, as it was with Hammarskjöld.** In another sense, the absence is surprising because in the thought of Hammarskjöld's principal tutor in his latter years, Martin Buber, 'Spirit' holds an important place. In the volume of essays which had so stimulated Hammarskjöld that he clung to the hope that someday he might translate several of them, stressing the contrast between Plato and Isaiah, Buber wrote:

'Isaiah does not share Plato's belief that the spirit is a possession of man. The man of spirit. . . . is one whom the spirit invades and seizes, whom the spirit uses as its garment, not one who contains the spirit. He [Isaiah] knows himself to be a man of spirit and to be without power. . . . The prophet speaks the word that it is his task to speak; he is borne by this task, proceeding from a divine purpose and pointing to a divine goal. The spirit moves him; not only his

---

* See above, p. 176.
** Cf. Henry P. Van Dusen, *Spirit, Son, and Father* (New York: Charles Scribner's Sons, 1958), pp. 1–29.

organs of speech but the whole man is taken up into the service of the spirit.'*

The Church holds no place whatever in Hammarskjöld's recognition, unless by implication in references to 'the sanctuary' in the 63rd and 73rd Psalms.(117, 204) It is well known that he seldom attended church services, although he never failed to search out notable cathedrals and sanctuaries in places which he visited and he is reported to have dropped in at some of the churches in New York. To be sure, he responded to invitations to address the International Committee of Y.M.C.As. and the World Council of Churches; but he established no relation to congregations of his own or other Communions in America, explaining that a United Nations officer must be free of partisan or particular associations. And he appears to have been wholly out of touch with his own Church of Sweden. The 'Room of Quiet' at United Nations Headquarters served as his private sanctuary; it is said that he unfailingly went there for a few moments before setting forth on his numerous journeys.

Clearly, Dag Hammarskjöld felt no need for participation in ordinary church life. W. H. Auden suggests: 'It is possible that his lack of participation in the liturgical and sacramental life of a church was a deliberate act of self-sacrifice on his part, that, as Secretary General, he felt any public commitment to a particular Christian body would label him as too "Western," but he gives no evidence in his diary of desiring such a commitment.' Auden then adds his own comment: 'In any case, I am sorry for his sake, because it is precisely the introverted intellectual character who stands most in need of the ecclesiastical routine, both as a discipline and as a refreshment.'** Perhaps Auden is right. On the other hand, it is quite possible that, had Dag Hammarskjöld maintained even a minimal formal association with conventional ecclesiastical practice, we would never have had *Markings*—and the remarkable faith there declared.

viii

On faith's final question—the destiny of the human spirit beyond physical death—Hammarskjöld's 'Road Marks' speak only once.

* *Pointing the Way*, pp. 187, 200.
** 'Foreword' to *Markings*, p. xxii.

What he says there is the more noteworthy because it stands near the close of his period of deepest dejection, toward the end of 1952; it immediately precedes his most agonized cries of desolation. It concludes the luminous 'marking' which had reported his 'vision of a magnetic field in the soul, created in a timeless present by unknown multitudes, living in holy obedience, whose words and actions are a timeless prayer'*. Then:

'—"The Communion of Saints"—and—within it—an eternal life.' (84)

With this may be placed an even more intimate confession in a private letter to one of his closest friends whose father had just died. It was written in the rather special circumstance that the deceased had been a Christian minister of very conservative sectarian loyalties while his son, the recipient of the letter, was without positive religious allegiance. The letter was written in early 1943 during one of the intervals of 'silence' in Hammarskjöld's 'diary': 'The atmosphere and light around Death has seemed to me to be one of the greatest miracles of Life. I suppose it is because in Death itself the whole striving and innermost "daimon" of the deceased emerge with a strength and clarity as never before. And therefore the death of a good person becomes a proud manifestation of Life, a "Quand même" of the spirit that elevates and relieves.'

Whether the deepening of his own basic faith across the years, and his fellowship of thought with mystics and Psalmists, altered his attitude toward life's 'ultimate destiny', we may never know.**

---

* Above, p. 94.
** These and other uncertainties regarding Dag Hammarskjöld's private life may be clarified through access to his personal correspondence, filed along with his public papers in the Royal Library in Stockholm. Helpful light might be shed by any letters of condolence written during his last decade.

VI · EPILOGUE

Inner Person–Private Man–Public Servant

A S THIS STUDY DRAWS TOWARD A CLOSE, two questions press
for illumination:

First, what, if any, was the bearing of Dag Hammarskjöld's
interior life upon his public career?

Second, what, if any, is the meaning of Hammarskjöld's spiritual
pilgrimage and its outcome for men and women of today?

1

To the obverse of the first query—the bearing, if any, of Hammarskjöld's public career upon his interior life—we have discovered clear
and definitive answer. From the moment when he was notified of his
election as Secretary-General of the United Nations—and probably
no less through the earlier years if precise datings of individual 'Road
Marks' were available to us—by far the bulk of his most striking,
profoundest and most self-revealing reflections were set down in
direct reaction to specific events in his career and the Cause which he
served—flaming sparks struck off at white heat from the anvil of
history.

But, was the reverse equally true? What, if any effect did his inner
life have upon his public career?

On the right answer to that question, Hammarskjöld himself
entertained no doubt whatever. Repeatedly, he insisted that any
value the world might credit to his efforts was a mistaken attribution;
all that he was, worth noting, was wholly the operating of Divine
Purpose and Power through him. Whatever of consequence resulted
was not his achievement; it was God in him. From those first passionate assertions in response to his United Nations election: 'Not I,
but God in me.' 'I am the vessel. The draught is God's. And God is
the thirsty one.' 'The gift is God's.' '. . . to know that in God I am

[209

nothing, but that God is in me.' [90, 91, 92]—through his year-end comment following months of testing negotiations over Suez almost four years later: 'Your own efforts "did not bring it to pass," only God. . . . you were simply the instrument by means of which He added one tiny grain to the Universe He has created for His own purposes.' [143]—and his retrospective reflection as his first term as Secretary-General drew toward its close: 'For someone whose job so obviously mirrors man's extraordinary possibilities and responsibilities, there is no excuse if he loses his sense of "having been called." ' [154] —and his response to his re-election, when he quotes from an unidentified source: ' "The best and most wonderful thing that can happen to you in this life, is that you should be silent and let God work and speak." ' [156]—to his last recorded prayers less than two months before the end, a single note dominates: he and his efforts are merely agencies of the Divine.

To be sure, all this is Hammarskjöld's own interpretation. Is there objective evidence in its support?

Yes, especially in the qualities of character which dumfounded and humbled those, friend and foe alike, associated with Hammarskjöld in his public work. His biographer, writing shortly before his death and searching for 'The Sources of His "Power" ', concludes: 'The ascendancy that he established above all turned upon. . . . a kind of "moral magistracy". His authority was rooted in integrity and sheer intellectual power. . . . Above all, Hammarskjöld's influence rested on his reputation for probity.'* Henry Cabot Lodge, whose early relations with Hammarskjöld had not been easy, once said of him: 'He is without vanity and desire for magnification of his public personality.' When the United Nations General Assembly paid its corporate tribute, in virtually every one of the more than thirty eulogies, two characterizations recurred as though they had been preconcerted: 'Integrity' and 'Dedication'—in the words of Lord Home of Great Britain, 'unswerving integrity' and 'utter devotion'; and of Adlai Stevenson: 'resolutely impartial, resolutely even-handed and resolutely firm'.

The secret, the wellspring of such commanding character? An unexpected witness, Professor Eric Goldman of Princeton, presently on leave in Washington as special consultant to the President, while

* Lash, *op. cit.*, pp. 206, 209.

confessing his inability to share Hammarskjöld's religious faith, gives the answer: 'Unmistakable is the fact that his deep religious commitment helped a great deal toward his striking effectiveness as Secretary-General of the U.N. Hammarskjöld genuinely felt himself above the need of any self-conscious neutrality. He did not have to serve either East or West; he served God.'* Hammarskjöld himself had once recorded the explanation in a quite specific context**: 'He had no need for the divided responsibility in which others seek to be safe from ridicule, because he had been granted a faith which required no confirmation. . . .' (110)

2

What, if any, is the meaning of Hammarskjöld's spiritual pilgrimage and its outcome for each of us?

The answer is to be discovered at the two poles around which every human life revolves—and which Hammarskjöld himself was so fond of distinguishing as the 'private man' and the 'public servant'—in his case, behind and beneath and within both of which, as we said at the beginning, in the most intimate and continuous interrelation with both—at once a reflection, a mirror of the 'public servant' and the 'private man' and at the same time the determinative prime mover of each—was the 'inner person', known only to himself, the real Dag Hammarskjöld.

With respect to the 'private life' of Everyman, here is a man of affairs, summoned in duty to some of the most exacting and responsible offices for the peace and good order of mankind, who was also a man of the world, acutely sensitive to every movement and nuance of present-day thought, counting among his closest friends persons of the *avant-garde* in the arts and literature and drama and philosophy, thoroughly schooled in contemporary intellectual fashions and dogmatisms—truly a 'Renaissance man at mid-twentieth century'—who was also a mercilessly honest and therefore sometimes tortured soul in pilgrimage from an inherited traditional Christian belief through an 'intellectual hesitation which demands proofs and logical demonstration' to 'convictions without any compromise with the demands

---

* Review of *Markings* in *Book Week*, Oct. 18, 1964.
** For a fuller quotation from this 'marking', see above, p. 133.

of that intellectual honesty which is the very key to maturity of mind'. In this age of 'revolt against parents' and 'chasms between generations', here is a man who moved out from an upbringing of strong and devout loyalties into a world of sophisticated skepticism without trauma or *Angst*, and from within that world back, not strictly 'in a circle', but to a far richer, more comprehensive Christian Faith.

It may be contended that Hammarskjöld's is the normal and normative three-step advance of the truly mature mind—from uncritical credence through honest doubt to firmly founded faith. Dag Hammarskjöld did not differ from his generation in the terms of the pilgrimage. On the contrary, he was thoroughly, peculiarly representative of the most advanced thought of our day. He differed from his contemporaries in that he was unwilling to rest in the miasma of unbelief. He pressed a way through, not by withdrawal from life but by agonizing search and self-scrutiny within the maelstrom of events until they led to secure assurance: 'He who has once been under God's hand. . . . how strong he is, with the strength of God who is within him because he is in God.'

In face of this man's pilgrimage, let no one—however steeped in the dominant relativisms, agnosticisms and negativisms of our day—let no one maintain that the ablest and most honest contemporary mind is unable to affirm informed and confident religious certitude.

The conclusion of the pilgrimage is often not far from its starting point. T. S. Eliot hints at something of the same 'logic of spiritual development' in the familiar lines from the concluding section of *Four Quartets:*

'What we call the beginning is often the end
And to make an end is to make a beginning.
The end is where we start from. . . .

We shall not cease from exploration
And the end of all our exploring
Will be to arrive where we started
And know the place for the first time. . . .'*

With respect to the 'public life' of Everyman, we return once more to Hammarskjöld's own dictum: 'In our era, the road to holiness

* "Little Gidding." Used by permission of Harcourt, Brace & World, Inc.

necessarily passes through the world of action.' [122] We have suggested that of this truth, his life is the proof, his 'Road Marks' the evidence.

May not the obverse be equally true: In our era, the road to action adequate to the demands of these times necessarily passes through the world of holiness? Only a spirit tempered in the fires of unflinching and indomitable inner struggle, more than that a spirit firmly grounded in profound and secure faith in God, can yield character capable of supreme leadership for this tortured, frantic, unhappy age. This, at least, was Dag Hammarskjöld's clear and strong conviction. We have cited his testimony, as well as the objective evidence, to the truth of this conviction for his own life. But he held it to be true for all men. Let this be his concluding word to us:

'It is not sufficient to place yourself daily under God. What really matters is to be only under God. . . .' [110]

'. . . a living relation to God is the necessary precondition for the self-knowledge which enables us to follow a straight path, and so be victorious over ourselves. . . .' [149]

NOTE

Dag Hammarskjöld and Martin Buber

IT WAS JUST FIVE DAYS after his reinduction for a second term as Secretary-General of the United Nations that Dag Hammarskjöld initiated communication with Martin Buber. On April 15, 1958, he wrote to Buber in Jerusalem:

'Dear Professor Buber,

'You do not know me personally, but I am afraid you have not been able to escape knowing about me.

'My reason for sending you these lines is that I just read the newly published American edition of your collection of essays, "Pointing the Way."

'I wish to tell you how strongly I have responded to what you write about our age of distrust and to the background of your observations which I find in your general philosophy of unity created "out of the manifold." Certainly, for me, this is a case of "parallel ways."

'Once in a while I have my way to Jerusalem. It would, indeed, give me very great pleasure if on a forthcoming visit I may call on you.

'Yours sincerely,
'Dag Hammarskjöld.

'Professor Martin Buber
Jerusalem.'

Apparently, *Pointing the Way*, first published in English in 1957, was Hammarskjöld's introduction to Buber's thought. Three times in the preceding two years—in April-May 1956, in May 1957 and in December 1957—Hammarskjöld had been in Jerusalem but had made no effort to make contact with Buber.

[215

A day or two after his letter to Buber, Hammarskjöld discovered that the Jewish scholar was lecturing at Princeton. Hammarskjöld wrote him there, inviting Buber to visit 'us' at the United Nations, and suggesting the afternoon of May 1. Hammarskjöld's secretaries were under strict instructions that under no circumstances were he and his guest to be interrupted. Several important messages were impatiently brushed aside as the two men continued in intense conversation for more than two hours.

Hammarskjöld may already have been preparing his major address on 'The Walls of Distrust' for delivery at Cambridge University on June 5. In any event, he incorporated into that address the extended quotation, cited above,* from Martin Buber's farewell address in Carnegie Hall, New York, in 1952, 'Hope for this Hour,' which appears among the concluding essays in Pointing the Way.**

Hammarskjöld's next visit to Jerusalem was in September 1958. This may have been the occasion of his first call at Buber's home, reported at a Press Conference as 'one out-of-the-way tourism with a strong personal accent'.

However, it was on his next and last visit to Jerusalem in January 1959 that Hammarskjöld and Buber had their longest and most intimate conversation over dinner in Buber's home. It made a profound impression on both men. Buber gave an account of it in his Nachlese, quoted above. Hammarskjöld spoke of it to the Press on his return with a disclosure of his hope to translate three or four essays from Pointing the Way, 'the moment I get time'. Almost certainly, Hammarskjöld had revealed this intention to Buber and had won his provisional approval.

In June of the same year, 1959, Hammarskjöld submitted to the Nobel Prize Committee in Sweden a four-page memorandum on Buber's qualifications for consideration for the Nobel award. It is a characteristically detailed, discerning and scrupulously objective account of Buber's work and influence which reveals as much about its author as about his subject.†
The document is concerned principally with Buber as a candidate for the Nobel Prize in Literature, but concludes with this appraisal and recommendation:

'Under such circumstances, it seems evident that Buber could without doubt be considered as a Nobel Prize candidate. But the reservations too are clear: he is an 80 year old person, whose life-work is sealed, and his

---

* P. 187.
** Pp. 223–24. Cf. Servant of Peace, p. 186.
† A copy of this Memorandum, translated from the Literary Supplement of Ha-Aretz, Tel Aviv, through the initiative of Dr. Maurice Friedman, is also lodged in the Dag Hammarskjöld collection in the Princeton University Library.

creation touches only indirectly upon the field intended by the Nobel Prize [for Literature]. His greatest virtue is probably his being the interpreter of an important culture, whose son he is, and this in such a high degree of purity and intensity, that already in his life he is prominent as a symbol of this culture.

'In spite of the admiration for Buber evident in these lines, I would hesitate to see him awarded the Nobel Prize for Literature. A more natural form of appreciation would be to award him the Peace Prize.'

Here is a moving illustration of Dag Hammarskjöld's conscientiousness, perhaps almost overconscientiousness—an unshadowed 'integrity' in judgment of a man whom he admired profoundly no less than in negotiation between Nations. He greatly desired to recommend Buber for the award in Literature, and that is the main thrust of his Memorandum. But, in the end, he cannot quite bring himself to urge this and, as an alternative, suggests the Peace Prize.

After an interval of two years, Hammarskjöld resumed the correspondence with Buber in a letter dated August 17, 1961:

'The last few days I have been reading some studies of yours which I had not seen before. . . .

'After having finished reading these studies, I feel the need to send you again a greeting—after far too long a time of silence, understandable only in the light of the pressure of circumstances. In what you say about the "signs," about the "questions" and the response and about the Single One and his responsibility, with reference also to the political sphere, you have formulated shared experiences in ways which made your studies very much what you would call a "sign" for me. It is strange—over a gulf of time and a gulf of differences as to background and outer experience— to find a bridge built which, in one move, eliminates the distance.

'This is all I wanted to tell you and I do not believe that any further comments would add or clarify anything.'

Then, almost as an afterthought, Hammarskjöld adds this paragraph:

'I still keep in my mind the idea of translating you so as to bring you closer to my countrymen, but it becomes increasingly difficult to choose and of course I can not envisage any more extensive work. Also, the more I sense the nuances of your German, the more shy I become at the thought of a translation which, at best, could render only a modest part of its overtones.'

This letter was written just one week before Hammarskjöld's last 'marking'.

Buber responded at once with a handwritten letter from Jerusalem dated '23 August 1961':

'Dear Mr. Hammarskjöld—
'I want to thank you for your letter.
'It is, for me, even more than what you said in our first talk, a token of true. . . . understanding—rather a rare gift in this world of ours.

'Were I asked, which of my books a Swede should read first, I should answer: "The most difficult of them all, but the most apt to introduce the reader into the realm of dialogue, I mean: *I and Thou.*" As you may not know the Postscript to the new edition, I am sending you a copy, together with a paper on language I gave last year.

'With kind regards,
'Yours,
'Martin Buber.'*

Both this letter and the copy of Buber's book must have been posted Air Mail for, three days later on August 26, Hammarskjöld acknowledged their receipt and replied: 'I am certain that I am reading you correctly if I see reflected in your reply a silent "Aufruf" that I try a translation of this key work, as decisive in its message as supremely beautiful in its form. This decides the issue and, if I have your permission, I shall do it even if it may take some time. I am, in fact, today getting in touch with the main Swedish publishing firm asking them whether they would accept my offer. . . . If this all works out, may I tell you how much it would mean to me also by providing me with a justification for a broadened and intensified contact with you personally.'

In less than a fortnight, Hammarskjöld had a favorable response from his Swedish publishers. On September 12, he so informed Buber. Thus, in less than four weeks' time from Hammarskjöld's almost casual suggestion, the author's permission had come from Jerusalem, the publisher's agreement from Stockholm, and the translator was at work.

September 12 was the day when Hammarskjöld enplaned in New York for the Congo. Thus, his letter to Buber about the detailed arrangements for his translation must have been the last, or almost the last, he ever wrote. This project occupied the forefront of his thought as he embarked upon his last and fatal mission.

As already reported, he took the copy of *Ich und Du*, newly received from Martin Buber, as his only book on the trip, other than his bedside copy of à Kempis' *Imitatio*. More than that; it appears from this corre-

---

* Hammarskjöld was already familiar with *I and Thou*. He had included a fairly extended discussion of it in his commendation of Buber for the Nobel Prize.

spondence that the twelve pages of translation which Hammarskjöld had completed were probably, in whole or in part, completed while he was en route to and during his stay in Leopoldville.

Incidentally, this exchange of letters should serve to silence the persistent rumors that Hammarskjöld started for the Congo shadowed by a premonition of impending death. One does not undertake so formidable a project in translation if he expects to die in a few days, or weeks, or months!

Not only was Martin Buber's thought, and his task of making it available in Sweden, in Dag Hammarskjöld's mind as he set off for the Congo. His last words of which we have knowledge were on the same theme. George Ivan Smith reported to Buber on October 3:

'. . . In the course of the funeral service at Uppsala, Dr. Linner told me that before Dag boarded the aircraft, almost the last conversation he had with Linner concerned your work. He was translating some of it into Swedish while he was at Leopoldville and, almost certainly, in the aircraft on the way to Ndola.* Linner said that the last words he remembered Dag saying before the aircraft took off referred to your work and to medieval mystics. "Love, for them," he said, "was a surplus of power which they felt completely filled them when they began to live in self-forgetfulness." ' **

* This is a slight error. Linner states that, contrary to a widely circulated report, Hammarskjöld left the book and his unfinished translation in his bedroom in Leopoldville.

** Cf. Hammarskjöld's radio credo: 'Love . . . for them meant simply an overflowing of the strength with which they felt themselves filled when living in true self-oblivion.' Servant of Peace, p. 24.

NOTE: The correspondence between Hammarskjöld and Buber, consisting of six letters from Hammarskjöld to Buber and one handwritten letter from Buber to Hammarskjöld, supplemented by letters written to Buber after Hammarskjöld's death by the latter's nephew, Knut Hammarskjöld, and by George Ivan Smith of the United Nations Staff, is in the Buber Archives in the Jewish National and University Library, Jerusalem, Israel. It has been made available through the prompt and generous cooperation of Dr. C. Wormann, Director of that Library. Duplicates of the correspondence are in the Dag Hammarskjöld collection in the Princeton University Library which has kindly supplied me with copies. They are reproduced here with the permission of Governor Bo Hammarskjöld in Stockholm and of the Library and Professor Ernst Simon in Jerusalem. This material reached me after the text of this book was already in type; hence, this Note. I am greatly indebted to Dr. Maurice S. Friedman, now at Sarah Lawrence College, Bronxville, New York, editor and translator of Pointing the Way: Collected Essays by Martin Buber (Harper Torchbook, 1963) who informed me of the existence and location of this correspondence and has given me his impression of the relations of the two men's thought.

NOTE*

'It is easy for me to honestly and sincerely declare that I do not believe these rumors to be true. . . . When I heard about them, it was my thought that these rumors formed the continuation or the backwash from the New York gossip which also got into the Swedish press that the well-dressed head of the U.N. was included among the town's most sought-after bachelors on the part of American society women and that he fled from the interest of this sort of women. From there it is no far cry to wondering why the man did not get married. In our society a man subject to the searchlight of publicity is hardly permitted to remain un-married without some people taking up the question of what can be wrong with him. . . .

'In our circle we sometimes joked about Dag's lack of interest in women as we often did about bachelors in general. But there is no doubt but that he was attracted by persons of the opposite sex. . . . On the surface he seemed to be rather shy and somewhat reserved when in the company of women, especially with respect to those who appeared to be "interested" in him. However, with the wives of his friends he was a gallant and popular conversationalist, perhaps inclined to be rather too "highbrow" sometimes. . . . His greatest interest lay at the cerebral level, and he much preferred to live with books and problems than to spend time so-cially talking nonsense and gossiping. . . . By no means insensitive to female charm, he appeared to enjoy most being together with more mature women with a greater experience of life. . . .

'We occasionally spoke of marriage but more as a theoretical problem of how difficult it would be to combine the necessary consideration to-wards a wife with the kind of working life we pursued. The explanation he is said to have given the Queen Mother as to why he had not married appears to have the hallmark of probability and to contain a good portion

* Excerpts from a personal letter of Judge Henrik Klackenberg to H.P.V.D.

of the truth. He knew that his mother had suffered from the fact that his father, owing to his super-human burden of work, had had so little time for her, and having in mind the great and demanding tasks with which he himself had been entrusted, he did not wish to cause such suffering to another woman. . . .

'His self-chosen state of celibacy could give him a serious feeling of loneliness. He felt shut out from a central feeling of human communion, and it is difficult for me to imagine that he sought physical "ersatz" elsewhere. This would not have been in accordance with his personality or the spirit which expresses itself so convincingly in Markings: "For him who has responded to the call of the Way of Possibility, loneliness may be obligatory. Such loneliness, it is true, may lead to a communion closer and deeper than any achieved by the union of two bodies. . . ." (120)

'About rumors of homosexuality, . . . I have searched my memory for observations in this direction without finding anything I can consider remarkable. . . .

'To an unusual degree Dag became the friend of his colleagues and in fact these were mainly men. In his intimacy with them he found quite a lot of human communion it seemed at that time (but one becomes frightened when one reads the expressions of loneliness and isolation to be found in Markings). Formerly it has never occurred to me or, as far as I know, to anyone else to interpret these friendly relations as romantically coloured homosexual sympathy or tenderness. If some cocksure experts want to interpret things this way, let them. For me they have no value as proof and I can only wish that such relationships could become more widespread on the job, both in the public and private sectors. . . .

'I can honestly and unhesitatingly bear witness to the fact that during the whole of our long and occasionally fairly intensive time together, I cannot recall any action or gesture or even any word of Dag's which could have indicated a sexual inversion. No thought of homosexuality ever occurred to me and from Dag's period in Sweden I have never heard rumors in this direction. In Swedish public life there were some highly publicized cases of homosexuality on the part of prominent people concerning which we had lively and frank discussions. To me it is a completely absurd thought that I could have had these conversations with a person with homosexual leanings himself.

'It has felt strange for me to discourse in this way about a person who always stood out to me as being a strong-willed and morally well-disciplined nature, a man without effeminate leanings in his emotional life and with a markedly virile pattern of reactions. . . . To me these rumors about Dag Hammarskjöld appear equally idiotic as would a claim that this lover of paintings and fine describer of nature was color-blind!'

APPENDIX

Correlation of Dag Hammarskjöld's MARKINGS and Events of His Public and Private Life

I. Public Events and Corresponding 'Markings'

Date	Event	Page in 'Markings'	Page in this book
Apr. 1–10, 1953	Election as Secretary-General	89ff.	124ff., 184, 191, 194, 196, 209
Dec. 4, 1954ff.	Commission to seek release of American airmen by Peking	102	130f.
Aug. 1, 1955	Release of American airmen	108f.	191, 132f., 101, 175, 204, 213
Mar. 20, 1956	Security Council debate on Middle East	125	
Apr. 8, 1956	3rd anniversary, UN election	126	183
Apr. 22, 1956	Visit to Middle East	127	145, 135
June 4, 1956	Report to Security Council on Middle East	131f.	191, 178, 184
July 26– Nov. 28, 1956	Suez Crisis	137ff.	136, 178, 79, **139f.***
Feb. 22, 1957	Statement to General Assembly on Near East	149	143, 213
Apr. 7, 1957	4th anniversary, UN election	150	84, 143, 177, 179
Sept. 26, 1957	Re-election as Secretary-General	156ff.	146, 149, 177, 210
Apr. 10, 1958	Induction, Second Term	165	**150,** 179, 184

II. Dag Hammarskjöld's Birthdays and Corresponding 'Markings'

Date	Event	Page in 'Markings'	Page in this book
July 29, 1955	50th birthday	107	132f., 184
July 29, 1956	51st birthday	136	135
July 29, 1957	52nd birthday	155	146
July 29, 1958	53rd birthday	166	74, 76, 160
July 29, 1959	54th birthday	174	222, 145, 161

* Principal references are in **bold-face type.**

[223

III. Special Days in the Christian Year and Corresponding 'Markings'

Date	Event	Page in 'Markings'	Page in this book
Dec. 25, 1954	Christmas	102	131
Dec. 24–25, 1955	Christmas Eve and Christmas Day	117ff.	82, 134, 74, 79, 145, iii, 37, 157, 175, 188f, 213
Mar. 30, 1956	Good Friday	126	196f.
Apr. 8, 1956	Sunday	126	183
Aug. 26, 1956	Sunday	137	136, 178
Dec. 24–26, 1956	Christmastide	143f.	140f., 143, 145, 32–33, 178f., 183
Dec. 31, 1956	New Year's Eve	145f.	140f.
Feb. 24, 1957	Sunday	149	143, 213
Apr. 7, 1957	Sunday	150	143
(Apr. 19, 1957)	Good Friday	151	197
Oct. 6, 1957	Sunday	157f.	102, 149
Dec. 24, 1957	Christmas Eve	161	150
Feb. 16, 1958	Sunday before Lent	163	183
Oct. 5, 1958	Sunday	167	161
Oct. 12, 1958	Sunday	169	161
Oct. 19, 1958	Sunday	172	161
Aug. 9, 1959	Sunday	176ff.	163
Oct. 25, 1959	Sunday	192f.	83
Nov. 1, 1959	Sunday	193ff.	165, 195
(Apr. 17, 1960)	Easter	197	165
Dec. 24, 1960	Christmas Eve	198	165
Mar. 30, 1961	Maundy Thursday	204	197
May 21, 1961	Whitsunday	205	100, 166, 169, 176, 199f.
June 18, 1961	Sunday	212	167

IV. Comprehensive Chronological Correlation

1953

Page in 'Markings'	Date	Page in this book	Date	Event
191	Apr. 7		Mar. 31	Election, Secretary-General, UN
			Apr. 5	Easter
		124ff., 184, 191, 194, 196, 209	Apr. 8	Left Stockholm for New York
			Apr. 9	Arrival, New York: Press Conf. Foote,* 27
			Apr. 10	Inducted as Secretary-General: Statement. F., 28
			May 13–June 9	Stockholm, Geneva, Paris, London
			May 26	Address to Staff, Geneva. F., 30
			July 10	UN Correspondents Assoc. F., 31
			July 24	Rededication, Bernadotte Plaque. F. 31
			July 29–Aug. 4	Paris, Geneva, Paris
			July 29	48th birthday
			Sept. 11–13	Washington. Amer. Pol. Science Assoc. F., 34–39
			Sept. 14	Amer. Assoc. for UN, F., 40–48
			Oct. 15–18	Stockholm
			Oct. 21	For. Policy Assoc. F., 49–55
			Dec. 4	UN Staff Day, Geneva. F., 32–33
			Dec. 16–18	London

1954

Page in 'Markings'	Date	Page in this book	Date	Event
			Mar. 1–4	Caracas
			Mar. 11–19	Stockholm, London
			May 23–27	Paris, Geneva, Paris
			July 4–19	Paris, Geneva, Malmo
			July 29	49th birthday

* Servant of Peace: A Selection of the Speeches and Statements of Dag Hammarskjöld, edited by Wilder Foote (New York: Harper & Row, 1963). Hereafter abbreviated 'F.'.

Appendix IV (Continued)

Page in 'Markings'	Date	Page in this book	Date	Event
			Aug. 20	Address, World Council of Churches, Evanston. F., 56–61
102	Dec. 10	131	Oct. 19	Museum of Modern Art. F., 62
			Dec. 4ff.	China Issue in UN General Assembly
			Dec. 18–21	Stockholm
			Dec. 20	Inaugural Address, Swedish Academy. F., 63–79
102	Dec. 25	131	Dec. 25	Christmas
102	Dec. 30	131	Dec. 30–31	New York, London
			1955	
			Jan. 1–13	London, Paris, New Delhi, Canton, Peking, Canton, Hongkong, Tokyo, Honolulu
			Apr. 20–May 1	Stockholm, London, Geneva, Paris
			May 19	Press Conf. F., 132
			May 22–27	Paris
			June 13–14	Baltimore. Johns Hopkins Univ. Address. F., 80–85
			June 19	Stanford Univ. F., 86–91
			June 25	Univ. of Calif. F., 92–98
			July 8	Annual Report. F., 99–100
			July 10–Aug. 10	Zurich, Geneva, Zurich, Copenhagen, Malmo, Copenhagen, Geneva, Paris
107	July 29		July 29	50th birthday
108ff.	Aug. 1	132f., 184 191,101,132–33,175, 205, 213	Aug. 1	Release of American airmen
			Aug. 8	Atoms for Peace Conf, Geneva. F., 101–2
			Aug. 27–30	Bogota
113f.	Nov. 19–20 (Sat. & Sun.)			

Appendix IV (Continued)

Page in 'Markings'	Date	Page in this book	Date	Event
117	Dec. 24	82	Dec. 24	Christmas Eve
118	Dec. 25	134, 74, 79, 145, x, 37, 157f., 188, 213	Dec. 25	Christmas Day
			1956	
			Jan. 16–Feb. 23	Athens, Istanbul, Ankara, Lydda, Cairo, Lydda, Amman, Beirut, Teheran, Beirut, Damascus, Baghdad, Bahrein, Karachi, Bombay, Bangalore, Delhi, Rangoon, Bangkok, Djakarta, Sydney, Canberra, Sydney, Aukland, Wellington, Aukland, Honolulu, Fiji, San Francisco
			Feb. 27	Press Conf. F., 132–34
			Mar. 7	Press Conf. F., 134–36
			Mar. 20	Security Council on Middle East
125	Mar. 21			
126	Mar. 29			
126	Mar. 30 (Good Friday)	196f.	Apr. 7–May 5	London, Rome, Beirut, Cairo, Gaza, Jerusalem, Beirut, Amman, Damascus, Rome, Paris
126	Apr. 8 (Sun.)	183	Apr. 8	Rome, Third Anniversary, UN Election
127	Apr. 22	145	Apr. 22	Beirut
			May 14	Williamsburg. F., 103–7
			May 20	New York Univ. F., 108–13
			May 29–31	Montreal. International Law Assoc. F., 114–17
131	June 4	191	June 4	Upsala College. F., 118. Report on ME, Security Council

Appendix IV (Continued)

Page in 'Markings'	Date	Page in this book	Date	Event
132	June 10	178, 184	June 28–July 26	Copenhagen, Warsaw, Stockholm, Helsinki, Moscow, Prague, Vienna, Belgrade, Zurich, Geneva, Beirut, Cairo, Geneva
			July 20–Nov. 28	Suez Crisis
136	July 29, Aug. 16	135, 184	July 29	51st birthday
137	Aug. 26 (Sun.)	136, 178, 184		
138	Aug. 30	136		
			Oct. 4	Annual Report. F., 119–22
			Oct. 31	Security Council Statements. F., 123
139	Nov. 1–7	139, 140	Nov. 4	Security Council Statements. F., 125
			Nov. 14–18	Paris, Rome, Naples, Abu Suweir, Cairo, Rome, Paris
140	Nov. 17	140	Nov. 17	Cairo
			Nov. 22	French & British withdraw from Suez
141	Nov. 25 (Sun.)		Nov. 28	Conclusion, Gen. Assembly debate on Suez
141	Nov. 29	140, 143, 201		
143	Dec. 24	145, 183	Dec. 24	Christmas Eve
143	Dec. 25	32–33, 140f, 178, 179	Dec. 25	Christmas Day
144	Dec. 26	140, 178, 141		
145	Dec. 31		Dec. 31	New Year's Eve

1957

Page in 'Markings'	Date	Page in this book	Date	Event
148	Jan. 21	143	Jan.	Home leave
			Jan. 21	DH's mother died—Jan. 21, 1940
			Feb. 2	UN Assembly Resolution on Israel
			Feb. 22	DH Statement in UN Assembly
149	Feb. 24 (Sun.)	143, 213	Mar. 20–27	Brussels, Athens, Cairo, Beirut, Rome, Paris

Appendix IV (*Continued*)

Page in 'Markings'	Date	Page in this book	Date	Event
150	Apr. 7 (Sun.)	143, 84, 177, 179	Apr. 4	Press Statement. F., 136–37
			Apr. 7	4th anniversary, UN election
			Apr. 10	Amer. Jewish Com. Address. F., 126–31
152	Apr. 28 (Sun. after Easter)		Apr. 28	New York–Lisbon
			Apr. 29–May 11	Lisbon, Barcelona, Nice, Rome, Zurich, Geneva, Beirut, Jerusalem, Paris
152	May 25			
153	June 20			
153	June 23 (Sun. after Trinity)	146	June 23	Mid-summer night
			June 29–July 18	Copenhagen, Malmo, Geneva, Paris
155	July 20	146		
155	July 28 (Sun.)		July 29	52nd birthday
			Aug. 22	Annual Report
156	Sept. 3	146, 177	Sept. 3	Parents' wedding anniversary
156	Sept. 26	146–49, 177, 210	Sept. 26	Re-election, UN Secretary-General. F., 148
157	Oct. 1	149, 197		
157	Oct. 6 (Sun.)	102, 149	Nov. 3–Dec. 6	Rome, Beirut, Amman, Jerusalem, Damascus, Beirut, Rome, Paris
			Dec. 19–28	Copenhagen, Stockholm, Cairo, Gaza, Beirut, Rome, Paris
			Dec. 20	Presidential Address, Swedish Academy. F., 151–59

Appendix IV (Continued)

Page in 'Markings'	Date	Page in this book	Date	Event
161	Dec. 22 (Sun. before Christmas)		Dec. 22	Stockholm, Copenhagen, Cairo, Gaza
161	Dec. 24 (Christmas Eve)	150	Dec. 24	Gaza
			1958	
			Jan. 16-17	London
163		183	Feb. 4	Address, International YMCAs, Cleveland
	Feb. 16 (Sun. before Lent)			
165		150, 179, 184	Mar. 22–Apr. 4	Stockholm, Helsinki, Moscow, Prague, Zurich, Geneva, London
			Apr. 2	British Parliament. F., 170
	Apr. 10		Apr. 10	Induction, Second Term. F., 165–69
			Apr. 29	Security Council Statement. F., 171
			May 1	Press Conf. F., 175–76; 179–81
			May 4–9	Brussels, Paris, Geneva
			May 19–20	Miami. Governors' Conf. F., 182–83
			June 1–5	Copenhagen, Oslo, London
			June 5	Cambridge Univ. F., 184–87
			June 12	Press Conf. F., 187–88
			June 18–27	London, Beirut, London
166	July 29	74, 76, 160	July 29	53rd birthday
			Aug. 8	Statement to UN Assembly on Lebanon-Jordan Crisis
			Aug. 26–Sept. 12	Paris, Rome, Beirut, Amman, Beirut, Rome, Geneva, Beirut, Cairo, Jerusalem, Beirut, Baghdad, Amman, Jerusalem, Beirut

Appendix IV (Continued)

Page in 'Markings'	Date	Page in this book	Date	Event
167	Oct. 5 (Sun.)	161		
169	Oct. 12 (Sun.)	161		
172	Oct. 19 (Sun.)	161	Dec. 19–Dec. 31	Stockholm, Copenhagen, Beirut, Gaza, El Arish, Khartoum, Addis Ababa, Mogadiscio, Afgoi, Jerusalem
			1959	
			Jan. 1–9	Jerusalem, Amman, Riyadh, Cairo, Benghazi, Malta, Rome, Paris
			Jan. 29	Rockefeller Institute. F., 194–99
			Feb. 2, 5	Press Conf. F., 261–67
173	Feb. 8 (Sun. before Lent)			
173	Feb. 9			
			Feb. 28–Mar. 28	Paris, Rome, Karachi, Calcutta, Rangoon, Bangkok, Vientiane, Phnom Penh, Kuala Lumpur, Katmandu, Delhi, Srinagar, Moscow
			Apr. 2	Press Conf. F., 266–67
			Apr. 30	Press Conf. F., 267–68
			May 1–5	Copenhagen, Malmo, Lund, Stockholm
			May 2	Students Assoc., Copenhagen. F., 200–211
			May 4	Univ. of Lund. F., 212–19
			May 6–15	Frankfurt, Geneva, Caracas, Panama
			June 27–Aug. 1	Malmo, Rome, Cairo, Geneva, Malmo, Paris
174	July 29	xiii, 161	July 29	54th birthday
174	Aug. 4	145, 161f.		

Appendix IV *(Continued)*

Page in 'Markings'	Date	Page in this book	Date	Event
175	Aug. 4	162	Aug. 22	Annual Report. F., 220–28
175–76	Aug. 7	163f.	Sept. 10	UN Correspondents Assoc. F., 229f.
176ff.	Aug. 9 (Sun.)	163f, 78, 88f., 176		
189ff.	Sept. 13	164	Nov. 11–21	London, Bangkok, Vientiane, Bangkok, Tokyo, San Francisco Stockholm
192f.	Oct. 25 (Sun.)	83	Dec. 19–21	
193ff.	Nov. 1 (Sun.)	165, 195	Dec. 21–Dec. 31	Paris, Lisbon, Palmas, Dakar, Monrovia, Conakry, Accra, Lomé, Lagos, Yaounde
			1960	
			Jan. 1–30	Yaounde, Tiko, Kaduna, Brazzaville, Leopoldville, Stanleyville, Usumbura, Dar es Salaam, Zanzibar, Mombasa, Nairobi, Entebbe, Mogadiscio, Addis Ababa, Khartoum, Cairo, Tunis, Ribat, Tangier, Madrid, Lisbon
			Jan. 10	Press Conf., Dar es Salaam. F., 268f.
			Jan. 14	Congress for International Coop. in Africa. F., 231–33
			Jan. 26	UN Econ. Commission, Morocco. F., 233
			Feb. 4	Press Conf, Africa. F., 234–41; 269–70
			Feb. 18	Press Conf. F., 270–71
			Feb. 26–28	Stockholm, Copenhagen
			Feb. 27	Swedish Tourish Assoc. F., 242–50

Appendix IV (Continued)

Page in 'Markings'	Date	Page in this book	Date	Event
197	Easter (Apr. 17)	165, 199	Apr. 27–29	London, Geneva
			May 1–2	Chicago. Univ. of Chicago. F., 251ff.
			May 12–17	London
			May 19	Paris Statement. F., 273–74
			June 2	Press Conf. F., 271–72
			June 6	International Coop. F., 274–92
			July 9–Aug. 11	Geneva, Rome, Nairobi, Mogadiscio, Nairobi, Johannesburg, Leopoldville, Brussels
				55th birthday
			July 29	Annual Report. F., 293–313
			Aug. 31	Statement, UN Assembly. F., 314–17
			Sept. 30	Statement, UN Assembly. F., 317–19
			Oct. 3	Statement, UN Assembly. F., 319–24
			Oct. 17	
			Oct. 24	UN Day Concert. F., 379–80
198	Christmas Eve	165		
199	Nov. 26			
200	Dec. 2			
201	Dec. 3			

1961

Page in 'Markings'	Date	Page in this book	Date	Event
203	Feb. 13–Mar. 13 (Lent)		Jan. 4–12	Leopoldville, Pretoria
			Feb. 15	UN Security Council. F., 327–28
			Feb. 15	Ash Wednesday
204	Maundy Thurs., (Mar. 30)	197		
205	Whitsunday (May 21)	100, 169, 176, 199f.		

Appendix IV (Continued)

Page in 'Markings'	Date	Page in this book	Date	Event
			May 29–June 1	London
			May 30	Oxford Univ. F., 329–49
206–7	July 7, 1960– Spring 1961	102, 167		
208	June 8	166, 167		
211	June 11 (Sun.)			
			June 12	Press Conf. F., 349–53
212	June 18 (Sun.)	166f.		
213	July 6			
			July 8–15	Geneva
214	July 19	176f., 202–3	July 24–27	Rome, Tunis, Bizerte, Tunis, Rome
			July 29	56th birthday
216	July 30 (Sun.)	167		
217	Aug. 2			
219	Aug. 6 (Sun.)		Aug. 17	Annual Report. F., 354–75
221	Aug. 6 (Sun.)		Sept. 8	Last words to Staff. F., 376–78
			Sept. 13	Leopoldville
			Sept. 17–18	Death, Ndola

Index

(Principal references are in **bold-face** type)
(References within single quotes are to Hammarskjöld's words)